The Real Questions

Eden to Big Apple

Anthony Arkell

Abele Publications

ISBN 0-9543558-0-6

Published by Abele Publications, Hillside, Albion Street, Chipping Norton, OX7 5BH.

Copyright © 2002 by Anthony Arkell

The right of Anthony Arkell to be identified as the author has been asserted by him in accordance with the Copyright, Designs and Patents Act 1988.

All rights reserved. No part of this publication may be reproduced, stored in a retrieval system, transmitted, in any form or by any means, electronic, mechanical, photocopying, recording or otherwise, without the written prior permission of the author and the publisher.

Printed in Great Britain by Antony Rowe Ltd

Cover Design by Emma Lidgey,

using detail from a painting: The Lark, 1882 (oil on canvas) by Pal Szinyei Merse (1845-1920), Magyar Nemzeti Galeria, Budapest, Hungary / Bridgeman Art Library,

and photography by Emma Lidgey.

To my family

Acknowledgements

I am most grateful to those who have given me help with this book: Christopher Long who read the first draft and offered advice; members of my family, and particularly my wife who listened years ago, has read the text several times, and has had to take second place to a word processor for some time.

And, in memory of my father who would, I know, have been delighted to read this book.

CONTENTS

		Page
Foreword by	Christopher Long, CMG.	
PROLOGUE	Sex rules the race	1
CHAPTER 1	Sex, abundance and choice	4
CHAPTER 2	Some questions for all of us in the 21st century	9
CHAPTER 3	In the beginning	12
CHAPTER 4	What is Rent?	20
CHAPTER 5	The Royal meaning of Real and the Real meaning of Royalty	26
CHAPTER 6	Rent as government revenue	30
CHAPTER 7	Property taxes wont do	34
CHAPTER 8	Planning	39
CHAPTER 9	Congestion	46
CHAPTER 10	Capital	52
CHAPTER 11	Property	57
CHAPTER 12	Why are you paid so little? (And why is he, or she, paid so much?)	61
CHAPTER 13	Interest rates	78

CHAPTER 14	What do the well-paid spend their money on?	87
CHAPTER 15	What does government do? What should it do?	93
CHAPTER 16	Taxation: what is it trying to do?	100
CHAPTER 17	Law, crime and punishment	110
CHAPTER 18	Free trade	117
CHAPTER 19	Agriculture - is it a special case?	128
CHAPTER 20	Europe	142
CHAPTER 21	German unification	155
CHAPTER 22	Currencies	158
CHAPTER 23	The Euro – European monetary union (EMU)	167
CHAPTER 24	Money	172
CHAPTER 25	Banking	181
CHAPTER 26	Recessions and stagnation	188
CHAPTER 27	World debt	199
CHAPTER 28	Political parties: where did they go wrong?	204
CHAPTER 29	Monopoly: just a game?	212
CHAPTER 30	Cyberspace	220

CHAPTER 31	Immigration	223
CHAPTER 32	War and peace	227
CHAPTER 33	Terrorism	236
CHAPTER 34	Partnership	241
CHAPTER 35	United States of America – a failed dream?	245
CHAPTER 36	Charity	251
CHAPTER 37	Churches	255
CHAPTER 38	Collecting the Rent: how to assess it	261
CHAPTER 39	Acceptance of ideas	265
CHAPTER 40	Patronage	270
CHAPTER 41	Liberty	274
CONCLUSION		277

APPENDIX 1	The power of Rent	281
APPENDIX 2	Population	284
APPENDIX 3	The enclosure of land	285
Abbreviations	and acronyms	289

Foreword

This is an original and timely book. Its author examines some of the fundamental mechanisms of the way modern societies function, focussing on the United Kingdom. In the language of modern management, he looks conscientiously "outside the box", asks challenging questions and offers fresh and often highly innovative answers. He tackles the big themes of poverty or prosperity, justice, individual freedom, the community, the role of government, ever-increasing tax burdens and much else.

It all has plenty of resonance for me, though I have perhaps had better opportunities to study other countries than my own during a 35-year diplomatic career which included service in Latin America, the Middle East, Central and Eastern Europe and not least Switzerland, a country from which I believe we can learn a great deal.

It is fashionable, but misguided, to underestimate the Swiss. Despite their critics, they persist in running one of the most successful societies on earth, while remaining quintessentially European and yet firmly outside the structures of the EU. How do they manage this? I suspect the secret is that they have their government firmly under the control of the people, and not the other way round. Elected representatives legislate, but the Swiss people always reserve the final decision, if they judge it necessary, for voting by referendum at local or national level. Income tax is collected at local level by the communes, who pass on (in a suitably grudging spirit) to the cantonal and federal authorities only the inescapable minimum. No-one forgets where the money comes from, or who it belongs to.

Britain is in many ways more blessed than most, but we do not lack problems. With the policies of the two major parties more and more inclined to converge in substance, and with increasing public apathy or even disenchantment with politics and politicians, there is a great need for those who can, as the author says, look beyond present systems and arrangements to contribute to an open and wide-ranging debate on how this vicious circle can be broken. I hope the ideas in this book will help to launch the process.

Christopher Long, CMG.

PROLOGUE

Sex Rules the Race

High above the snow-covered slopes on one of Zermatt's modern four-man chairlifts they were soaking up the intense spring sunshine, though the air temperature was low for late March, keeping the skiing conditions perfect. Some of the heaviest snowfalls seen in the Alps in recent years had left deep snow right to the end of the season. Part of the family was enjoying the Easter week taking every opportunity to be out on the ski slopes under cloudless skies. Elizabeth, the eldest, and John, the youngest, were with their father on the higher slopes near the Italian border. Catherine, his wife, was having a quiet day also enjoying the clear mountain air and sunshine, but not skiing that day. So Anthony had the two children to himself and was getting to know them again after the school term, and in Elizabeth's case almost permanent absence from parental influence now that she was established in London.

The two children had always got on well in spite of their ten-year age gap and having brothers and sisters between them, and both could talk for England. Following on from some other remark, somehow the question was posed "What is the most important thing in Life?"

"Food", said John with the appetite of a fourteen year old.

"No, Sex", said Anthony with all the gravitas of his fifty-plus years. This rather surprised the young ones who perhaps thought the subject risqué for their father to be raising in their presence, but they listened as he drew them in with his justifications.

1

"Yes food is essential to life, as is water and air, but sex is almost infinitely interesting at all stages of life. And how! It can and does affect all of us from early childhood to teenager; to twenties; then marriage; maturity; and old age. Even then it is a constant challenge in the face of changing circumstances. Throughout life the fact of sex and its effect on our lives are so varied that the basic necessities such as food, even when epicurean, pale into the merely mundane."

At this point the children had returned their attention to the ski slopes, as the chairlift came to the summit, but Anthony pondered what he had started and mentally enumerated the points as he enjoyed the clear winter atmosphere in the Alps in the next few days.

First love. Does anyone forget that intense feeling of being overwhelmed by another person for the first time? Then the early really sexual encounters. So powerful, and almost everything is subjugated to thinking about when and how the next tryst can be arranged.

How vivid is that fear of losing an intense relationship and finding that the girl prefers someone else. The nagging thought that although there are always more fish in the sea, no one else will be as magical.

Cupid's arrows, love, sexual attraction: call it what you will. We are obedient to the call by some deeply ingrained force. Artists strive to capture its nuances, and audiences at theatres and opera houses never seem to satiate their appetite for representations of the cruelties of the love lost, perhaps in the hope of catching a fleeting glimpse of love's glorious heights.

Awareness of the sexes starts at a very early age. Girls of three, or even younger, flirt with fathers and other males in the family circle. Teenage girls spend forever keeping up to the minute in fashion, and molly coddle their developing bodies. Choosing a partner, hopefully for life, is a daunting and challenging experience. It is a miracle that so *many achieve it and the heartaches are no worse. A mature relationship with the birth and bringing up of children is a long and varied phase of early middle life.*

Expression of all these sexual relationships has been reflected in the arts throughout the centuries. From Botticelli to Picasso in paintings; Romeo and Juliet, Abelard and Eloise, Zhivago and Lara - great passions of literature; Tristan and Isolde, Don Juan, Figaro, Manon Lescaut - powerful images of the opera. Our artistic heritage is rich with encounters both passionate and tragic under the influence of sex.

Although Anthony can't be denied the breadth and depth of humankind's feelings for the opposite sex, John was right in his way. Food, the very fuel of life is crucial, and it is a daily struggle to achieve enough of it for half or more of the people on the planet. In that situation food is the most important thing in life, for without it there is no life. Its scarcity in some areas contrasts with abundance in others. And as Anthony mused there is so much more to living.

In this book I attempt to make it more generally recognized why it is that even in the midst of plenty we have poverty, depriving the many of the opportunity to live a full life, and in many countries thousands, far too many thousands, are forced to surrender life itself.

.

CHAPTER 1

Sex, Abundance and Choice

Give me my Romeo: and, when he shall die,
Take him and cut him out in little stars,
And he will make the face of heaven so fine
That all the world will be in love with night,
And pay no worship to the garish sun.
- *Romeo and Juliet*

Human sexuality can take many courses leading some to great fulfilment, others to heart rending anguish. The inescapable fact is that at the root of it all is the fact of sex: the need for the species to reproduce itself and the only way that can be done is by the combining of DNA from two individuals to make a new one - a new generation.

This ineluctable fact underpins everything anyone has said, thought or written about human sexuality. And there has been plenty, although not everyone would agree on exactly what expressions of human activity are sexually based, or what interpretations are valid.

Consider the care both men and women take of their appearance. Whole industries are based on our desire to look good to attract each other, to out-do our competitors in presenting a good face to the opposite sex, and to our own sex as a warning that we are high up the pecking order. Clothes, fashion, cosmetics, health and beauty, all trade on the back of these primitive desires which have been sophisticated to astounding elaboration throughout history.

Consider the darker side of sexuality: the pornography, the films, magazines, books and other publications that trade on our basic desires.

Consider the aggression in gang culture of young males, an aggression directly descended from the animal kingdom where constant sparring of male animals - particularly in certain seasons - are fights to the death. Consider the implications this has for our own species.

Consider family life, and our desire for contentment in middle and later life resulting from the sharing of the responsibility of raising a family.

Consider jealousy and preferment in social, commercial, and political life.

Consider the controversy resulting from the fact that some males are more female than others; some females more male than others. It seems that we can all be placed on a spectrum ranging from very female to very male. This gamut of possibilities may be caused by hormonal balance and relative levels. Hormonal activity may be temporarily imbalanced and will undoubtedly be most influential in early adulthood. But it may well also have genetic origins. In the middle of the spectrum is the area of homosexuality. In some cultures this has seemed normal and acceptable, in our own culture in recent years we have seen a grudging re-acceptance of homosexuality as normal - or at least tolerable. Regrettably there is still the evangelism of the persecuted perpetrating on the rest of us the in-your-face presence of the 'gay' community. They need to learn that both hetero- and homo-sexuality is best kept to a proper place in society. What exactly that place is for either section is variable depending on the mores of the time, and therefore will always be debated, and tested by each new generation.

These are some of the very many areas of human life that are strongly influenced by our sexuality. Even our very spirituality may be affected by our gender and our position on the spectrum of sexuality. If so it is possible to argue that all human behaviour has an element of sexuality. What we can be sure of is that human behaviour cannot be described without recognising that fundamental influence. We can be sure that any hypothesis put forward to explain who we are and why we behave as we do which sought to deny our sexuality and put forward the contention that we were not sexual beings at all and merely reproduced asexually like aphids would not be taken seriously. Everyday experience, of course, says otherwise.

I have chosen to use the analogy of sexual relationships to demonstrate that a complex subject cannot be explained if it is taken as a premise that there is a fundamental lie at the bottom of the edifice.

We could equally look at other incontrovertible facts. Gravity is a fact of life for all things on earth, and indeed all things in the universe in so far as gravity is a force in the proximity of all the heavenly bodies. We may not be able to explain how it works but we can be certain we are all affected by it.

While the knowledge of quantum physics has expanded greatly in the twentieth century, we are still bound by, and have to live within the laws of physics. Nothing has changed except our knowledge of some of the sub-molecular processes. The same is true of all the natural sciences.

Biology at some times in the middle of the last century may have been overwhelmed by chemistry. Certainly it was in the minds of the chemists, but biology has its own laws, and if we have ignored these, we have been corrected by the hard lessons of trial and error.

Much of the knowledge gained so painfully in the nineteenth century is now a common and accepted part of our everyday lives. Yet in other parts of the world this is not the case, and the third world still lives in conditions not dissimilar to pre-industrial Britain. Yet life in the Western world is not Utopia. We regard ourselves as a rich nation. Yet many of us struggle to meet our monthly commitments, and only do so by working extremely hard, or for long hours in conditions which are rarely ideal.

Few of us have a real choice about what we can do with our lives. Even the fat cats of industry must fear that they will be cast aside and have no more cream.

Why is this so in a rich nation?

There is abundance of everything. It would be fair to say that we are a wasteful people. The throw-away culture is no longer remarked on because nearly all of us live it as a matter of course.

The area in which we are not so rich, in fact most of us are extremely poor, is in the matter of choice. How many of your friends can actually say they have a choice about what they do today, tomorrow, or for the next year?

Certainly some retired people. Within limits, if the dice has fallen well for them. But for every one who feels free in this way there are a score or more who budget every penny and even if the budget does run to a nice holiday in the sun, their freedom of choice is extremely limited for the rest of the year. And that's not so surprising when you consider that we live in a high cost society. Abundance, waste, throw-away convenience, but all at high price.

You may say that we are, for a change, in a low inflation era. The cost of new technology and consumer goods of other sorts is actually falling. Well that is something, but only in the context of the price structure as it was yesterday or last year.

Very few of us are particularly concerned about these questions, though the fact that politicians enter the public arena and grapple for years with some of the difficult questions of running a country, and in doing so thrust upon us through the media a whole host of opinions, even obsessions, keeps a dialogue of sorts alive. A huge indifference is more typical, and it is fair to say that the majority of the population is distracted by the everyday world of work and mass culture.

But some of us are different: those politicians for a start. They at some stage said to themselves that they want to see changes. They probably have big egos, and wanted to get into politics for the kudos of a role in public life, but it is at least reasonable to assume that they have a view of what they want to do if they do actually get any power.

Inevitably 90% of the population will do nothing except go with the flow, but the 10% who are more thoughtful will make the changes if they are equipped to do so.

What is so staggering is that in spite of an active broadsheet press, a radio and television service that is a quantum leap better than those in most other countries, and periodicals devoted to all kind of specialist topics, including economics and politics and current affairs, there is no meaningful debate on the questions which so fundamentally affect everyday of our working lives. And our lives long after we have retired. It is as if all the effort of commenting on our society, our community, our welfare and our economic lives was being conducted in a vacuum that does not address the fundamental data. Just as if the human behaviourists ignored our sexuality.

Just how affected we all are will be examined in the following chapters. And I will point out just why and how we are so blind to the obvious data.

CHAPTER 2

Some Questions for All of Us in the 21st Century

Economics has always had a bad name. Branded the "dismal science", "boring", "no consensus". Show me ten economists and I will show you at least eleven opinions on the same subject. Philosophy on the other hand always has a good ring to it. "Love of wisdom". Yet the two are intimately bound together.

The wriggling of economists with their different opinions is symptomatic of the fact that human society exists in a metastable state. The slightest upset to the status quo will have dramatic consequences. Therefore, modern economists perceive the need for very careful gentle manipulation of the levers. No wonder there are so many opinions for what is right at any one particular point in time. And of course being bound up with politics not many of the hands on the levers want the same result anyway! It is for good reason that Economics, Politics and Philosophy are studied together in university degrees. However, the graduates of all such degree courses do not seem to have helped twentieth century man come to any promising methods of ordering human affairs.

At any particular point in time the newspapers are dominated by controversy of one sort or another, and they can be blinkered to the point where the happening of the moment seems to exclude all or most other topics. Or perhaps the usual topics are discussed with a slant toward the subject of the moment.

In spite of this, serious topics that occur again and again are the ones that worry us all. Yes, sex and the antics of the famous, of course, but that is not so much a worry as an entertainment.

No, the things that concern us all are jobs, remuneration, education, housing, holidays, prices, investments, health, law and order and crime, travel and congestion on our roads and railways, pensions for retirement (at least for those of us getting near it, and those already retired). These can be said to be worries, because they affect us all most of the time or at some stage in our lives. So, the newspapers are full of topics relating to such matters. They may allay our fears or make us more aware of them! Happily many people also read about, and partake in the arts, sport, family life (which can also be a worry) religious churches and numerous other interests, which we could refer to as hobbies or special interests. Whilst not personal worries we may as a community have worries about the poor countries of the world; famines in Africa; poverty in South America, Asia, Africa, India, Russia and the former soviet states; wars in the Middle East, the Balkans, Africa and the former soviet states; terrorism in Northern Ireland and many other places and (after September 11th 2001) where it might strike again; mafia activities in many parts of the world - shall we just say corruption generally. And closer to home, the institutions of our own country: lawyers that aren't accessible to any but the extremely rich, or the very poor who can use legal aid; planners who allow the despoliation of out countryside; politicians who seem to have the wrong priorities, or are ineffective, or worse seems to only feather their own nests; our relationship with Europe, which seems to operate against our national interest, and to curtail our commercial and personal freedoms.

Some of us may be too young, too old, too busy, or have overriding worries of our own, but it is a fair bet that these matters are of concern to the majority of people, certainly to thinking people. What is so surprising is that there is such hopelessness in the response of most people when faced with such problems. They seem to see no way of overcoming either their own personal hurdles or the wider issues that affect the community, the nation, or the world.

It will be my aim to ask the questions that lead to better ways of addressing all of these apparently intractable matters.

CHAPTER 3

In the Beginning

Let us stand back a bit, and look at some fundamentals of life. Just as we looked at the fundamental fact of sex, we can set out the truisms of earning a living, or more broadly, the whole economic structure. But we have to be simple at first to understand economics. And we shall find that philosophy plays its part.

You and I, and all the people we know, and the millions we don't know at all, are all the same in the fact that we have to eat. We have to drink water. We have to be warm, or be clothed sufficiently to keep warm. We don't absolutely have to be housed as shelter from rain, storms or excessive sunshine, but most of us in fact do live in a structure of some kind, although this can vary from country to country and culture to culture.

If we were alone on a hypothetical desert island, we would have to solve all the problems of survival that I have mentioned above, and probably some more too, depending on what the conditions were like. Avoiding being eaten by termites, stung by a scorpion, or a host of other perils of the natural world.

We often talk of desert islands: there is the long running radio programme Desert Island Discs. In this the guest who chooses his favourite music, also has to say how he would survive, and make shelters etc, but the answers the guests give often assume a much less hostile place than a desert island. They think in terms more of a tropical island. So let us envisage for a moment an island blessed with quite an abundance of natural life, in the tropical region, so that seasons are pretty well absent. There would be rainfall, providing water. There would be vegetation, providing materials for structures, and there would be fruit on those tropical plants. There would be insect life, mammalian life and reptilian life, as well as fish in the surrounding sea. This would be a fairly typical tropical island, though I imagine that most idyllic ones that were once so pure have long since been populated.

Nevertheless we are imagining how things would be in the natural state. At this point there is no human activity, and therefore the plant and animal life is in steady state of balance. It might fluctuate, as populations of both plant and animal life naturally do in cycles of glut, when food for one species is abundant and can then support many more of that particular species. But as the food supply is eaten up, the larger population is forced to go hungry, and declines again. Or may suffer for other reasons. That species itself may as its population grows encourage an increase in the population of its predators so that more of its enemies attack it and the population is kept in check that way.

Even if you have never studied such natural subjects, it is easy enough to imagine how this tropical paradise would be. Constantly fluctuating, but overall stable.

Now imagine this is a kind of Garden of Eden. In other words we have introduced Man. He will be busy, but not very busy getting something to eat. He will therefore easily be well fed, and being in a tropical climate, he will probably not have to worry about either clothes or shelter. He would almost certainly be bored, because challenges of any sort, and certainly any intellectual challenges would be absent. If this were a twenty-first century Adam, who dropped in by plane crash, or shipwreck, he would have his cultural background with him, and might therefore devise all sorts of games or pastimes to keep him amused. Or he might try some new skills such as training the monkeys to talk or do other complicated things. But in terms of economic necessity he would be well off. He would probably make himself very comfortable, as do the guests, in their imaginations, of Desert Island Discs. He would almost certainly find the materials to make a shelter of some kind if only to keep the tropical storms from waking him up at night, and he would make some kind of hammock or bed to make his nights more comfortable. He might be able to fashion from clay, or wood something to carry water with, and he would find it easier to drink out of a vessel than use his cupped hands all the time.

In other words he would have a smaller or larger number of artefacts that would come into being as a result of his own labour applied to the natural resources he was lucky enough to find around him.

Again to make the water availability reliable he might construct dams and ponds to ensure the tropical rain did not run straight to the sea, but was retained for the whole period between one rain storm and the next. There would be other examples of his labour in conjunction with the natural world being combined to produce something useful.

To summarise, we have an island, and some sea, we have abundance of nature, and we have Man using his labour to make things from the animal, vegetable and mineral resources creating things that are useful or interesting to him.

Following the Garden of Eden story for a bit we can now imagine what it might be like to have Eve alongside our Adam. Very delicious is my first reaction, but we have to look a little deeper for any economic lessons.

Being Man and Woman, they would have not only a natural affinity, but also a natural complementariness. In sheer survival terms there is still abundance for two of them, but they might well have more ambitious plans to fill their days. They might decide to make a bigger shelter. And only because there are two people could they lift certain things that are too heavy for one. They might decide to make a boat of some kind, and would need to cooperate with the difficult tasks of construction that might be possible with four hands, but nigh on impossible with only two. Then moving the finished boat down to the sea, and more so up the beach again may be a task only two can accomplish.

So we still have the human population - of two - using their labour to achieve the making of artefacts from natural resources, but we also have co-operation of that labour. And we almost certainly right from day one or day two have division of labour, so that, typically, she might cook, while he might be seeking food, fishing or gathering firewood etc. This is very simple economics, but nothing stands still, and the Eden story continues with the sons of Adam and Eve, Cain and Abel, going their separate ways, and feuding.

But we will depart a little from that story, and imagine what happens when we introduce a few more people into the island. This would happen naturally anyway, as the children of our two grew up, but we can speed things up by assuming a peaceful import of new adults. Not a lot, just a few couples or family units. Perhaps the island is now on a shipping route of some kind, and some newcomers decide to stay and set up home there.

Suddenly things have changed quite a bit. Family Two will not want to settle too close, nor too far away from Adam and Eve. Why? Not too close, because each unit will want some privacy; not too far away because they will value each other's company at times, and putting it more in economic terms, they will want to co-operate. The heavy work for a start; now two men will be better able to do the tough jobs than a man and woman team. The practicality of certain tasks may call for problem solving. And the division of labour again, so that one person out of perhaps ten adults can teach the children. So they will form a small community of dwellings scattered around, not too far and not too close to each other.

I have already hinted at how one adult might spend a large part of his or her time schooling the children. Other adults will find they have special skills or just likes and dislikes, so they will become the specialists for the community. In a small community, they will almost certainly not be exclusively devoted to one skill, but they will be the one person the others call for when a particular happening occurs. Treatment for an injury or illness, waterproofing a boat or a roof, making a tool for fishing or hunting. Each member of the small community might have their own aptitude.

There will be more specialization as the community grows. If as we have postulated the island is on some shipping route, there will be a harbour or at least an anchorage where people and goods can land. This will be the same place every time, because by experience it will be found to be the best place to do so. It will have a natural advantage. It might even be improved by man-made effort, for example by making a breakwater.

The community of people will tend to live within easy access of this naturally advantageous place. Even more so the people with special skills, if their skill is regularly used, will find it more convenient to be near that focal point or centre of the community.

We can envisage quite an advancement now in the operation of that small community. We can assume that in the early days everyone did all the necessary things and that specialists only acted as such occasionally and perhaps were rewarded with a gift of some kind for the help they had given.

But now the specialist is seen to be primarily a specialist, and will be 'paid' for his services. Indeed some new-comers may see that they can set up near the port or centre of the community just so as to be a specialist. For example the man who brings in goods from elsewhere, and who trades them for other locally produced goods. He is in fact a shop-keeper and import and export trader.

This may seem a big leap in economic terms from the Adam and Eve existence, but it is still a simple community compared with the complexity of twenty-first century life in most parts of the world today. Such communities on islands or as isolated communities on larger land masses were common place throughout many centuries. You can think of tropical and not so tropical islands; or of the small market towns of rural England right up to the beginning of the last century; of the walled towns of the feuding Italian states and elsewhere in the twelfth century and later.

The islands of course had the natural boundaries of the sea. The rural towns had no strict boundaries, but there were very strong forces at work that made the people build their shelter next to the existing community, and within reach of the centre and the services of others provided in that centre. These were nothing more than economic forces. It could be argued that in particular the walled towns of medieval England and renaissance Italy were man made boundaries. But this was a reaction of the community to the threats from outside. The people of the community solving for themselves one of the problems of survival just like our lone islander having to avoid termites and scorpions.

The effect of building walls round a town reinforced the nature of the community.

What is that nature? What general conditions can we identify in this more varied community? We identified the elements of labour and natural materials when one or two people made things for themselves on an idyllic island.

In the walled or un-walled town we have the same elements of labour and natural material. The materials were and are usually brought in from the surrounding countryside (on an island the natural resources are all or nearly all within the boundary made by the sea), but the labour is much the same as it was before. Human effort, with division of labour, which takes more and more diverse paths as a community develops, is essentially what a man or woman can do - physically or mentally.

The additional element in economic production that the usual treatise on economics then identifies is capital. This in the form of capital goods is best seen as the making of things that can be used to make other things, or wealth for consumption. I want to come back to capital much later, because there are considerations much more important to look at while we have the idea of a small bounded community in our minds. It is worth pointing out what is of course obvious: in the final analysis we are a not so very large community on a not so very large 'island' or planet, bounded by the size of that planet, and held to it by the gravitational pull and the hostility of the space beyond. In the twenty-second century this may not seem such a barrier, but right now it is for practical purposes an absolute.

Think smaller again. Back to the island or small town. Think of one you have been to recently. Perhaps holidaying on a Greek island, or visiting a small rural town in South West France, for example. Picture the port as centre of the community. The shops and banks, and restaurants are here. Walk just a hundred yards down a side street, and the lesser services such as hair stylists, laundry, and mechanics can be found. Further away the shops give way to residential accommodation.

Now imagine you decide to emigrate and 'set up shop' to provide some service in such a small community. You will need to carefully explore the town and see what property or un-built-on space is available. Probably quite a choice, but you can be sure the properties near the smart centre will be more expensive to buy or rent than the properties in the side streets. Not only because they are grander, but more per square metre for similar looking properties, too. Of course, is probably your reaction. But why? You want to be where the other successful businesses are because you want to have the crowds passing your door to see your business, and come to buy your goods or services. Not all enterprises need that flow of people to pass the door but most will, and even the small artisan, a potter say, who makes pots which are shipped to other places to retail, will have the advantage of being able to sell some pots at retail prices from the premises if he is in the centre.

Also those business people need to have things and services supplied to them. The restaurant near the fresh fish and the fresh vegetable markets is better able to serve excellent meals than one a long way away from those markets. All businesses need to bank their takings, and proximity to a bank is useful, as is being near the train station, bus station or port.

So you, like others before you, will be prepared to pay for the better location rather than the secondary site, other things being equal.

It is this fundamental fact, which is self evident to all of us, that is nearly always overlooked in economic considerations. It can be seen to have affected the way societies have developed from a very early time. And it is because it is ignored in nearly all societies today that we have some major economic problems that exercise the minds of economists. Because they deny or appear ignorant of this simple truth they are like people trying to explain human behaviour, who have failed to notice that there are two sexes.

CHAPTER 4

What is Rent?

Throughout the rest of this book I will come back again and again to the danger of ignoring the simple facts embodied in the last chapter. I will explain why they are so important and look at many of the problems of economic life and consider how things would be different if only we all recognized this fundamental fact of economic life. It affects us all. Some of us gain because we are on the receiving end of society's failure. Many more of us lose because we are on the wrong end.

But first we have to understand exactly what it is that is missing. After all I said it was perfectly clear to most of us where we would want to set up our new business, and why. What is it we as a society are missing?

There is a danger in all those who seek to study economic and social systems and societies in getting confused by the ideas of their particular time and fashionable notions. While most of us think we live in a sophisticated society and have jobs involved in a very complex world with many interactions, in truth we are all at its simplest concerned to create wealth, so that we can consume what we want to consume. And of course have enough time to do so, and time just to be.

Broadly we can think in terms of wealth creation as part of our life, and consumption, as the reason to set about creating the wealth in the first place. While it must be true that we humans are an ingenious species and will find things to occupy our talents even when abundance is all around, we can regard that busy-ness as part of the consumption. We do it for fun. Some people will indeed just work for fun. Many perhaps, but all these considerations are not important, because in the whole, taking all the people in any society, we are obliged to be wealth creating so that we can consume. There is no endless Garden of Eden for us all to enjoy with no effort. Indeed one of the main elements of such a paradise is lost as soon as it becomes populated by more than two.

We have all heard people say that we live on a small island that is hopelessly overcrowded. In reality this is far from the truth, because so much of even crowded parts of the world are empty. Although the population of the third world is still rising steeply, it is probably still true that the whole population of the world can stand on the Isle of Wight. They will be standing very close to each other at today's population, but could comfortably fit into Wales. Some calculations demonstrating this point and comparing the densities of urban populations are given in Appendix 2. This at first surprising finding does emphasise the point that the rest of all the land mass of all the continents would then be empty, so talk of any one country being over-populated is certainly wide of the mark. That does not mean that there are not population density pressures in many parts of the world. There most certainly are. But instead of wringing our hands and complaining of congestion – and failing to see why that is so – we can with a little clear thinking understand why, and what can be done about it.

In any community as we saw in the last chapter we will be setting up businesses where it is most advantageous to do so, and we will tend to do so at the centre of the established community, or as near to it as we can justify. As the community expands those advantageous places become more sort after and therefore more expensive. We must not lose sight of the fact that all of human activity is constantly changing and 'the centre' may change gradually, or suddenly, partly or wholly, for a variety of reasons. That does not alter the fact that there is always a tendency to start new things at what is perceived by the individual to be the most advantageous place, and that will be towards the centre, even if that centre is a moving target. And sometimes some people will make wrong decisions.

We have already seen how natural barriers such as coasts can put a limit on a community. Another example would be the rivers surrounding Manhattan Island in New York. But the community itself may impose artificial ones such as Green Belts around cities. We shall see later (with historical details in Appendix 3) how the enclosure of land in the eighteenth century and at earlier times exacerbated the pressure on cities and we still live with the consequences today. Probably no one thinks of this as an artificial pressure, but it was crucial to the development of large metropolitan areas and remains a structural part of the economic system we have devised for ourselves.

Now, earlier we noted that labour and natural resources of the planet are combined to produce the wealth that we as whole are intent on producing. Other things being equal therefore we should expect the product to be the same price wherever it is produced, but we have seen that it is advantageous to do things or produce things in the centre of activity. And we have also seen that there is a cost of doing so which is not labour and not raw material. It is the cost of being there. But it is not the cost of being in a building, though that does have a cost because it is part of the capital: one of the 'tools' that make up capital, which we will look at in more detail later.

No, this other cost is the extra cost for being in exactly the same, or let us say identical, building as the one further out of town, but at the better location.

Location. You have heard the estate agents' mantra: Location, Location, Location; the three things that matter when buying a property. Or renting a property, i.e. using a property. And why do we all gladly pay this extra? And whom to?

We have seen why. It is in our own interests to do so, but the reason, the real reason is because the community of people already there made it advantageous for us to be there. We would not go to that location if we could not sell our wares or services to the community there. Or tap in to the pool of workers there. We want to be there because the community of people are there. A ghost town holds no attractions for us. It is not the nice buildings we go to the best locations for, but the very fact of the community's existence.

And to whom do we pay that extra charge for being there? We pay it to the owner of the building, or more accurately, to the owner of the land who is the same person in nearly all cases. We will also pay a community charge or commercial rates to the council, but this is allegedly for quite different reasons. The council is, more or less, giving us something in return for that charge. The refuse collection, fire service, police, etc. It is a crude method of charging and has been a political football on occasions, but it is more or less a service charge, or if not wholly that, because we pay more than we use in services, then it is an impost or tax on the building we use. The larger the building the more we pay.

I will look briefly at the enormous question of taxation in later chapters.

But first it is essential to understand the nature of this payment to the owner of the land. (We, as the business operator, may also be the owner, but in that case what we have done is paid a large sum of money to acquire that title from the previous owner.)

The nature of that payment is Rent. Economic Rent, a term of clearly defined exactness. And it has to be clearly differentiated from the other meanings in common parlance. We may 'rent' a car for example but that is merely a hire charge. We may pay 'rent' to a flat-owner to have somewhere to live, or to a landlord for business premises, but that is mostly a payment for the use of the building, and its fittings, but does include an element of true Economic Rent. I shall use a capital R in this text to remind readers that I mean Economic Rent when I use the term Rent.

And what is its meaning? It is the value to the user of being in a certain place occupying that particular land (or sea) and all that lies beneath it, for example the minerals.

Immediately it can be seen, as another example, why some land is favoured over other areas. The minerals, or oil, or fresh water below the land may make holding a piece of such land vastly more profitable compared with, say, agricultural land. While this is not usually in areas of high population, its value falls into the same category of Rent because if there were no community of people wanting the minerals including oil the land would have no value. Furthermore it is a natural gift, as is all the land and sea. Though of course the entrepreneur will be entitled to his reward for extracting the oil, or other natural resource and for making it available to the community who wants it.

We have now seen how land in particular places is more valuable than other parts. We can see that this is a gift of nature: minerals or geography such as a natural port, and we have seen how these naturally good bits of land, and the ordinary average land, in both cases have value only if there is a community who want to use them. We should therefore conclude that these values, the Rent, is the property not of just you or me, or whoever the 'landowner' maybe, but of all of us - the community as a whole.

This recognition profoundly affects the whole structure of society. It is our duty to recognise it, and not to allow it to be otherwise controlled or 'owned' by any one person or body. Not even the government! In fact, certainly not the government!

In today's world there is only one way to keep the Rent in the community's hands. That is to assess the value and pay an annual charge to the community (as defined by the relevant accountable democracy) for the 'title' to use it. 'It' being the land. Not the buildings or other structures on the land. That should be private property, and whether the structure is a car park, i.e. virtually no structure, or a multi-storey office block costing millions the Rent should be the same. That is because the community is creating the Rent, and in similar, say adjacent, locations the value created by the community is the same. The holder of the land will therefore other things being equal put as much productive structure on the site as possible. So it is unlikely that a mere parking lot would be at use in a city centre location. But a multi-storey car park might well be next to a large office block in central London. And the owners of both would be able to charge the users a market price for office space or the parking space. If the owners cannot make a profit charging the market price the site should be re-developed to provide something people did want and would pay for.

CHAPTER 5

The Real meaning of Royalty
and
the Royal meaning of Real

Property, particularly bare land is sometimes known as real estate, or in the USA as realty. This is a corruption or derivation from the word royal. Our word realm, meaning kingdom, has the same etymology. The reason for the terms realty or real estate derives from the fact that the title was long ago in distant centuries in royal ownership, or more accurately perhaps, guardianship, and although many of the kings did not behave as they should, abused their position, and perhaps did not even understand their role the king was deemed to be guardian for the whole community.

In biblical times and in early centuries in Europe, through the dark ages and into the medieval era the 'kings' were often no more than tribal warrior chieftains. Nevertheless, wherever the tribal communities were settled and led by a strong chief, or king, that leader had power over and 'rights' to the whole territory. The old testament of the Bible makes frequent reference to the land belonging to a particular tribe or race. There developed methods of allowing usage of their land for individuals to work on, but there was also developed the concept of it reverting to the original ownership at set intervals. At the end of the forty-ninth year, in the fiftieth year, or jubilee, being the most far reaching of these occasions. This clearly was not a perfect system, particularly if it were applied to the fast changing world of the twenty-first century.

Underlying the rules they set for themselves remained the concept that the leader held the ultimate right to all the land for all 'his' people.

The concept of Divine Right of Kings, which pertained until the Middle Ages, also embodied the Divine Duty of Kings. *Dieu et mon droit* has been the motto of royalty down the centuries. The just monarchs did not abuse their 'divine' link. They recognised that their divine position was trusteeship for God. They held in their power all that was God-given, but they held it as trustee for the whole community.

The rot set in when in return for service of some kind the monarch gave away in perpetuity the title to tracts of land, and created what we now call freehold. This may have seemed harmless enough, and was clearly extremely useful as a means of rewarding powerful people who had served the king's purpose in a military or some other way. With scattered and sparse populations kept in check numerically by disease and the harsh existence under which they lived, land was plentiful in all parts of Europe. Now that all the land is under the 'freehold' title of someone, the consequences of that early convenience of medieval kings has dire consequences. The repercussions have been commented on by philosophers and economists when the pressures built up in the seventeenth, eighteenth and nineteenth centuries, but then and in the twentieth century politicians believed they could ignore the fact. And with rare exceptions the explanation of the 'disease' was not sufficiently lucid to force recognition.

The true meaning of the term 'real estate' is not perhaps widely appreciated, but lawyers make a distinction between 'real' property and personal property. Having made the distinction they then allow both to be privately owned, even though the former is 'royal' property, and their division is to them of no more significance than to divide what can be moved from what cannot be moved. The legal system has done much to perpetuate this error that the 'real', or 'royal', can be private property.

It will I am sure now be clear why I have called this book 'The Real Questions' because I shall raise now questions of importance to all members of society, and in all of them we can see the unfortunate results of allowing Rent, which is due to the community on all 'real' property, to be appropriated by the title holder of property as if that holder were the absolute and outright owner in perpetuity.

I might have used the title The Real Question, because it is in fact one concept, one error, which distorts our modern civilizations. But so many facets of our lives are affected that each is a subsidiary Real Question. How each 'question' is corrupted by the failure to recognise the concept of Real, and of Rent, is explored in the remainder of this book.

If the monarchy needs a role, or more to the point if we need a role for the monarchy, it is the ancient one of holding what is God-given, what is of the natural world. As holders and defenders of something that is so fundamental, the monarch will be of supreme importance in the society. He or she will not be political but, as now, above politics. Politicians are and must be subordinate to that position, because the politicians elected by the people should only be allowed to operate under the principle that what is God's, what is given by nature, what belongs to no man but to all men, is held by the monarch for the whole community's benefit.

The monarch need not be fantastically wealthy. The fact that monarchs became so in Europe and other continents resulted from the misappropriation of land to themselves instead of holding it always and inalienably for the community. However, the monarch should not be denied personal property as any other person may hold personal property. It would not be surprising to find that considerable personal wealth had built up over many centuries. In addition the monarch, as head of state, should be in receipt of monies with which to perform state duties, as the Head of State would in a republic and this is provided today in the UK as annual payments comprised in the Civil List.

CHAPTER 6

Rent as Government Revenue

Most people who have had the concept of Rent properly explained to them have the initial difficulty of being unable to believe that a small element of industry's costs, re-named, and re-directed can change very much, if at all, the functioning of society as a whole. In some ways that's a good start. Industry will not be affected much. No new horrible taxes to get to grips with.

But as we study one subject after another, we will see that making the first change, leads to major beneficial changes. Or put the other way round failing to recognize the existence of Rent and failing to collect it for the community has led us and most nations into some horrendous difficulties. Let us first postulate that government does collect the Rent that is due to the community, every year. We can consider how it is assessed, and how it is collected in a later chapter (38).

You will remember it is the value on an annual basis of the land. And you will recall too that land only has any value at all if there is a person or a community of people who want to use it. And the larger and more sophisticated that community the greater that value will be. And Rent will be assessed on each title holder. In central areas it will be a large value, in most areas used for housing and agriculture it will be lower, and in small towns and villages it will be much less than the great city centres. In the far north of Scotland and remote parts of England and Wales, which have no productive potential in the present market it will be nil.

The government if it collects Rent now has a regular annual income stream, and while it is not static from year to year it is predictable. Because of this income stream all the current taxes of government can be reduced to zero.

This may sound a ridiculous dream, but as will be seen in Chapter 12 the Rent payable will rise as the imposts or taxes on production fall. And all other taxes are taxes on and dis-incentives to production. Remember too that Income tax was only introduced in 1799 and was then stated to be a temporary measure to finance the wars. It has been folly to perpetuate it. And even more folly to make it almost universal so that there are now few people who do not pay it. Certainly all workers pay its cloak and dagger version, National Insurance.

So we remove all taxes on income. Immediately we can dispense with an army of tax collectors. Not only that but half the accountants are calculating your and my taxes, and making sure we pay the right amount. And for the big corporations and wealthy individuals there are another legion finding ways of tax avoidance. They can all go, too. Not on the scrap heap, you understand, but into helping the wealth creation process.

Corporation tax is just another disincentive to wealth creation. There is no reason to keep that any more than income tax. And Capital Gains Tax has long been regarded as a very inefficient tax. It is now even more complicated to assess, and its collection costs are way out of balance with its revenue. It is only kept alive at all by recent governments because its abolition would make it child's play to avoid income tax.

The Inland Revenue could dispense with probably 90% or more of its staff, and concentrate the few left on collecting the Rent, which is predictable and easily collected.

Probably an equal number of people can be redeployed in the private sector from tax related, non-productive work to wealth creation related work. However, it is highly probable less accountants will be needed, and less professionals of other disciplines, such as lawyers. But we live in fast changing times, and if in the twentieth century manufacturing labour was 'asked' to re-train, so in the twenty-first century we should see more re-training in the average working life of the white collar workers. Even though they have spent years obtaining expensive qualifications.

It is helpful to look at commerce and industry's costs from another point of view. They may be costs to the enterprise, but having made a product or service and sold it and having a quantity of money for it, one can ask how the wealth created is distributed. Part will go to pay for the raw material, if it is a product that is being studied, part will be claimed by the labour involved. Another claim as we have seen is the Rent. These three can be regarded as the primary claims. But we can see that other secondary claims can be 'invented' by misguided governments. Taxation in all the guises that are mentioned above are such secondary claims, and because the total wealth from that production, or that days work is finite, if taxes take a bite, there is less available for the primary claims. And the one that suffers is labour. So all taxes depress the rewards of labour. And make it more likely that production will cease because it is not worthwhile for labour to work. In today's welfare state of course there is the choice of whether to work or not to work, because the dole is paid if available work does not pay labour sufficiently well. This leads to a classic vicious circle. Briefly, it can be recognized that taxes force enterprises to go out of business and shed labour, which then become a cost on the state, which then has to find more tax revenues, which further depress production.

Similarly, import duties - another government invention - are an additional cost on materials, and any attempt to modify the free trade of materials across frontiers, or within a community, are additional claims on the wealth being created, and therefore depress production.

In this short chapter I have tried to show that Rent not only should be collected by government because the Rent is due to the community, but also to briefly describe in outline how that revenue will be sufficient to replace all other forms of government revenue. Furthermore since taxation depresses productive activity, and in particular reduces the level of wages in the community, the government often finds it is having to spend money to prop up the unemployed or to pay for services that the low paid cannot afford themselves. By contrast, collection of Rent encourages people to be as productive as possible in any given location, and fully equip themselves to create wealth. All of that wealth is available to pay labour after materials, and any charge for the use of equipment, and the Rent have been paid. I shall raise the question of the level of wages in chapter 12. There it will be seen that the wages are not only higher because they are not reduced by taxation, but also high because everyone has the choice of being an employee or, with equal opportunity, to make a good living for themselves. And enough people will in fact exercise that option to keep the level of wages high for all.

CHAPTER 7

Property Taxes Won't Do

Another form of taxation, and called Property taxes in the USA, are just that: taxes on property. You might think that these are a good idea since property is usually regarded as partly a structure and partly land, and therefore such taxes are collecting at least some Rent.

But in fact property taxes - rates or council tax in the UK - are a disaster.

You build yourself a house, or improve the one you already have, or build or improve a commercial building and what happens? The council wants to know all about it, and re-assesses your rates. So these property taxes are largely another tax on production. The result? Production is less likely to happen.

We can easily see from what we have studied already that the government should assess the Rent value of all the land, whether it is used or not. It is irrelevant to government whether the land is used well with good buildings, or not all, or only with small or bad, or unsuitable buildings.

That should be the government's position. If it is, then from the title holder's point of view, the more suitable the structure on the site, the better use can be made of the site, and there will be a tendency for all sites to be as appropriately developed as possible, and this will lead to changes as and when necessary.

The present system of property taxes has more bad consequences. Not only does it tax the building not the site, but also in most cases the council stops charging when a building is empty. And charges therefore no Rent on land forming the basis of either empty buildings or vacant plots of land. So what results? Large portfolios of land, or land banks, are held out of production, often for years, so that at some future date when it is more advantageous, the developer can make a larger profit.

Holding land out of production creates an artificial shortage and so makes the price of land expensive for the land that is on the market, and thus increases again the cost of housing, and industry's costs.

Not only that but the community is losing revenue that would under an Economic Rent system be collected from the unused sites.

And more consequences, too. Because the land is free to the title holder, its true worth - which is the annual Rent - is capitalized in a freehold price. In round figures we can assume a capitalized price is the value of holding that land for a generation, plus a bit, because a generation is as far as most people plan ahead, and plus a bit because the seller assumes that the land will be more valuable in future years.

If a typical house has a plot with a market price of £25,000, the annual Rent is likely to be in the region of 1/40th (40 years being a generation plus a bit); that is £625. There will be large variations from this average for larger and better sited properties, but in percentage terms there are few of them. There are of course houses that are smaller, or on poor sites, and on some of these the Rent will be very low or even nil. These capital sums created where none should exist create distortions in the market, and force most people into long term debt to finance high capital costs.

The list of bad consequences goes on. Having encouraged and allowed the value of sites to be capitalized, and bought and sold there has grown up a speculative market. The total market is of course enormous. Even without the speculative element the huge market creates an unnecessary burden on society as a whole. Such a market needs people to trade in it, and banking resources to finance it. The young need to put themselves in substantial debt to enter it, and the old find themselves pressurized by the young to surrender houses or other assets before they are ready. Governments don't like the elderly passing large amounts of capital to the young and so invent Inheritance Tax.

But, on top of that it is a speculative market, in the sense that holders of land, whether occupied or not continually speculate whether it will be more or less valuable in the future. Since the quantity of land available is fixed, and the tendency is for populations in desirable areas to increase, and for the wealth of that population to rise due to the general tendency of wealth creation to better the standard of living of the community, the almost certain outcome is that the value of a given site in real terms will rise over a period of time. There is a strong desire therefore for individuals and organizations large and small to hold on to land or land-based assets unless they have a good reason to sell it. In spite of some costs of holding land, such as maintenance of buildings on it, there is a presumption that the net cost is negative. This expected gain is an inducement to do nothing, even if the activity on the land is not very successful, and therefore the amount of land actually traded is less than it would otherwise be. This results in higher capital prices for the land that is on the market because by the law of supply and demand prices will rise if the supply is low.

As I have already noted if the Rent is collected by the government, the cost of holding under-used land is a real and recurring cost, and unused land will come onto the market as soon as it is unused or unprofitably used.

In undesirable areas, if there are perceived to be such, the land will historically have had a capital value. The holders will also do nothing hoping that the local economy will eventually improve. They will however cut their costs as much as possible, which always means that they neglect the building. This then falls into disrepair, whether used or unused, and the undesirable area becomes even more undesirable. Another vicious circle is spun, with consequences we can see all around if we travel to disadvantaged areas.

If the less favoured area had been properly treated by the government, Rents should fall, maybe even to zero, and the local enterprises would find their costs falling, so that the goods and services provided there would be cheaper than elsewhere, and would sell better than before. The local enterprises would begin to thrive again, and new businesses would be attracted to the area by the lower costs. Over a short period of time the total activity would increase at a fast rate, and new business would mean new people. Therefore a growing population, which in turn would lead to new demand for goods and services. Compare this scenario with the cumbersome and expensive Regional Development Agencies (see Chapter 16).

And then there are bribes, politely called grants, to UK and more often foreign companies, to set up industries in the regions drained of activity. Grants to persuade industry to go to areas not at the economic centre, and hence over-burdened by Rent, uncollected by government, but demanded (as large capital sums) by private individuals or corporations. At the same time the economic centres are under-charged in respect of Rent - the government does not collect any - and are consequently seen as attractive places to be, so widening the gap between what are perceived to be desirable and undesirable areas. A gap that government attempts to bridge by bribing industry - usually foreign industry - to set up plants or offices with money collected from you and me.

Not only are the less active areas not relieved of the Rent, in capital form, going to private individuals, but also the government, as we have seen makes it virtually impossible to trade in these depressed areas, because of the alternative revenue-raising taxes that successive governments have dreamt up. Instead of collecting Rent, government revenue all comes from taxes on labour and taxes on production, so depressing activity.

I have shown that 'rates' and, residentially, council tax are property taxes, and target not Rent but the improvements and buildings on a site. They are not collected at all on vacant sites, and sometimes not on vacant buildings. It can be seen that depressed areas become more depressed, and active areas are prone to land speculation making capital values higher that they would have been. Land is held out of use in both depressed and active areas, decreasing the supply coming onto the market and so increasing prices. The high capital values associated with active communities impose other burdens particularly the financing of long term debt that is another burden on both commerce and private people, particularly the young. These property taxes also discourage full use of a site, penalizing those who make improvements.

CHAPTER 8

Planning

It is quite surprising to recall that there were no planning laws in the UK until 1947. Obviously the need for planning rules and restrictions on where houses and new factories could be built had been building up for decades before that. The complete freedom to build anything anywhere during the industrial expansion of the nineteenth century had led to some horrendous despoliation of the countryside, and the urban environment as well.

While the planning regime could be much improved, it is unrealistic to imagine a land area with a high population density being without any planning laws. But it is worth remembering that the major civilizations of the world, including the rapid and relatively recent spread of European populations across America from East to West happened without any planning restrictions. And the results were not always bad. As we have already seen the medieval communities were contained inside their walled towns for defence against neighbouring or nomadic enemies. But in more peaceful times, where there was no pressure on land usage, the new arrival wanting to build a house would do so, if he had the money, in a way that is pleasing to himself. And since architecture is prone to fashion like other visual arts, the new houses will usually blend with the surrounding ones already there. In addition, a major factor was the locally available materials that also led to a harmonious blend of the new with the existing architecture.

Expanding communities with no shortage of land, and having a confidence that their industries will be both profitable and long lasting have tended also to build their places of work, whether factories or commercial buildings in a style as pleasing as their own dwellings. This was certainly true of most of Victorian architecture that remains today. It is of course relevant that later generations have preserved the more pleasing and replaced the eyesores.

But the real blots on the landscape have been the result of desperate people unable to find money to build well enough to please themselves. And where governments have been responsible for either housing or commercial buildings the perception in government departments has always been to build as much as possible for as little as possible. The results have been predictably ugly. Think of the pre-fabricated dwellings thrown up after the 1939-1945 war or the tower block of the 1960s. In early times desperate people coming to the cities to find work because there was none in the rural economy, created slums on the outskirts of larger towns and cities, and the same thing is happening in South America, South Africa, Eastern Europe, and Asia today.

Western Europe's governments and the planners in relevant departments will think that as a result of planning laws such problems have been eradicated from our towns. Yet all is not well in planning departments. The communities of the small towns and villages are vocal in their criticism of change. The decay of inner city areas is profoundly worrying, not only to those whose lives are blighted by having such a poor environment, but also to those inside and outside politics who seem unable to find a solution to the problem of regeneration of cities.

While the inner cities are in decay and under-utilised the countryside continues to be despoiled - forever - by the spreading suburbia. At the same time the economic health of the rural areas is being destroyed. Even areas designated 'green belts' are not safe. There is an unholy alliance between planners and developers, aided now by 'Environment Ministers' of New Labour. All for slightly different reasons fall victim to the ridiculous methodology of predicting what might be 'needed' and then falling over themselves to fulfil their own predictions. Critics see through their folly, but do not suggest what is the root cause of the problem. For the developer it is easy profits. They have bought land with hope-value. They paid the original owner a little more than agricultural value; waited a year or two or longer; then obtained planning permission, by fair means or foul, revaluing their green fields from some £4000 per acre or less to £500,000 or even £1m per acre, and rising all the time.

The planners are just doing a job! But don't they love being all-powerful and being courted by the developers. The politicians also are seeking the limelight and they too are lobbied by the mega-developers. They too are bankrupt of any sensible policy.

When we consider how things would be different if government collected the proper Rent in all situations we can see that the communities themselves will be not only able but also keen to be a part of the planning process. Urban regeneration would cease to be a problem, because the Rent in such areas would be so low that industry, commerce and individuals would be attracted to the area. The community would be regenerated, and the houses, shops, offices and other workplaces would be built, or redeveloped to suit the new community. The simple reason being that it would be more desirable to be there than elsewhere. The market would dictate that.

An equally important consequence flowing from the proper collection of Rent is the disappearance of any windfall gain from obtaining planning permission. Under the present system the sums involved are very significant for an individual gaining permission to build a house on what was agricultural or unused land. But the motivation behind the retail and commercial organizations to achieve a successful planning outcome is many times greater. Because the financial rewards are so large, the expenditure by, for example, a supermarket company wishing to build an out of town development, can be millions and can be protracted over a long period of time. It is of course not just that company spending millions. If the application is refused and the company appeals the appeal may involve a public enquiry. The cost of these, involving as it does, experts, lawyers, and civil servants, all handsomely remunerated for their time, also runs into millions. Who pays? We do: your income tax and mine goes to fund the whole jamboree.

If the government collects the proper Rent, and the market is allowed to set the value of that Rent, then there will be no financial gain to the new home owner, or the new supermarket owner when, and if, the community allows the development to go ahead. Why? Because Rent is the value the community itself creates for each piece of land. As agricultural land that supermarket site of a few acres commanded very little Rent. But if the supermarket uses the land, the owners will be able to make a profit after paying the market Rent. The Rent will be many, many times what it was as agricultural land because the potential to trade and earn profits as a supermarket are many times greater. Put another way the millions the company, or in the case of a single dwelling, the thousands the house-owner stands to make on receipt of planning permission is a reflection of the Rent - capitalized - that the market is dictating.

Under a revised system where all users of land pay the proper Rent annually, there is no advantage in obtaining planning apart from the obvious one that you or I may need a place to build a house. And the company who thinks it can make a profit by expanding its operation, will need space somewhere on which to expand.

Gone, now would be the pressure on the community, which as we have seen is expensive for it to defend. Gone is the temptation to bribery of officials inside the planning office. Gone is the ability of the company to finance an army of executives to obtain a planning permission at any cost, because the reward is now removed. Gone is a whole industry of planning consultants, specialist barristers, and planning department civil servants.

The planning process can now be quite simple, except that local democracy requires the community as whole to be interested.

Like all parts of the civil service there is a conflict between the perceived need of having well trained executives to run departments, and the desirability of having a frequently changing body of disinterested volunteers. However, in the case of planning the expertise required is not so specialized that most members of the public could not bend their minds to it. Compare for example the fact that society demands random selection of jurors. Again, local government is already peopled by volunteers. Planning is so important to most communities that we should expect communities to devise safeguards so that a permanent staff of experts does not become a cabal. At the very least the planning authority should be composed of persons who have to be elected, and who cannot serve for more than, say, three years; one third of their number being replaced each year. If they require the services of experts, those experts should also be unable to serve the same community for more than three years. Such forced movement was common in both banking and the armed services. It is a safeguard against anyone becoming too friendly, or indeed too influential.

In any case the experts should be, and be seen to be, merely advisers. The elected members must be prepared to do a lot of the actual work themselves, not simply rubberstamp the work of experts. The members need not be unpaid. Planning of development in communities is one function of government that must be taken seriously.

It also needs to be locally based. Diktat from central government should play no part, except in so far as government must legislate that Rent be collected properly. This function should in any case be performed by a separate department from the planning department, but both locally.

Local planning departments' medium term plans should be submitted to central government but for the purposes of coordination only. The centre should not be able to overrule the local democracy. It does mean that local people need to be vigilant in questioning and calling to account their elected members of the planning department.

NIMBY was, and still is, an acronym for 'not in my back yard'. Those living in a good rural spot, or a quiet part of town want to preserve this. If in power they find every reason in the book to put the nasty bits of any community in someone else's back yard. So they might, but no one on that committee will be there for long. It would be incumbent on all members to come up with reasonable solutions to planning needs. In a chapter (19) on agriculture I explain how the market itself will dictate which 'green' land if any is to be released for building. The same will be true of redevelopment of 'brown' sites in towns.

There is now and should be still an appeal procedure. But not an appeal to central government. Appeals should be chaired by equals from other communities. More important than that the two sides of any argument should be formulated with compromise in mind. As explained in more detail in a chapter on justice, civil disputes - and planning would be one such whether a title holder against the planning committee, or two factions of the committee itself - should be settled by an outside arbitrator choosing one of the two - or more - proposals in its entirety. Yes, that means no compromise by the arbitrator. Thus will all protagonists aim for the most sensible compromise solution themselves, because if they put forward a reasonable compromise it will be chosen - in its entirety - instead of the less sensible competing ones.

When Rent is collected the resultant change in people's perception towards the benefits of owning property and obtaining permission for an advantageous use of a site, is so earth-shatteringly different that it is at least partially adopted in some cities in parts of the world. Full collection of Rent is essential for this change in the way society is ordered. While the benefits are obvious in the context of planning the effects elsewhere in the economic inter-relationships are more, much more important. The watchword is freedom - freedom for each of us to labour to our full potential and to be free to be a human spirit. A bold claim, but no exaggeration, as I will elucidate in subsequent chapters.

CHAPTER 9

Congestion

Anyone who has to travel to London from the suburbs or from further afield every day knows congestion is one of the questions that society needs to address. The trains are full, often late or cancelled altogether. The roads are at best full of slow moving traffic; at worst bad weather or an accident causes a complete standstill. Parking is expensive and difficult to find. The underground is dirty and unreliable.

The time wasted in daily commuting is a drain on human energy. The financial cost if that can be calculated is astronomical

The talk from politicians is of doing something about it, but nothing ever gets done. And from the current thinking the wrong things will be done if they do finally act.

We have seen that building more capacity on the roads simply encourages more vehicles. There is talk of better train services that compete successfully with the road service. To do this the trains would have to be cheaper, faster, as flexible, and available 24 hours a day. Even then the person used to the comfort of his own space and his own in-car entertainment will need persuasion. If the train does get that good, it too will suffer the same problem as new roads. New capacity will be swamped by new demand.

The trains can appear to be more competitive if road travel is made not just frustrating but very expensive. "Road pricing", meaning charging for the use per mile, or by entry to a city centre, is on the agenda. But as has been pointed out such changes would have to go hand in hand with increased capacity on the trains.

Congestion of course is made acute by the very size of metropolitan areas such as Greater London. Indeed the whole of the South East of England is now seen as over-populated. But it is the way it is populated that is the problem. Manhattan Island in New York has a much higher density of living and working space than any part of London. So it is not density as such that creates the problem.

Now, were Rent to be charged on all land in England it would be clearly an advantage to exploit the highest Rent land in the City of London by building skyscraper blocks for both living and offices, as in New York. This makes the best use of the land. The Rents may be high but the use made of the available land is then exceptionally good in terms of the area of working or living space per acre of ground. With proper planning, open spaces can and should be accommodated between the modern buildings, and the heritage of the past in the shape of churches and museums, opera houses and other listed buildings would mean a beautiful and congenial place to live and work. Such a city should be composed of both types of accommodation; working and living, and the places of work should not be peopled by commuters living miles from the cities. Again this is a function of planning. There is a rule regarding new office development submitted to planning at the present time that insists that enough parking spaces are provided for the capacity of the workers. This rule is a nonsense if the objective is to discourage parking in inner cities. Instead the principle of matching office space to living accommodation in the city as whole should be applied in a similar way. The Rent due from living space and an equivalent area of office space will differ. That is to be expected just as in the countryside the Rent on agricultural land will be much less than that on living space. But that is exactly the function of planning, to plan to allow appropriate types of land use in an area. The market will then set the Rent for each type of land use.

If this policy coupled with proper Rent collection is applied, the City of London - and other commercial parts of London, and other major cities, will become beautiful, efficient, and self-contained. Something akin to this has happened in the Docklands area of London.

The collection of Rent would ensure it happens because no owner can afford to pay a Rent on an under-utilized plot of land.

It may seem that the sprawl of suburbia is doomed to remain so and congestion and commuter problems would remain. But not so. Once the centre is self-sufficient because working and living space is matched, secondary centres of activity all over Greater London would develop, by the same combination of collecting Rent, and planning matching living space to commercial space. It has been said that London is a collection of villages, and indeed in some parts that is still very evident. The challenge will be to develop these secondary centres with more commercial space to match the living accommodation around them. It will take time, of course, but the sooner started the better. In an ideal situation no one will need to commute far. Many will walk to work. It will be easier to buy and sell houses to re-locate nearer a changed job because inflated prices for London houses and flats will be a thing of the past.

That is not to say that no travel would be required between regions of the metropolis. For social, pleasure and commercial reasons there will always be movement. But it will not be on top of millions of commuters making a journey daily simply to move from a dormitory suburb to a place of employment.

In the rest of the country the same forces will be at work. The Rents will be lower in other cities and towns. Businesses and people will gradually move to these areas, and as they do so previously unused parts of the country will thrive. As they thrive, so they will become more attractive. As a result of these natural forces and of Rent being collected, coupled with the whole community having a say in the planning requirements of their own community, there will be a whole range of thriving, and if we are wise, congenial places to live and work. Some small villages, some towns on the scale of market towns, some major cities; all will thrive and depressed areas will rejuvenate themselves.

The countryside will be preserved. Not in aspic, nor as merely a theme park for city dwellers, but as necessary for agriculture, and forestry, rural industry, housing for the working population, and yes some holiday accommodation and other get-way-from-it-all amenities for visitors. The market will decide what is the best and worst places for these farming and forestry industries, and in so far as new housing is needed it will be sensible to locate it where the market indicates agriculture and forestry are not viable. Because cities and towns will be better used, the derelict 'brown' sites in towns will be replaced with attractive new structures for living and working. It is unlikely therefore that there will be pressure on 'greenfield' sites. Indeed with a steady or falling population, and with much better use of urban space there should be no need at all for building on productive agricultural land, nor on land of outstanding natural beauty.

Certainly there will be no pressure in the South East and other areas where congestion followed from the non-collection of high Rents, because the tendency will be to populate, in sensible proportions, the area of the country with low Rents. Congestion in and around the Great Wen, a problem even in William Cobbett's day, will be a thing of the past.

Transport between places will be required, but with un-congested living, and minimal or no commuter traffic the provision of road and rail links becomes a matter of developing a service industry like any other. The industry requires space, and capital, and the operators of it should be private enterprises like any other service industry. The capital is no problem. When a service is required, finance is always forthcoming. The space will command a Rent like any other space. The operators of the enterprises will recover the operating costs from a paying public like any other service. To some extent the operators may have a quasi-monopoly position, but the rail will compete with the road, and both with airlines on longer journeys.

The roads unfortunately have a history of being free at the point of use. This will have to change, and the operators will have to find ways of making it change, because they have to recover the cost of building and maintaining the roads. Those costs include the Rent for the space. These Rents will be high in city areas. The possibilities of charging for access and use are numerous, and it will follow the course of road charging elsewhere, namely tolls on motorways; and also methods still in their development stages, such as in-car meters triggered by external devices. I am sure that in the computer age appropriate methods can be quickly and efficiently introduced if put in private hands.

In so far as there are monopoly concerns, the operators should be franchised for a period of years, and have to re-tender at each renewal date. It is important that enough operators and potential operators are in the market to make this a genuine tendering process. It works reasonably well in television broadcasting, and has begun to be used successfully in the area of local train operators. And, with transport monopoly is held in check because there is competition anyway between different methods of making the same journey.

To conclude, collection of Rent will have the effect of making efficient use of urban land. It will also redistribute the population evenly throughout the villages, towns and cities of the nation, all of which will be rejuvenated. Congestion that resulted from pressure on the South East will diminish and cease to be a problem.

Planning must play a crucial part. And planning should be in the control of the local communities. It will be in the interests of each community to match by planning decisions the volume of living space to working space. Commuting as we see it now will disappear. Transport will be provided by private companies who will recover the full cost of the service from the users. If necessary, monopoly will be kept in check by regularly offering numerous different franchises.

CHAPTER 10

Capital

The word capital is derived from caput, the Latin for head, and refers to the head (or number, as in the phrase head count) of cattle that formed the wealth of nomadic or semi-nomadic people. Cattle formed the basis of existence for such people providing daily provisions such as milk and cheese, less often meat when the calves or older animals were killed, and a sufficient supply of leather, and hides for shoes and clothing, as well as other items such as horns for drinking vessels and musical instruments. The bones were also used for small tools. The number of cattle a man owned determined his status or wealth in the eyes of his neighbours, and cattle were traded and given as dowries. Clearly, they were not mere tokens of wealth. As I have briefly noted they were the very basis of support for a man and his family, particularly for nomadic peoples. When people settled in one place and began to cultivate the land there became available other means of support, such as growing vegetables and cereals. Nevertheless cattle continued to be an important part of the food and material supply of rural people right into the twentieth century.

The point about cattle was that they were the means of supplying the needs of a man. They had to be husbanded. They were not lying around for the taking, and the goods derived from them mentioned above, did not just drop off them ready for use. Work had to be expended on them. To rear calves; to milk the cows; to kill the animal for meat, and skins; to tan the hide for leather, all required both skill and considerable human effort.

In modern economies capital takes many other forms, because we make and keep available for use all manner of tools with which to perform task to create goods, which we can then consume. Some of the tools will provide services rather than goods. What is not capital, though people often refer to it as such, is money in the bank or share certificates of a company. These at worst are mere bits of paper, because as we will see it is possible for money to become worthless. At best they are tokens acting as claims on wealth held by someone else.

It is important to distinguish between true capital and other things that people have become used to calling capital because we have seen that in a pure economic sense there can only be four legitimate primary claims on wealth at the point of production. Rent on the site being used; labour who receive wages or salaries; raw materials - the cost of the inputs; and interest on the capital employed in the production of the goods or services.

Interest is the name given to the return on capital. Unfortunately it is also used as a term for the return you or I receive for putting our money in a bank or building society. That is in fact a distortion of a pure economic model. Interest from a bank may be regarded as the return to a large number of small depositors who jointly through the bank provide funds for another person to buy capital goods for his industry. As a primary claim on production the interest on that capital is then paid to the holder of the capital in the first instance, but since he has borrowed money from the bank to buy the capital goods, the bank receives some or maybe all of that interest, and gives a proportion of it to the depositors. That would be fine in a pure system. But money is a much more complex subject, and the link between funds deposited in a bank and capital goods in industry is by no means direct. It is in fact a tenuous link. When money is examined in more depth (Chapter 24) we shall see some of the problems that have been created.

Another item that people regard as capital is the land they own. To put it more clearly the land to which they have a title. The reward in the name of interest on money that does not represent capital goods being productively used is certainly a confusion. But the greater harm is undoubtedly done by society regarding their title to land as capital.

As we have seen, there should be no return to the holder of a title to land, unless of course he uses the land productively in which case he will create wealth, and the wealth, or the claims on that wealth will be divided so that Rent is paid, labour is paid, materials are paid for, and interest is paid on the capital goods used. We should note here that profit is not mentioned. Profit is commonly used to describe the surplus after all the costs of production have been paid. But in truth it is a relatively meaningless term because all the wealth created can be paid out to the four elements that were involved in the production. If the entrepreneur chooses not draw all that is due to him from the enterprise when the other three categories have been paid, he is not paying some of the labour that was due as wages. The "profit" therefore is deferred wages. And may be deferred for the good reason that more capital and more materials need to be financed next year. In an unfettered economy where there are no taxes on production, it is unnecessary to declare what is a profit. We shall see also (in chapter 12) that what is due to labour as wages may differ very markedly from the way we regard wages and salaries in today's Western economies.

Very likely, today, in many enterprises, the only 'profit' being made is the Rent that government has neglected to collect.

While discussing what is capital we can see other dangers. If there is confusion in the meaning of this term, then there is confusion in the meaning of capitalism. The term is referred to with venom by the communist and 'left'-orientated political parties. This results from the fact that wages are forced to a low level (see again chapter 12). The providers of capital are the owners of the enterprise, the government does not collect any Rent, and the owners particularly if competition in that industry is poor collect probably a part of what is due to labour, and a large Rent, which is not due to them, on top of a legitimate interest due to capital. The first fault is a result of there not being a free market for labour - or more accurately not a market in labour that is free. The second fault is obviously society's fault. The interest, the third element is rightly due to them. It will usually if not always be at a level that reflects the degree of risk in providing that capital. If these distinctions were clear, capitalism would be seen for what it is and the venom direct only at what is wrong. Otherwise it appears that capital is getting an unfair reward. This has given capitalism a bad name. But capitalism should mean that owners judge and determine what capital is required in the economy. The state should not make that judgement, as in communist countries, and as was proposed by the now defunct Clause 4 of the Labour party. Then the market will decide what is the proper return to capital, so long as the community - the government - collects the Rent fairly and efficiently from all enterprises.

In chapter 12 I will explain why the market will also determine what is a fair level of wages, i.e. the proper return for human effort.

The use of capital – tools that help people produce wealth more efficiently that they could do so by hand – has often been identified as one of the causes of unemployment. Nothing could be further from the truth in a free society. The Luddites, in 1811 and for the next decade or so took into their own hands the destruction of new equipment in the textile industry, which appeared to threaten their jobs as hand weavers. The term Luddite has thereafter been attached to all who denounce the introduction of new methods of labour-saving by mechanization, and nowadays by computer technology. I can have some sympathy for the displaced workers, whether the first Luddites or today's workers suddenly on the scrap heap. But yet again we have to blame the non-collection of Rent for these happenings.

It is quite clear that men and women in free association with each other and in free competition with each other will use capital only if it enables wealth to be created more economically than without it. In which case the return to wage-earners will rise. Less of them will be employed than before in a given situation perhaps but being free to associate with others and free to compete the displaced, too, can enter the same or a similar market place, or can become involved in a quite new industry. (In the chapter 12 it can be seen why this does not happen in the industrialized societies today.) This displacement of people by new technologies and their re-employment elsewhere may seem unrealistic to those who have suddenly been made redundant by closure of long established industries, the mines and the large car-plants, which can leave whole towns, even counties, under- or un-employed. Yet given time even those communities recover. And that is in today's flawed economy. Many of the problems of industries like the mines and the megalithic car-plants would not have arisen at all if Rent collection had kept a more discerning work force in being. That is not to say that large-scale units of production in those and other industries are inappropriate. But wage rates, ownership, interest rates, and currencies, free trade and taxation all are factors bearing on the viability of industry small and large. Each of these topics is examined in subsequent chapters.

CHAPTER 11

Property

"Whereas it has long been known and declared that the poor have no right to the property of the rich, I wish it to be known and declared that the rich have no right to the property of the poor"

- *John Ruskin, 1819-1900*

    Things, by and large physical things, that a person owns, might best be the description of what people think of when the word property is used. In recent times there is talk of intellectual property. Such properties are obviously less tangible. But the concept of copyright has been around for a long time indicating the ownership of original work. Even such works are normally manifest in some physical form.

    It is a fundamental human characteristic to be able to acquire and hold property. A man or woman needs clothes. They and their family need a roof over their head. They need to be able to accumulate and store food for future use, so that they can eat in seasons when food is not readily available. All these things are property of a person, or sometimes jointly of a few people.

    It is enshrined in the laws of most societies that men and women have a fundamental right to hold these things, to call them exclusively their own, and to be able to claim a legal title to them.

    Societies that have not allowed such ownership have come and gone from time to time and have found that something fundamental in the human psyche is being denied. Communes on a small scale, or communism on a national scale as promulgated in the former Soviet bloc have eventually found that the concept of holding communally all the things that are needed for existence of humans living in a civilised society just does not work.

There is pride in ownership. People take care of what is their own. They will treasure what they have paid for, but squander what they have been allocated by some nameless authority. Even communal assets in a modern Western city are given little respect, often being the objects of vandalism.

It is clear from the previous chapter that human effort needs capital to perform tasks efficiently. These may be simple or complex tools used by an artisan or a sole trader. More often the ownership is held by a larger entity. But in both cases it is clear who has title to the physical assets, and equally important who has the right to use them.

In the same way we all have and wish to have assets that are in the nature of consumer goods. They are not capital in the sense that they are tools for the creation of wealth. They are the end result of the production process and are held by the owner for the benefit they bestow on him or her.

Many of these pieces of property could not exist without at the same time having a space in which to hold them. All physical things take up some space, and apart from clothes on one's person, and a few tools or possessions one might carry, all valued possessions that any of us have will be taking up space. This will nearly always be space that we can call our own – a house, a garden, a flat or a shed.

These larger pieces of property are not able to exist without the land they are on. The house has its foundations in the land, and in any case is so large as to be for most practical considerations too large to move. Similarly the garden is little else but land, though it may have had a very large amount of human effort applied to it. The flat is even less moveable than the house, and the shed while moveable occasionally always needs some land on which to place it and make it of any use.

Everything that has been mentioned so far in this chapter is legitimate property that can be held by individuals or corporate bodies. But the beginnings of the confusion about property can be seen when talking about houses and larger structures. The legal system tends not to make the distinction between the house, flat, factory, or even garden and the land on which it is situated. In common parlance we all tend to go further and think in terms of buildings and the associated land when we use the word property. We are inclined to use other words when we mean mere possessions that are portable: goods and chattels, belongings, personal effects, gear – and a whole host of other slang words.

The legal convention is to talk of 'personal property' for those things that are moveable and 'real property' for those land-based assets that are the structures I have already referred to.

Regrettably the legal profession confuses things further by including within the term 'real property', all land holdings, whether or not they have any property attached to them. This is not to deny that nearly all occupied and used land has had some human effort applied to it. But real property in the legal sense might include an island or mountainous moorland that is untouched by any human interference.

Clear thinking is now needed. The right to hold property is a fundamental of the human condition, just as much and more so than a bird needs materials to build a nest.

It cannot be denied that all these possessions need space. But that space, that land under our house, under our garden, under our factory or office is not capable, morally, of being owned.

The distinction is based on what is the result of human effort and what is not. The land was not. The garden would not be a garden without human effort. The overall result of that effort may be a thing of beauty and much valued by the owner. The land was always there and cannot, morally, be bought and owned as property. It can, of course, be held by one person for his or her use and quiet enjoyment. In the same way we can and do hold the house, flat or factory.

Such concepts of exclusive use and quiet enjoyment are already part of English law where leases are granted. These can take many forms. But in all cases the fundamental flaw is not that the tenant or leaseholder should be granted rights of occupation and quiet enjoyment – that is obviously essential. The fundamental wrong is that the payment for the use of the land is not assessed regularly and brought up to date with that which would apply in a free market. And, even more wrong is that the payment goes not to the community but to a freeholder who believes that he has absolute title to the land.

We have already seen what distortions and hideous consequences flow from the failure to make the distinction between what is property that men and women can legitimately – morally – hold and what is common to all. What belongs to all of us, collectively, if held by one person for that one person, has to be paid for annually by way of a Rent that accords with the free market Rent.

In the following chapters I explore what other distortions follow from the community's fundamental failure to see what is essentially personal property, and by contrast what is not and can never, morally, be so. At first sight these distortions may appear to have little if anything to do with space, or land, or the physical environment. But the error of believing property can include land is so deep rooted and has been part of the affairs of men and communities for so long that a whole miasma of wrongs have been woven into our commercial and personal lives. Each error has compounded the difficulty. Each palliative measure leads to more absurdities.

CHAPTER 12

Why are You Paid So Little?
(and Why is He, or She, Paid So Much?)

Why work? The answer is complex, and involves necessity, creativity, ambition, duty, love, ability, kudos, and for each individual other motives that are specific to him or her. But probably in all of us there is a certain laziness too. At least in so far as we prefer to have some leisure time, and none of us want to be needlessly "made" to work.

The self-employed will wish to balance their working time and their non-working time to their best advantage. That is to balance their desire for results of their labour, and the time to enjoy the results.

For the employee of organizations large and small the choice is more limited. In a particular job, the rules may be set rigidly. Certainly a high percentage of the working population is employed in such conditions even if they are top management. It is generally recognized that the unionization of labour from the nineteenth century onwards was a result of harsh employment conditions. So harsh as to be forcing labourers and their families to be living at or below the poverty level. Later legislation caught up with what had been achieved by labour unions, and in today's labour market we have not only protection against the use of child labour and other abuses of the nineteenth century, but also a whole raft of conditions-at-work legislation, from health and safety, to length of the working week and minimum pay.

Gradually unions gained more and more concessions, and by the 1970s in the UK they had wrested from parliament and enshrined in the legal system a privileged status that did not apply to any other trade organization.

Since the Thatcher revolution of the 1980s broke that stranglehold on industry, the conventional wisdom is that the demands of labour have been held in check by the uncertainty of employment, which has resulted from the relative ease, compared with the 1960s and 1970s, with which employees can hire and fire, and the recessionary conditions in the early 1990s. These feelings of insecurity for employees have been exacerbated by the faster changes in technology making some jobs, and indeed some whole industries, redundant in a short space of time. Government too has stopped featherbedding industries that ran at losses while in state control. Most have now been privatised and will fail if the product or service is not required by the market.

In addition to unionisation and legislation wage rates have been underpinned by the welfare state paying unemployment benefit. This has led to undesirable consequences. Not least the difficulty of getting people back into work. This is partly psychological, and partly structural - the so-called poverty trap.

Now a New Labour administration has seen fit to have a minimum wage level. Both unemployment benefit and a minimum wage are seen by socialist parties as essential to the avoidance of poverty wages that were a feature of Victorian Britain.

Cast your mind back to London of the mid nineteenth century; the time of Dickens' novels. The Enclosure Acts of the previous century had made employment in rural Britain uncertain, and the Agricultural revolution followed by the Industrial Revolution had made employment more likely in the towns and cities. But there was no free market for labour. Although activity was greatly enhanced by new technologies, the total number of employers was numerically small, though often they were large employers of labour. The displaced persons were numerous. There was no choice for those people except to take whatever employers in that location were offering as wages. There might be only one large employer in some areas. Mobility of labour was poor, because transport was primitive, and time-consuming, and knowledge of alternative employment was difficult to obtain.

Virtually all land was enclosed so subsistence living as peasants was no longer an option. There was some common land, but this could only be grazed in common with others who had sheep or cattle. Tilling the common land was not allowed, and in any case the crop would not have been secure from other users or their livestock.

Labour therefore was only able to obtain from employers the least that any man, woman or child was prepared to work for. That meant that the general level of wages for all was at or around the level that the most desperate was prepared to accept. So, the wage levels tended to be very low: to the point where employees were offered only what might keep them from starvation, or even less. And if that was true for the single and fit young man, the wage was impossibly low for a man supporting a wife and children. And the old and infirm could be expected to command a lower wage than the young and the fit. Such pressures led to the use of child labour, now outlawed in the UK, but still prevalent in third world countries.

Conditions without all today's technology would have been harsh in a simple economy anyway. In theory new inventions should have made the rewards to labour higher. To take a nineteenth century example, if cloth could be produced twice or ten times as fast using new looms with the same or less people manning it, the wages of those people should have been higher. There are numerous parallel examples in the twentieth century: robot mechanization in car manufacture; computerization in accounts offices; the internet in marketing; the list could be endless. But in fact neither wages nor working hours have improved over the decades of the nineteenth and twentieth centuries except in so far as unionisation and legislation have improved the lot of the working classes.

Some commentators on conditions in the developed economies of the Western world at the end of the twentieth century may disagree with this analysis. Let us be clear what is actually happening. The population as a whole is composed primarily of those who have no or very little access to land. What little space the majority do occupy is the site their house or flat is built on. And we have seen how even this has to be paid for dearly over half a lifetime by way of mortgage payments. But the places of work are in the hands of an extremely few people or corporations. The majority have therefore to seek work from those people or companies in much the same ways as previous generations offered themselves for work at the hiring fairs. The employer is all-powerful.

In a simpler situation than we find today one can imagine a single person in 'ownership' of a whole area. Consider for example the mill-owner in Lancashire, or the mine-owner in Cornwall. Only by his consent could other people be there, and only by his consent could they work. However, one person against a multitude of disadvantaged people would not be popular, and in such a society we would expect the owner to feel vulnerable. He could be murdered or incarcerated by the overwhelming numbers of those he was exploiting. So the tendency will be to favour some of the population and appoint them to managerial positions to control the workforce comprised of the common people. Whole hierarchies of managers and officials will tend to become the norm.

If we expand this example so that not one but two, or ten or two hundred owners control a much larger area, those owners will tend to confer together and find ways of reinforcing their dominant position by making themselves less vulnerable. Not just from brute force, and not just by favouring the few as their henchmen, but also by passing laws. It will be the owners who will be the legislators. They have the need of laws, and they have the time and freedom to be the legislators. The laws they pass will be ones that favour their interests.

But let us not lose sight of the fact that the powerful owners of land control all the managerial and professional classes even today. Whether the land was for the important primary industries of agriculture, mining, and iron and steel foundries dominant in earlier decades, or is land for today's industries of pharmaceuticals, financial services, leisure, retailing, and light industry, the picture is essentially the same. The armies of white collar workers, the managers, the directors, the accountants, the legal advisers, the research scientists, the salesmen: they are all jostling for position in the hierarchy to serve the ultimate owners. Some of them will be so high in the hierarchy that they begin to feel free, begin to feel that they are the bosses. There are indeed 'fat cat' managers and directors who have almost a sinecure position at the top of some privatised utility company, powerful City institution, or globalised manufacturer or trader. By a certain amount of 'unionisation' of their own they can temporarily protect themselves in their privileged roles. But their position is not secure. They are ultimately there by the grace of the owners. This may be a weak mass of shareholders who are badly organized and unable to talk with one voice.

If the particular public company has really weak ownership, then the executives may well usurp the profits of the owners and pocket the benefit as million pound plus salaries for themselves. But that will not last long if the company is thereby weakened and made a target for take-over by a better-run competitor. However, this is not really the point. It makes no difference whether the true owners control the situation, and set the terms for the hierarchy of employees employed there or whether the top management do the job in their place. The conditions for the employees are no better or worse in either case.

What we see then in today's job market is a struggle for supremacy in trying to become the best servant of the ownership. It is quite a circus. The well-educated young of today are obsessed by what is on their CV. They are constantly aiming to improve their qualifications in a particular profession. They cultivate contacts. This on the face of it gives them a route to the best things in life. But stress is a word on everyone's lips. There are failures. Not all will get to the top of their chosen tree. You may argue that the career progression of the young will lead to them becoming owners themselves - by management buy outs or by successful managers setting up new companies themselves. It happens, but again only the few make it and those few make it against the odds because the conditions set are weighted against the working man and in favour of ownership. Not ownership of capital, but 'ownership' of nature's resources. Ownership of the truly-defined capital will also protect the enterprise and enhance its exploitation of the 'ownership' of Rent, but ownership of capital by itself could not do that.

The complex economies of the West today may seem far removed from the land based industries of yesteryear. Yet all industries however sophisticated are still land based. Even the cyberspace industries are only tools to allow other industries to happen better - or at least differently!

The London based elite operating in or for the financial sector may think the space they occupy of little or no consequence, but they not only occupy some of the most sought after - and therefore high Rent - space in the world, they also are there only to service industries elsewhere. Or to service the owners - shareholders - of industries elsewhere.

London and such centres in other countries are only a part, the top of the pyramid, of the whole inter-related economy. The majority of the workforce is employed in smaller cities and towns and it is these people who can fairly ask 'why I am I paid so little?' and ' why is he, or she, paid so much?'

The average wage earner is underpaid and overtaxed. As a result most family units will have two wage earners. This will have other consequences. But another pertinent question will be 'after all the technological advances and even after struggle by unions and legislators, who have claimed to improve the lot of the workforce, why after all this are two people working full time long hours for wages that will seem meagre after paying the everyday bills for a small family?'

Women entering the workforce should not be discouraged. But it should not be essential for a family to survive.

I can conclude this chapter with a re-statement of how free labour - that is when people have access to land for the payment of a small annual Rent - will earn for themselves (with collaborators and employees of their own) good wages. The level of those wages will be enhanced by a well-equipped workplace, so clever use of capital goods will be prevalent. The range of human desires for goods, services, leisure pursuits, games, frivolities, sport, travel, arts, learning, is endless. There is therefore always scope for enterprising people to employ themselves and others. And, there will always be some who would happily be employed by others. Their wages will tend towards the level of wages that they could earn for themselves. We see therefore a free market for labour.

In this chapter I have explained why this is not so when government fails to collect Rent, and why many people then work very long hours for a meagre reward, and with high stress levels. Others seek to climb the hierarchical pyramid and some succeed in persuading the owners to pay hugely inflated salaries to them as their henchmen. But here again the stress levels are high.

All individuals are different. Some have extraordinary talents. We can think of well known musicians, and artists, and we all know personally people less famous who we regard as particularly gifted in some way. All are different, but we claim as a society, quite rightly, that all should have an equal opportunity.

Yet we have seen that the opportunity for all to have access to the gifts of nature is denied. Air and water would, a few decades ago, be cited as examples of things essential to life to which all of us had free access. Nowadays that is not so certain. The air quality in urban, and often rural areas is poor, and water is becoming an expensive commodity. Even so all of us can breathe, and can get water, though this can be difficult, and in dire circumstances one might have to rely on rain.

The other necessities of life: food, clothing and shelter have to be bought in the market - market in its widest sense - and that market is not a free market. The socialist would have said the means of production were concentrated in the hands of a relatively few people. And this was the problem. But it is not the tools of production (capital), but the land that everybody needs some of - however small an amount - to go about his business and to live on, that needs to be equally available to all.

I hope it is clear from earlier chapters that if the Rent due to society is collected, the opportunity for all of us to occupy a little bit is greatly improved. Even if the bulk of the land is still occupied by relatively few. In fact in terms of productive potential all the land will be equal once the differential Rents have been collected. And since all of us have the potential to do something (the disabled, the old and the very young are discussed later) we can all make a living.

With the experience of earlier generations in your mind, and the present conditions where it is nigh on impossible to get credit from a bank for some of us, it may be hard to see how some people could get started. But we have to see all the changes that would take place, once the market for land is a free market. Furthermore it must not be thought that everyone is suddenly going to become a one-man enterprise. Many, perhaps most people will still be employed by some organization, or another sole trader. The point is that there is a free interface, on the one hand, of people choosing to work for themselves, building up enterprises which will grow to employ others, and on the other hand, being employed for good wages and salaries by others. The wages will be good, because if they are not it will be in the interest of the employee to go and work for someone who pays better, or go and work for himself. That does not sound very different from the job market you know today. Nor should it be. It is only the crucial difference that the opportunity to use land is equal for all, and at marginal locations it is very cheap or actually free. As we have observed elsewhere it is very probable that many parts of even a populated country such as Britain would have many areas commanding no Rent at all. And equally important after the proper collection of Rent all locations are equally productive.

On top of this there will now be no disincentives to work in the shape of Income Tax, National Insurance, and all the other taxes which discourage production, and so it will be much easier for new enterprises which are based on sound ideas, and sound financially, to flourish and grow to employ, on good wages, well trained and suitable staff.

It has been gradually become recognized during the last few years of the twentieth century, that economies are more healthy, grow faster, are more resistant to recessions, and generally more flexible if taxation is low. If therefore all taxes on production are removed, the ideal will have been reached.

It is necessary to examine a little closer the opportunity of a good existence on free or cheaply used marginally located land to really understand how the general level of wages in the community will rise. With no government imposts of any kind, except Rent and on marginally located land that will be virtually or actually zero, the entrepreneurs in society will be keen and able to make a very good living for themselves. It is tempting when we think in terms of land, particularly marginal land, to imagine a poor peasant planting a few vegetables and scratching a living. Nothing could be further from the truth. There will of course be the agricultural and horticultural enterprises. But the range of opportunities for other talented people is endless. Literally, anything any of us is employed to do now which is involved in producing goods or services will attract the talented to start up a rival enterprise. There will be exceptions that are clearly government services such as the armed services but this does not alter the basic argument. By far the greater part of a healthy economy soundly based on competitive private industry will be in a state of flux where new competition is being set up, and mature businesses amalgamated, bought out, or closed down if inefficient. At every turn there is opportunity for many people now employees.

By no means all new start up businesses will be away from established centres, and not all will be small in terms of people employed. Some retail and service industries need the central locations to gain trade. But when they consider whether to start up in a central location or a marginal one, or somewhere in between, they will have to cost out the advantages of each. They will do so taking in to account the Rent that will be high in the central locations, and low or nil on the marginal sites. If they can run the business with the lower overhead of little or no Rent, then to be competitive with others in the same industry they will choose the less central site. It can be seen therefore that they will be a tendency for enterprises whether manufacturing or services to spread out, and be universally spread throughout the country, so creating jobs in the outlying regions, and so employing people on good wages. Good wages because those new employees will have the same choices as everyone else. They can use their skills to set up on their own, or with others, and make as much for themselves as their employer was paying them. This possibility, which is always a real possibility, underpins the level of wages generally, and ensures that the level of wages is always high. The general level of wages will in fact be what an averagely skilled person with current technology can make for himself on a site where the Rent is being paid. And since the Rent if properly collected makes all sites equally beneficial to work, the level of wages throughout the geography of the community will be roughly equal.

It follows there will be no unemployment black spots where a downward spiral of no work, no purchasing power, therefore no services, therefore less employment leads, and has led for decades, to depressed areas. Areas that not only need dole payments to those living there, but massive regional aid that is never enough. And because the market is not allowed to work properly the aided projects often fail. Even when kept going the area is seen as one of low employment, and wages are low because employers only need to offer little and still get applicants.

It can be seen now – when Rent is collected – that wages are not only high - as high as any average person can earn on his own or in cooperation with others - but also average wages will be equally high wherever their employment is. This makes for a very powerful economy. Men and women are now not reduced to taking the least that men and women on the poverty line are likely to accept. Or in today's welfare state a wage in line with the dole payment they could get if unemployed, or the New Labour 'Minimum Wage', but are actually getting the most that can be earned in that type of work on any site anywhere in the community. And what is more keeping all the proceeds of their labour. No taxes will take away what they earn, because the government has raised all the revenue it needs to finance the things it needs to do from Rent collection.

I will examine in Chapter 14 what the labour will do with its earnings and why. I also look at what government will need to do with Rent it has collected (Chapter 15).

Advocates of Rent collection are few and far. Where it has been adopted, it is usually a half-hearted movement addressing itself primarily to the property aspects, which I have covered in earlier chapters. But the real power of Rent collection revolves round the relationship between Rent and wages. This is so important and affects the whole of the philosophy of the economic system and all its ramifications that it needs to be stated very clearly. For this reason it is necessary to state here at the risk of irksome repetition, the relationship between Rent and wages, under the possible conditions that might prevail in any territory.

For those that find numerical data helpful this text is supplemented by Appendix 1, but I hope that the concept is clear anyway from what has already been said and from what follows.

The simple economy where land is plentiful:

>Here, in an undeveloped territory such as the pioneers of the American west enjoyed, we would expect wages to be high because the entrepreneurs and workers will settle the land and apply capital as efficiently as they know how to produce a range of goods and services which they will trade with each other. The best sites will yield a total return to the

users somewhat higher than the less good sites, but since land is plentiful, each person can make a good living for himself and his family. As the economy develops the living to be made, or wages, on the periphery is still good, but the earnings to be made on the sites in the centres of population are substantially more. While the Rent on the periphery is nil, and all the return to the occupier is wages, the Rent at the centre whether collected or not is high, and always increasing as the community develops. The return to these occupiers is therefore partly wages and partly Rent (unless the community decides to collect it).

The developed economy where all productive land is in occupation:

There being no surplus of land on which new labourers can work, the situation has changed for ever. While the previous scenario was typified by the vastness of the New World in the eighteenth and early nineteenth centuries, this new scenario is typical of virtually all parts of the world today. This is because even though some areas of the world are under-used, they are 'occupied' in the sense that an owner somewhere is stopping any newcomer from taking up occupation and making a living for himself. This is of huge significance in a community that now has new entrants to the workforce being born or arriving as immigrants all the time. For what can they do? They can only offer themselves to employers who already are there. These employers may or may not want to employ more people. It is clear that the more people looking for jobs and the less jobs there are available the more the tendency will be for wages to fall. Even low wages may not tempt the employers to take on more labour. As wages fall, the profits from the existing enterprises will rise because wages will be seen by them as a cost of employment. As their profits rise, there will be a tendency for employers to be content will less activity, and less risk of employing others, particularly where employment legislation makes the risks of employing people onerous. They will also concurrently with the growth of the community see the prices of the assets they hold as land and buildings increase. This will tend to encourage the employers to do less employing and more trading in assets. The risks will seem less. As has been seen in graphic reality, in our own communities in the nineteenth century, and in 'under-developed' countries in our own time, wages can fall to very low levels indeed. In truth, they will fall to the level that will just avoid mass starvation. That is unless unionisation or legislation intercedes. Both will be expensive to achieve. At the same time, the level of production in the community will be the same or roughly the same. The increasing numbers of people will be a positive factor, even if the tendency of employees to employ less as noted above is a negative one. The wealth created has therefore remained high, but the wage level has dropped. The Rent appropriated by the employers has therefore become greatly enhanced. It will be evident that the wage level will drop not just at the periphery of the community, but throughout it. As we observe in practice, when work is scarce, the unemployed tend to move to the centres of activity - the big cities - in the hope of obtaining a minute fraction of the action going on there, or if not, to at least be on the streets begging from the affluent who pass by. The very presence of the unemployed depresses the wages of the whole community. There will be many in the community with payslips higher than the average, because as I explained earlier much of the Rent uncollected by the community will go to build a hierarchy of managers to support 'owners' appropriating the Rent. The government will have no revenue from Rents so will invent many methods of raising taxes which will depress productive activity and distort markets.

The developed economy where all land is used, and where the user pays an annual Rent to the community:

The situation could not be more different from the previous scenario. Whether the population is growing or not the newcomer to the community can always find a place to make a living. All he has to do is to pay the going Rent. All others are also paying the annual Rent, which will be high in the centres of activity and low or nil at the periphery or marginal sites. It is the 'wage' that can be earned by one or more people, well equipped with capital, on any of these sites that will dictate the general level of wages. And because it is the Rent that varies from place to place the wage level will tend to be the same throughout the community. There will still be variation due to different skills, of course. Some of these skills will be managerial, but gone will be the distorted hierarchical pyramids, which now exist because 'owners' use uncollected Rent to pay inflated sums to managers to protect their interests. The unemployed will not flock to the cities for work, or simply to beg, because now they can work anywhere for roughly the same wages. If anything they will tend to migrate to the lower Rent areas to set themselves up as cheaply as possible. Or if they are choosing to be employed by others they will have no particular need to go to the densest centres of population because the general wage level is uniform throughout the community. Furthermore their living costs will be less where Rents on residential accommodation are low so providing another reason to avoid the established centres. The owners of enterprises will seek to maximise their profits by using the available site as efficiently as possible, using the best techniques, the latest capital equipment and employing the best people they can find to collaborate with. Clearly this is a recipe for a thriving economy. Even in such a thriving community wages will not either rise or fall because they will always tend to the norm dictated by what the average man can earn for himself - well equipped and with or without the collaboration of others. There will be a perpetual interface between the self-employed and the wage-earner keeping the level of wages for both in balance. Of course, there will be other rewards and risks in being self-employed, or joint owner with others to own a business. So the total return to the self-employed, or owners, may over time be greater. These rewards are the return on capital he will have saved and built up in the business, and the goodwill in the business. But the wage level for both employed and self-employed will always tend to the same norm so long as all have access to sites, and all sites are equally productive. What keeps sites available to all is the collection of all the Rent. This not only ensures that unused sites are available in the market place, but also and equally important, that the sites at the centre of activity are no more advantageous to occupy. The revenue that the community receives from Rent collection obviates the need to impose taxes. Taxes whether on income or profits, or indirect taxes on sales or added value are all taxes on production and depress the level of wages. None of these is needed so industry and commercial activity is encouraged to flourish.

CHAPTER 13

Interest Rates

In the last chapter I looked closely at the level of wages in an economy as it is now, and as it should be when Rent is collected by the government. In this chapter I raise the questions about interest rates, and we will see that this mechanism as used today has a relationship with wages and the level of unemployment. I go on to examine how things would be different if Rent were collected.

What determines the level of interest rates?

Up until 1997 in the UK it was the government, and nowadays it is the Monetary Policy Committee (MPC) of the Bank of England. That is the simple answer, only, of course.

That committee or whoever makes the decision in any economy is constrained by external factors. If they make the wrong decision there will be howls of anguish from one interested party or another.

In recent years the strength of the pound sterling has given the MPC the problem that interest rates seem too high for the exporters of goods and services from the UK, because a high interest rate tends to produce a high exchange rate. Exporters therefore find their prices in the world markets too high. Or, put another way the costs of labour in the UK market - when converted into US dollars or Euros or Yen - make it difficult to make a profit at prices which are acceptable in the world markets. At the same time a high exchange rate makes imports seem cheap to home-market importers, and therefore tends to encourage consumption of imported goods by UK consumers. This makes similar goods made in the UK less competitively priced than the imports.

On the other hand a lower interest rate which other things being equal will produce a lower exchange rate encourages manufacturers, retailers and consumers to increase their activity, and leads to an increase in the money supply, and hence to inflation. Since the MPC has the statutory duty to target a rate of low inflation, and inflation is generally thought to be a bad thing, there is a fine balancing act to be performed. Why the money supply increases and why inflation has been a bugbear of the twentieth century is explained in Chapter 24.

Another consequence of low interest rates is a heightened affordability of property. So house prices increase. Again there is a poor return on cash held in bank accounts; so alternative investments such as share prices are sought instead with a consequent rise in share prices. In general there is then asset inflation, even when inflation measured by the Retail Price Index (RPI) is low.

In summary it can be simply stated that high rates lead to a decline in activity. Low rates lead to inflation of all kinds, but particularly asset price inflation.

How much of this quandary is the result of failing to grasp the fundamental relationship between labour, and natural resources?

Since the power of the trade unions was broken in the 1980s wage inflation has been held in check by encouraging competition for all goods and services in the home market, and by maintaining what is euphemistically called the "natural rate of unemployment". And since inflation - which is a bad thing - is only measured by the RPI, the MPC can get away with keeping the RPI inflation low, and ignoring asset inflation. They can also keep both the workforce and the entrepreneurs on tenterhooks by frequent changes in the interest rate level, so that no one complacently demands higher wages that in uncertain times might mean no job, or loss of your job to one of the unemployed. And entrepreneurs are not sure whether to invest rapidly to take account of good times, because the uncertainty means that no one is sure the bad times are not around the corner.

In other words there is a deliberate policy to keep unemployment up to "the natural level" so that wage inflation is kept in check. This in turn keeps the RPI down, and if the economy is balanced to be just growing at a "reasonable" rate then it doesn't matter, under the terms of reference set for the MPC, if asset prices rise. This is not nowadays thought to hurt anyone unless it is excessive and might lead to a bursting bubble that then causes shock waves that depress activity. If this does happen the authorities have tended to drop interest rates smartly to build confidence again. Since politicians think only in the short timescale, they seem to be able to ignore the long term effects that asset inflation will have.

When the MPC and politicians talk of the "natural level of unemployment" what we are seeing is the average working person without much capital, usually meaning the lower paid and the young, being targeted to be kept on their toes to perform, yet to have no increased reward for their labour which has helped to make the economy as a whole perform better. Those who gain are the holders of assets. This may seem fair in the case of the entrepreneur who has risked much to make his enterprise perform, and who as a result sees the profits rise, and the share price rise. No such merit attaches to the holder of property. He may do little, usually nothing, to increase the value of the property, and yet in the benign scenario outlined above his assets will gradually but quite rapidly increase in value. Nor too has the speculator in shares done much to deserve sudden and large rises in share prices.

Now, as we have already observed this injustice in society is perpetuated by the failure of governments to collect the Rent that is due to the community as a whole. If property could not increase in value in this way, asset prices would not be the beneficiaries of the policy adopted by the MPC (under the guidance of the government).

More importantly, the labour market would not have to be artificially kept at wages which do not reward it for the increase in production because a concomitant effect of collecting Rent is that labour is free to make a choice between working for someone else - whether that someone is a large corporation or a one man band - and working for himself, with or without partners, under conditions which are no less favourable than are available to all other men and women.

In this scenario what will determine the level of interest rates?

Given sound money, which is of course a big if, but it is one I assumed in the first scenario, interest rates would be set by the demand for banking facilities from entrepreneurs. Potentially there will be more of them so demand might be strong. But their demand for credit will be balanced by their assessment of risk involved in the enterprise being undertaken.

Let us suppose for a moment that demand is really strong because so many people and collections of people as entrepreneurs need bank finance. Then the banks will make banking decisions and agree or not with their clients that the profits in future years will repay the bank borrowing, or will not. If they agree, the credit advanced by the banks will increase, and depending on exactly what the rules of banking are, the money supply will increase accordingly. If the money supply is fairly "elastic" the interest rates will not be forced higher because all the new money will be repaid to the banks by the profits of the businesses in future years. If it is less elastic, because it is tied to some arbitrary standard, such as was the pound when currencies were linked to the gold standard then in times of high demand there will be a high price for money; interest rates will rise. But we are in a world where few if any people recommend a return to such an artificial standard, so we can assume that the bankers know their job, and will create new credit to satisfy the demand for money. Interest rates will therefore remain at a natural level. This really is a natural level: natural in the sense that it will depend on the performance of the sovereign state's performance as a whole.

This can best be seen by supposing that the conditions suddenly change in, say, some mythical sovereign state. Imagine an island that was devoted to an economy of growing bananas. A new condition is introduced so that banana growing is suddenly twice as profitable. Maybe as a result of new strains of banana, a new island-wide irrigation scheme, or simply because the demand for bananas from the markets the economy supplies has pushed the price up dramatically. In any of these cases there will be a tendency for labour - free labour - to produce lots of bananas. The profits from doing so will be seen to be good for all new production schemes. The labour, wearing hats as entrepreneurs will go to their banks wanting to borrow to finance the capital to start new production. The banks will say yes, seeing the profits to be made. Even with enlightened banking there will be a tendency for the rate of borrowing to rise. Now this is a sovereign state, and the rise in interest rates for the "bana" - the unit of currency in that state - will encourage the interest rate to rise from 1 bana to £1 (say) to 1 bana to £1.1. Also the interest rate being higher than in other countries depositors of money - other banks for example - will tend to lend money to the island's banks. Their motive will be to get a high rate of interest and they having learnt of the change in that island's economy will expect the nation to continue to prosper and the exchange rate not to go back to 1 bana to £1.

The effect of this inward flow of money is to tend to push the interest rate down again a little. Looking at the same picture from the banana growing peoples' point of view they may think they could borrow more cheaply in pounds. They too will have noticed the change in the exchange rate and will predict that the new profitability in their economy will keep the exchange rate as high or even higher, so some of them will decide to borrow in pounds and expect to gain a small advantage in lower borrowing costs. Depending how many decide this, there will be that much less demand for borrowing in banas from the local banks, and again the local interest rate will fall slightly. This in turn will tend to push the exchange rate down a bit.

It is clear from this simple example that there will be a natural interest rate that will depend on the activity in different sovereign states. In a more complex economy the activity will depend not only on natural improvements - or deteriorations - but also on the dead weight of the government if it sets wrong conditions of, for example, taxation or tariffs, or employing a large percentage of a nation's work force in non-productive governmental bureaucracy.

What cannot happen in the island nation is the money borrowed from banks ending up in the finance of inflated asset prices. Because property will still have the same value after the boom as it had before. In so far as the community is more prosperous as a result of the people exploiting the new opportunity, then there may be a heightened demand for housing and commercial property - and of course land to grow bananas. But this will increase the Rent to be collected by the government, so the properties will change hands in the open market at the same price: in the case of houses, the cost of the relevant house's construction.

If this sovereign nation has a central bank, it will be the lender of last resort to the other banks, and it will need to set an interest rate at which it is prepared to lend to the commercial banks. But there is no need for this to be a fixed rate. It can vary on a daily basis.

Since property based assets will not vary in price whatever the state of the economy if Rents are adjusted frequently, the only beneficiaries of the new wealth created in the nation will be the people creating the wealth. And since there is a free interchange between people being employed labour and those people employing themselves, and probably others: there is a balance between the benefits of being employed or employing, then, there will be a natural increase in the level of wages hand in hand with the level of the value of enterprises, i.e. share prices. Neither of these will lead to a dangerous inflationary spiral, because the new levels of wages are properly underpinned by the new level of prosperity. Of course, since the wage level has risen, there will be a knock on effect in employing labour in other occupations, and the price of for example bread may rise.

Therefore one would expect the RPI to rise. This may or not happen, and may happen briefly only, if at all. But even if it should happen this would be a relatively benign change: wages will generally have risen so the population will not mind paying the new higher prices. But there will also be other changes that will always tend to bring the prices of everyday goods down again. These goods make up the RPI, and the RPI will therefore not change at the fast rate that wages changed when the banana boom happened. These changes are such that if in any enterprise wages increase as a proportion of other costs, then more effort will be put into supplying the same goods more cheaply using better techniques. More sophisticated methods using better machinery and less labour will produce the same goods, say bread again, so the price of bread will be less dependent on wages. All these subtle changes will tend to keep the RPI steady or falling as in general goods are produced more efficiently.

What about the retired? Their incomes will depend on their savings, which are being used by the generation behind them, and they have just experienced those savings in the shape of share prices rising in value. So the retired will find no problem with a change that is one underpinned by real changes in wealth, even if there are fluctuations in the RPI. And anyway, as I have explained the RPI will tend to fall over the longer timescale, because new methods of production make it possible to produce goods more cheaply.

In this chapter I have demonstrated how in a free economy in balance with other nations and having sovereignty over its own affairs the interest rate will set itself. The exchange rate will set itself. Prices of everyday goods may change, but only in harmony with the real wealth-creating potential of the nation We have to conclude therefore that the quandary that governments have got themselves into when they perceive there to be contrary forces needing both lower and high interest rates is only self-inflicted. It is yet another consequence of failing to collect Rent and therefore failing to allow its people to be economically free.

I have shown also the need for a freely floating exchange rate. Furthermore there is a need for nations to be of a sufficient size to properly reflect what is happening to the wealth creating peoples making up that nation. From this point of view the smaller the better because the more homogeneous the population and its conditions the more the currency will reflect the true state of the nation. However it has to be accepted that a sovereign government needs to be competent and if it is not to be a burden on its people, the size of the nation should be sufficiently large to support a slim government machine.

A nation of free people will, I believe, elect only slim and efficient governments, and although the governing classes of nations large and not so large like to think there is an advantage in being large, and having great influence in the world, there is in truth little benefit except militarily. The rest is vanity. And only a military advantage if the other nations of the world are hostile. Small nations in this case need to make treaties and to combine with others to have effective world police forces such as the UN. They should resist at all costs the amalgamation of sovereignty. Because sovereignty ceases to exist when it is pooled with disparate peoples. And democracy ceases to be effective if an elected government cannot set conditions for its own people, and ceases if in turn the people cannot reject that government for setting the wrong conditions.

The consideration of interest rates has led to some far reaching conclusions. If we as a nation ignore these we do so at our peril, and we will always have far greater problems than that of merely setting the level of interest rates.

The following chapters examine some of the questions most affected. But first I want to concentrate on how well paid labour can be self-sufficient.

CHAPTER 14

What Do the Well-Paid Spend their Money on?

If a survey of the spending habits of the middle classes is made, it will be seen that there are patterns of behaviour that repeat themselves as each generation proceeds through life.

The newly married couple with a first child put their money where their attention is. This is a new and quite different experience for them. They have real responsibilities now. All the paraphernalia for a baby takes high priority. A new house, or an extension to an existing small one may soon follow. A change of car to accommodate the extra luggage every time the family moves, or even just getting the baby to the shops, may seem a real necessity.

As the new parents become established, and perhaps now have two children, choice of schools will be uppermost in their minds. Funding for those will also be planned. This will take the form of help from an older generation, or more probably regular saving schemes, to provide for large school fee payments every year from ages 8 to 18, or even longer.

At the same time the family will continue its everyday existence of eating, entertaining with friends, holidaying, and of course working to pay for all these things.

This young family is replicated throughout the middle classes, which make up the largest proportion of the entire population. So with the older families, they will have three perhaps four or more children by now, and be established in a bigger, probably more pleasant house, in a country village perhaps with room to have a good garden, a swimming pool, tennis court, paddocks for ponies, or some of these things depending on their hobbies and how much they have been able to afford. Some will prefer to stay in cities to be nearer work, perhaps, or just from choice of life style, and will spend their time and money on cinema, theatre, and museums to enlighten growing children. Travel to have a break from city life; one, two or more holidays probably abroad, will be a feature - almost a necessity.

Both the younger and older families will have less conspicuous expenditure. Life insurance in case of sudden death of the bread-winner. Medical and accident insurance in case of expensive health needs or prolonged absence from work. Insurance for the house, their possessions and car. Probably also, as they can afford it, some investments in quoted shares, or let property which will act as savings for later in life to supplement what will probably be a job-related pension scheme.

It all adds up to a substantial annual outgoing, but it is regarded as quite normal for much of Middle England. There will be great variations on the pattern depending on inclination, earnings, and whether the couple is blessed with a stable marriage or not. Or some other disaster may make life difficult.

The fact is that millions of ordinary people are content to live a middle class existence. They provide for their own families all the necessities and comforts of everyday life. Each has its own idea of luxuries, hobbies, sports or cultural activities.

The very wealthy in fact probably don't live in essence a very different life. They may have more leisure time if they are semi-retired, but their actual expenditure, although in money terms it might be 10 or 100 times greater, is still involved with eating, housing, educating children, travel, holidays, etc. They almost certainly waste much of their time and their money doing too much of all those things.

The mature parents might now be more adventurous in their travels, be pursuing new heights of career, service to the community either local or national, have the joy and expense of the rights of passage which feature in all families, such as 21st birthdays, and later, weddings. They will probably try and find more time for leisure pursuits, and may even have a complete change of career or lifestyle. They will have their worries too: health, retirement plans, personal relationships, to name but a few. Meanwhile their grown-up children will be concentrating on tertiary education, qualifications, job hunting, travelling the world on a gap year, making friends, falling in and out of love, spending more than they earn - and learning the lessons. Soon they will settle for a job, a partner, a permanent place to live, and will themselves become that new young family.

Having planned for retirement, the later years of a family's life will be spent comfortably doing what most interests the individuals using savings and pension income to provide for the expenditure, health permitting. Some 'retired' people will have part time work for the interest it gives them rather than for the monetary rewards.

There is no perfect life. Each will be very different in detail, but in common they have responsibility for themselves, and their families in so far as the necessities of life are concerned. There is a natural desire to take on these functions. A dignity that is denied to those who cannot, and who have to rely on others to provide for them. What our mothers and fathers may have thought of as new fangled luxuries may be commonplace now. Times change of course, but in the context of each age each individual and each family should be able to provide for themselves.

What is surprising in the context of what most people are capable of is that there is a whole class of people unused to providing more than the food and clothing for themselves. They live in a state house which is allocated to them, send their children to a state school, which they don't choose themselves, rely on state medical services, which are unable to provide help when needed, rely on a state pension which will in time prove to be inadequate even for the basic necessities of life. Many in this position are unemployed and so are living on a state determined hand-out instead of a wage. This is poverty. This is loss of dignity.

For far too many it is the norm, yet it should be very rare. And if it were rare and applied to only a few people incapable of looking after themselves because of some early-life misfortune, even those few would be made reasonably comfortable by a caring community.

The state of affairs, when 99% of the population, not just the affluent middle class, is self sufficient, and comfortably so, we have come to think of as an impossible dream. In truth, had the industrialized world developed in a system where all men and women were free to work, we would be looking at today's aberrations as an impossibly awful nightmare.

It is perfectly obvious that we live in an abundant world, and more particularly we in Western countries live in an abundant society. I have outlined how free labour will be well-paid labour. And in free markets all the normal desires and needs of the typical family will be provided by the market. Why not? If there is a shortage of medical care, more hospitals will be built by entrepreneurs only too willing and able to exploit the opportunity. More doctors and nurses will be trained, again by private institutions offering training services. Shortages will call for higher wage rates so encouraging more to train. So also with teachers and schooling. In both cases the capital for new buildings and new equipment will be forthcoming from the entrepreneurs and the financial markets, because the demand for new and better services is being seen, assessed, and so provided.

I have deliberately chosen to mention the two services that both major political parties in England seem to shrink from making private. But the fact is all needs of the individuals in the community and all normal desires will be catered for. It only needs for some people to see the need or want in society for that need or want to be satisfied. But it needs all people to be free to service that want for the market to operate. And for all people to be free to earn good wages to pay market prices.

What stops the individuals in today's society from entering the market to make the supply happen is low wages, expensive access to natural resources, high taxation on effort and the results of effort, poor banking practice, congestion in some parts and decay in other parts of the nation, law and order break down, and other symptoms flowing from these faults. These are all weighty questions in the UK today and in most other Western nations. It is my intention to look more closely at all of these and allied matters and see how the fundamental error of failing to collect Rent has contributed to all these problems.

It is perhaps necessary when talking of abundance to refute Malthus' theory of population and poverty. Put simply Malthus (1766-1834) observed populations growing to the point where there was insufficient food to feed everybody and poverty was rife and acute. Such behaviour of plants and animals is described in Chapter 3 where it is noted that populations of a species with abundant food are checked by limits on that food and increases in predators. But the human population has no real predators so famine is the only check. Malthus observed both rapid colonization of North America and the widespread poverty in England and thought that human populations were therefore like those of simpler species.

With hindsight we can see that it is not so. Affluent human societies do not lead to an explosion of population. Particularly where free competition is checking the endeavours of individuals. Malthus' observations that North America rapidly became populated was in reality explained by a combination of immigration and the existing population having great opportunity to expand geographically and numerically without competition. The young could, early in their lives, leave their childhood communities and flourish in new communities. And there was no Rent to pay.

As societies are more constrained and have to find opportunities within an already populated community their endeavours are more cautious. A degree of affluence affects the majority of adults. The Rent payable will increase if people stay put in their comfortable society. They will, and do, think twice before adding to a family. Even in our modern affluent societies the well-off choose to limit their family size largely because they have learnt from experience that the time and effort required in bringing up children is a serious commitment, and many couples have other goals in life.

Where we still see unchecked population growth is in primitive and poor communities. They have little chance of other goals. Their education is poor and birth control methods are often unsatisfactory. Their history has taught them that many children may help provide their own support in old age; and they may need to produce two or more children to see one live to maturity.

Poverty in 'developed' countries may lead to population growth amongst the poor because of other factors: boredom; welfare making the financial cost of a child minimal; lack of other goals in life; incentives, though unintended, that provide housing more quickly for those with children.

It is likely Malthus himself would have come to a different conclusion writing today. What is clear is that there is abundance in today's world and populations, net of immigration and emigration, are steady or falling where the affluent can choose.

CHAPTER 15

What Does Government Do?   What Should it Do?

There are relatively few fundamental functions of government, although as we shall see there are a number of topics that are worth considering that might be called subsidiary functions of the main ones.

In a community that is to thrive, it should almost be self evident that government should not try and do too much. We probably all have had some experience in non-governmental organizations, whether at work or in local activities or charities. Most of us have therefore seen how bureaucracy stifles the real purpose of the organization. Nations and governments are no different, just larger and more vulnerable to stifling bureaucracy.

Once government tries to interfere in the things that are really the functions of enterprise, it quickly finds that it is fire-fighting to stop undesirable consequences of its interference. From what has already been said, it is clearly a prime duty of the government to collect Rent from all in the community. This is not an enormous task, and is very much easier than collecting other kinds of revenue. How this is done is outlined in Chapter 38.

Another fundamental function of a community is to protect its people and property from outsiders with war-like intentions. So armed services are essential.

A subsidiary function is to protect its own citizens from abuse of each other. In other words to have a police force. And a criminal system to handle wrong-doers.

There will be some in the community who are unable to look after themselves. The true causes of this are however very few. Permanent disability from birth, orphaned children, and that is about all. Other accidents of life are easily insurable. And as we have seen well paid labour is able to look after itself.

A few individuals will slip through the net and become destitute through failing to take reasonable precautions to safeguard themselves, or parents failing to provide for their children. However, in a well-educated and well paid work force there will be relatively few. The chance of this happening can be limited by incentives. The people in the community should ask themselves how best this can be done, and the costs of doing so, weighed up against the costs of providing emergency care for those who slip through the safety net.

Society certainly should not decide to make universal benefits for all, as has happened with promises of state pensions. These have turned out to be wholly inadequate and to meet people's expectations would be extremely expensive. Clearly insurance should play a major part for the unexpected. Any emergency care should be at a low level, and temporary if at all possible.

Democracy itself should be a fundamental necessity of any community, and therefore government has a duty to protect it, and nurture it.

To summarise, I have listed four fundamental functions of government that are essential: Revenue raising from Rent, and in no other way; defence of persons and property from inside and outside the territory; to look after those who really absolutely cannot look after themselves; and to ensure democracy is allowed to thrive.

That is it. These things can be looked at it more depth. But first I can enumerate some of the things that governments should not do.

They should not attempt to manage enterprises, or control the market in any commodity or manufactured goods.

They should not raise taxes with a view to robbing the rich to pay the poor. Indeed they should not raise any revenue apart from Rent, and the least well paid will not need support if they are allowed to operate in a free economy where wages are high.

Government should not penalise the rich. Many of today's wealthy, and the wealthy of earlier centuries became rich by collecting the Rent due to the community for themselves. But many others through talent and no doubt some good fortune are wealthy in their own right. That wealth will not last forever, and although it can be passed to other family members who may seem then to be rewarded for no great effort of their own, the wealth will be dissipated in a generation or two at the most, and the number of exceptionally wealthy entrepreneurs will be few. Even they will often feel the desire to dissipate their wealth in their own lifetime by making charitable gifts, being sponsors of the arts, or other types of benefactor. They will not be tempted to store their wealth in freehold property, because freeholds will become titles to possess but not to own, with an annual obligation to pay Rent. Therefore they have no value over and above the improvements on the site.

The few super wealthy who are rightfully so from their own good fortune are not a problem, and the probability is that the community will have a very large middle class, and only a small wealthy class because the opportunities to make fabulous wealth from genuinely new ideas come only infrequently. Bill Gates of Microsoft, is an example from the late twentieth century, but the pre-eminence of Microsoft in the long run is doubtful, and if it were to prove so, it would be the duty of government to break a monopoly as the oil barons of the USA were forced to split their holdings in the late nineteenth and early twentieth centuries.

The point is that most monopolies in the past have been based on territorial monopoly, and the exceptional benefit therefore accrued to the owners as uncollected Rent. The oil in the USA was an example. Had the government collected the Rent from oil fields and refineries the oil companies would not have become fabulously wealthy, and the breaking of the monopoly would not have been necessary.

Other monopolies have been based on clever inventions, protected by patents. But patent law gives the patent only a limited life, and thereafter competition will bring profits down to reasonable levels. That reasonable level will be a profit which gives a realistic return on the capital employed in the enterprise, which the individual, individuals, or more likely a wide circle of shareholders will deem acceptable when compared with the other opportunities open to them.

I will return to monopolies and the utilities and similar enterprises in Chapter 29. But to continue the list of areas that government should avoid, consider education. It was quite right and proper that the government made a law that all children between 5 and 16 be formally educated at school. It was pure dogma that then said the state must set up schools so that that should happen, and it was entrenched bigotry that tried to control what type of schools people should be allowed to send their children to.

Even with all the high taxation, and the high cost of educating children in elite private schools the middle classes have chosen to use the private system rather than an often inadequate state system. If the middle class were even wider, as it would be in a free economy, there would be ample private schools set up to educate the whole of the nation's children.

Nor should government seek to control or influence the morals of the community. Educated people will find their own moral standards. The churches will have some influence, the press and media generally will probably have more in today's secular society, but the government need not and should not pontificate on the standards of family life, the sexual activity of the young or the drug culture that has exercised the minds of many. It is doubtful that government can usefully interfere in any case, and taxes and import duties will create their own problems especially when applied to undesirable activities with a view to making them less practised. For what actually happens is that the higher prices caused by the taxes and tariffs, and also of course by prohibition, encourage smuggling by the suppliers and crime by the users who need to find more money to feed their habits.

Governments should not try to provide medical services. As we saw in the last chapter this service will be provided naturally in a free society. As we have seen from the experience of the last 50 years, state funded medicine has always been too little, and if paid out of taxation has a depressing effect on the wages of the whole population.

There are other lesser, but important functions of government.

If democracy is to survive and thrive, there must be a free press. Fortunately, it is one area of national life that has been allowed to be free. Not perfectly so perhaps, but the fundamental point has been recognized.

Clearly elections must be held regularly. Again, in the UK today this happens whatever the merits of the system used. Local government is too weak, but its functions should be better defined, and like central government kept to a minimum. As I have commented already the planning function must be local, very active and kept free from entrenched interests.

The legislature, the executive and the judiciary should be separate and independent of each other.

Governments must keep diplomatic contact with other nations, and must co-operate with other governments in the setting up of supra-national bodies such as the UN. If Rent is important in one nation it is important in all nations, and free trade can only properly be allowed if Rent is collected in all nations. Therefore there needs to be international agreement on such conditions, in the same way as the World Trade Organization (WTO) seeks (but conspicuously fails) to set a level playing field in today's flawed trading arenas. I will examine the difficulties of free trade in Chapter 18. There will always be opposition to free trade unless Rent is collected throughout the trading nations.

There are certain services within a nation that can only be provided by one or perhaps several entities serving the whole nation. The utilities such as water, gas and electricity are such services. So also are broadcasting, and, if we must have one, the national lottery. It is the duty of government to avoid monopolies. The services should be provided by entrepreneurial companies but should be subject to franchise agreements in much the same way as independent television is today.

There has grown up a culture of dependency over the last 50 years, and well before that the experience of deprivation for the masses. This will not change overnight. But surely it will change, just as in the Western economies, the percentage of people regarding themselves as middle class has been rising strongly with rising standards of living in recent decades.

Voucher systems for those paying Rent, which in practice will be most householders is worth considering. The vouchers could be of several kinds for different needs. Perhaps medical, pension, and accident insurance. But even voucher systems can be open to abuse, and the cost of funding the whole population's insurance needs even to a modest degree would greatly decrease the cash payments that could otherwise be made to all from Rent collected. However, it is a legitimate question to be explored. At least vouchers cannot be used for anything else, and there is therefore a probability that everyone in the community will have a basic level of cover. They have no reason not to use the voucher, except inertia, which is more and more unlikely as the community gets better educated and better paid, and becomes accustomed to being independent. It is all too easy to extrapolate our experience of a workforce crushed to accept low wages, and used to being told what it can have by way of medical benefits, education, pension, even housing. Because this is so politicians might be tempted to use vouchers as a half way stage between the nanny state and full independence. The danger is that vouchers will be seen to be a permanent feature. Not only that, they will be seen to be of too low value to cover peoples' expectations. I have to conclude that the temptation to use vouchers should be resisted.

CHAPTER 16

Taxation: what is it trying to do?

Muddled thinking typifies the whole of taxation policy. And the more legislation that is passed the worse it gets. Government revenue is clearly needed, otherwise governments cannot function. As I have commented already, the functions of government should be few and clearly defined. If society allows government to become overblown and take on roles to which it is not suited we have the dual problem of interference and the cost of financing that inappropriate action.

In the first days of income tax, a government short of funds to wage war against the French taxed the 'incomes' of the wealthy. These incomes were not wages as we think of income today, but net proceeds of operating large landed estates. Before that time government did not interfere greatly, and government expenditure was low, financed by the Crown under the feudal system in earlier centuries, and to a small extent by excise duties on traded goods entering the country. In earlier centuries one powerful nation invaded and crushed its neighbour, and physically removed treasure.

The income tax to finance the Napoleonic wars was intended to be temporary and was in the nature of a whip-round to the great and the good of the time who could easily be identified. Had greater thought been given to how each of those contributed the Chancellor of the Exchequer of the time might have requested payment in proportion to the value of the landed estates. In fact crudely he did do so because the 'income' of the estates was probably proportionate to the value of each estate. It can be argued then that the mistake in re-inventing income tax later (in 1842) was to equate income with the wages of ordinary people.

Nowadays we have direct and indirect taxation. The direct taxes include income tax, capital gains tax, corporation tax, and inheritance tax. The indirect taxes are so called because they are only paid when the individual takes some voluntary action. The largest revenue is raised from Value Added Tax, and some countries have simpler Sales taxes. Then there are stamp duties on sales of assets and, insurance tax, betting levies, car tax and fuel tax.

It is amusing if not wholly accurate to add together all these impositions and see how little of the money a person earns can actually be spent. Starting with the wages or salary earned, say £1000, it can be seen that all but a small fraction is eroded. For a start there is income tax at 40% and national insurance of nearly 22% (soon to be nearly 24%), leaving only 38%. VAT at 17.5% will take about 15% of the remainder leaving just over 32% and insurance taxes and other occasional taxes might reduce this further, say, to 30%. If you want your children to benefit inheritance tax will take 40%, leaving 18% or £180 from the original £1000.

While this set of calculations may not be mathematically or even logically correct, it does show how at every turn the tax system bites. And we are led to believe that the UK is relatively lightly taxed!

The purpose of these taxes is primarily to raise revenue but governments have and still do try and be clever by redistributing the wealth created by industry. However, it is clear that they have spectacularly failed to remove poverty. Another aim is to re-set the counters to zero for each generation. In other words, no individual should be super-wealthy as a result of inheriting a large fortune from a parent or a grandparent. So first Death Duties, then Capital Transfer Tax, and nowadays Inheritance Tax were created. The perceived need for these taxes on wealth moving from one generation to another was and is as a response to inflated asset prices. As we have seen assets are inflated in value very largely by the failure to collect Rent. The assets affected are obviously land based property, but also the claims on whole industries, represented by the share certificates of individual companies. That this is so is due to the pressure on wages when Rent is not collected, and the consequent increased rewards to the owners of industry.

There are other over inflated prices of assets. For example the very high sums paid for well known works of art. But all such markets in rare goods can be seen to be inflated as a consequence of the combination of rarity of the goods in question, and great wealth being in the hands of individuals or organizations.

Inheritance Tax and its forerunners have frequently been referred to as voluntary taxes, not because we can choose whether or not to pay them, but because we can choose to find ways of avoiding them. So much for the government's objective of stopping un-earned wealth from moving to a new generation. Clearly the problem could be minimized, if not eliminated, if Rent collection kept wages high and asset values low.

Redistribution

Rob the rich to pay the poor. Tax the rich to provide for the poor. Do our left leaning legislators think like his because of some admiration for Robin Hood in the twelfth century? Probably more influential were the conditions in the nineteenth century, and the intellectual efforts of the Fabians. They too saw the plight of the poor and instead of overthrowing the government by revolution chose to delay their efforts and gradually change society by encouraging the state to become a latter day Robin Hood. (They took their name from Fabius Cunctator the Roman general noted for his delaying tactics.) Until recent times their thinking has dominated the last hundred years or so, and it has been said in the twentieth century "we are all socialists now". Putting the Fabian policies into practice has at least demonstrated the folly of doing so. It is unfortunate that with all the intellectual capacity that they had between them the Fabians failed to address the root causes of poverty and instead chose to tax and spend: three words that came to symbolise the Labour party for nearly a century.

Taxation of a different kind, tariffs and excise duties, have also played their part in creating the muddle through treating symptoms rather than causes. The revenue raised is of course welcome to the government machine. Using ports as collection points, tariffs were an easy way to raise revenue, but another reason for tariffs is to protect markets from 'unfair' competition from abroad. I examine the whole question of trade, tariffs and free trade in Chapter 18.

There are then three main reasons why governments raise taxes. They think they need revenue from taxes; they think they can be redistributive by taking excess from the rich and improving the lot of the poor; and they think, or have been lobbied to think, that some industries need protection from foreign competition. Each of these premises is fallacious. And because they are fallacious lead to major distortions. For a start no one willingly parts with his or her money, so enforcement is needed. Evasion is of course illegal, and the cost of policing the system to minimize evasion is not inconsiderable. On the other hand avoidance - the legitimate method of evading taxes - becomes widespread, and costly for both sides.

Avoidance

It is only in recent years that the UK governments have realized that the tendency to avoid taxes is greater if rates are penal. And lower tax rates are usually accepted without large numbers of people taking avoidance measures. The net result is that the tax collected by the governments is greater in aggregate when rates are lower.

Nevertheless, there is a tendency for people with exceptional circumstances to avoid tax. For example when a business is sold and Capital Gains tax applies. Or when a wealthy individual dies and the family faces a large Inheritance Tax charge. Even the current 40% tax rate on incomes (in addition to National Insurance charges) is severe enough for those with large incomes to find ways of mitigating their tax bill. This can take the form of being a tax exile, or arranging to earn in more favourable tax climates. In extreme cases this has led to a flight of talent to more favourable tax regimes in other countries.

In the 1970s in the UK there were tax rates at 98% and even over 100% in one year. There developed an enormous industry of advisers to avoid tax. While the problem is now less crucial for wealthy taxpayers, the number of people employed on both sides of the taxation battle is still considerable. Not only is the taxpayer always seeking ways to minimize tax, and his advisers finding ways of doing so, but also an army of civil servants is intent on making sure tax is collected, and new legislation has to be drafted to stop any loopholes discovered, and to attempt to draft legislation without anomalies in the first place. Because governments tinker with the complex tax and benefit regimes every year, the taxation complexities grow. Simplification of the system is always being canvassed, and Chancellors of the Exchequer no doubt wish to simplify, but even recent Chancellors starting down that road find that they trip up over some unforeseen problem, and have to make amendments which complicate the whole picture again. If there were no taxes, there would be no problem!

I have actually read at least one newspaper article suggesting an end to Income tax. This would end Capital Gains tax as well, because CGT is only kept in place - and currently has the same rate as Income tax - because otherwise it is relatively easy as part of tax avoidance to convert income to capital gains. Very regrettably, the article suggested putting the whole burden onto VAT. But at least there was recognition of the tangled inefficiency of direct taxes. Not enough insight to see the depressing effect on wages, however.

Those who work in the field of VAT as advisers must weep at the complexity of that regime. It would take a book in itself to unearth all the Alice in Wonderland thinking behind the development and practice of VAT. It was one of the horrors imposed by the bureaucratic mandarins in Europe, and has since the 1970s in the UK grown into a savagely inefficient method of collecting tax, although the cost is partly hidden by the fact that every business in the country is an unpaid tax collector. The sums collected are large it is true, but the regime to enforce its collection from defaulting businesses is large, and as consumers we are all very aware of its penal rate and when possible many people attempt to avoid its imposition on major items of expenditure, leading to a black economy in house maintenance and similar expenditure.

How much better then to have no tax of either the direct kind - Income tax, or the indirect kind - VAT or other sales taxes. There are many types of indirect taxes in other countries, and in the UK we have special taxes on fuel, and cars, as well as VAT.

All these taxes are a disincentive to production because they are impositions on effort or on trade. None of them is easy to collect, and the fact that for years there is and has been such a robust avoidance industry proves that avoidance is possible.

No taxes. No problem. So the government would then get its revenue from the Rents due from all, or nearly all individuals, because the we all live somewhere, and most of those somewheres will be in part of a community that commands a Rent. And also from all businesses, or very nearly all businesses because most of these operate at places in the community where a Rent is chargeable.

And no avoidance. Partly as we have seen because when the quantum of tax is low people are content to pay, and equally importantly it will be unavoidable. Impossible to avoid unless you choose to mitigate it by using less of the space commanding a Rent created because the community exists. Some of us will choose to live in more marginal places and set up our businesses in more marginal areas, so freeing space for others and making the average Rent charge lower.

But impossible to avoid if we are in occupation, because if we are legally in possession of the title to a place, and are at a fixed geographical point we can be found. Yes, there will be some absent owners, but it would be easy to devise a method of notification that effectively lets it be known that unpaid Rent will mean forfeiture of title. Not of course on day one. But if persistent non-payment occurred it would lead to forfeiture, or payment of back Rent before the threat was lifted.

I conclude that the first premise – that governments think they need to raise revenue from taxes - is fallacious because all the revenue needed should come from Rent. Furthermore, the collection of taxes is fraught with major legislative difficulties, and puts great burdens on individuals and companies, depressing wealth creation and distorting markets.

The second premise - that government can play Robin Hood - has been disproved in practice. The poor are still with us, and the rich get richer. At the end of the twentieth century the gap was as wide as ever, and widening. In the dark days of the 1970s the Labour government only succeeded in depressing the whole economy so that the rich emigrated or stopped being entrepreneurial. The tax revenue fell, and the poor stayed poor.

Governments have also attempted to redistribute, not to individuals, but to whole areas. Regional Development Agencies hand out grants to enterprises who are thereby persuaded to relocate to less active parts of the nation. The EU is playing the same game on a larger scale by using vast sums to target whole member states, or parts of a state that someone in the bureaucracy thinks is worthy.

Even the Conservative administration under Margaret Thatcher invented Enterprise Zones in the run down parts of cities to revitalize the inner cities. These at least had the merit of exempting them from many of the tax burdens, and in a sense simulated what a free economy should be like. Except one of the exemptions was from planning control, and that is the one essential that should have been preserved. There was no mention of Rent of course. It could be argued at first that there was no Rent to collect in such depressed areas. This was probably correct, but not a situation that would have lasted once the community had been regenerated. It was, then, another example of government's muddled thinking.

How is it that when clear-headed people set out to address the problems of depressed areas they fail to see why some parts of a nation are depressed while others flourish? Regional Development policy has the remit to look at just that problem, yet they continue to throw money away treating the symptoms rather than seeing the cause of the disease, and acting accordingly.

The third premise that taxes such as tariffs and excise duties are a good idea is examined in a chapter that follows (Chapter 18).

There is a fourth reason why governments impose taxes: to discourage particular products, services, or activities.

Alcohol and tobacco are obvious examples. Petrol is another. In each case although the government claims it is aiming to influence behaviour, there is a strong suspicion that the motive is pure revenue raising.

Unless prices are prohibitively high alcohol and tobacco will go on being consumed more or less at the level which individuals prefer. Indeed if they are relatively cheap there is a tendency for them to be less socially elitist, and therefore less used. If there is a case for saying they are undesirable habits, the role of government, if it has a role at all in this area, is to make available evidence to show the harm, and then let individuals choose. But private research bodies and the media will do that job anyway. In some cases direct action will work: if smoking is dangerous in confined public places - as it is - then it should be only allowed in private or open spaces.

The case for taxing petrol is equally weak. Recently it has been suggested that greenhouse gases will be reduced by taxing petrol to discourage consumption. However, the demand for travel is relatively inelastic; i.e. does not vary with price, so the raising of taxes on petrol will have little effect on consumption. In so far as all polluters should pay a price to the community for the pollution they cause then the suppliers of fuel are in reality the polluters, and they should be the ones charged with clearing up. Since they are large corporations they will have the ability to make the necessary changes. What those remedial moves might be can only be hinted at, but one move might be to maintain appropriately large forested areas so that the CO_2 produced by the burning of fuels, is reabsorbed by the trees in the forests. Other nasties which petrol and diesel fuels produced can be limited by refining of the fuels to exclude sulphur, etc. Legislation is appropriate to set the standards. The result of making the polluter - the manufacturer of fuel - pay will in extremis result in the fuel cost rising so that other methods of transport are selected by the individual. Until that happens, and it is probably a long way away from present (untaxed) prices, then the use of fossil fuel should be freely available to cars, trains, planes, industry, domestic heating uses, and electricity generation.

CHAPTER 17

Law, Crime and Punishment

We have a legal system. We do not have justice. And the British system is emulated around the globe because of the former empire. As a young manager in India, where and when trade union disputes were frequent, I was constantly reminded by my Indian legal mentor of the need for Natural Justice. This book is about Rent, a phenomenon of natural law that cries out to be recognized allowing us all at least that basic element of justice in a society.

We have only to look around to see that we have certain other basic freedoms. But not absolute freedoms: in a society all our freedoms are constrained.

Consider for a start the fact that we do not, normally, have anarchy on the streets. We are able most of the time in most places to go about unmolested. This simple freedom is reciprocal. I cannot expect that freedom if I deny it to you and all others. By accepting that I should not take by force from my neighbours in the street, I expect to be treated in the same way myself.

To help reinforce this in those in whom it does not come so naturally, there are of course police and other enforcement procedures. But these are secondary. Primarily, there is a universal or nearly universal acknowledgement that we all need this basic freedom to move about. Similarly, murder is almost universally frowned upon. We all conform more or less to a whole host of procedures that allow civilization to exist in some semblance of order. Many of these are the result of childhood upbringing and early schooling. Others arise from religious teaching that, more or less unchanged, goes back thousands of years. The consideration given to others is in our own self-interest too. It would be impossible to rely on the police to be on hand everywhere and all the time to make sure none of us did something anti-social.

Acceptance of some things we in the UK adhere to may be less secure in other cultures. Even our neighbours in Europe are said to be less meticulous in paying their taxes and abiding by regulations than we are here, in the UK. As times change so does the acceptability of what we in the UK tolerate. Animal welfare might be an example. Foxhunting is part of a centuries old way of life. Yet now some find it repugnant. Homosexuality was illegal; now it is not only legal but beware anyone who criticises it!

The terrible truth about lawyers is that they themselves have developed rituals, and are a powerful cartel, and uphold practices and doctrines that go against natural justice. Each century has changed the legal framework slightly, but the profession is profoundly conservative, and very conscious of it own privileged position.

The sanctioning in law of absolute title to land is an injustice that has been perpetrated since Roman law, on which much of British law is based. But it is all of us who allow it to continue. In the same way as we consent to let others go about unmolested, to drive our cars safely, to pay our road licence, to pay our income tax, so we allow ourselves to be fooled that it is in our interest to allow some of us to own land absolutely, and by so doing deny others their equally just right to use it. We are not always so meek about newer ideas.

When Margaret Thatcher dreamt up a poll tax - a tax against all the known principles of taxation - we could all see straight away how unfair it was. Many refused to pay, and we threw it out, and then threw her out!

Incidentally, we should drive cars safely in our own self-interest again, but we should not pay a road licence or income tax. Both are ill founded.

We love to hate the lawyers, and that a system such as freehold property is profoundly unjust should be crystal clear to those who have been educated well enough to pass a law examination. But to repeat, it is really you and me and all of us who allow this wrong to continue. We, through the democratic process of electing a government, should be formulating the laws that we will accept, and rejecting those we will not.

In a democracy this requires that a political party has in its manifesto the framework of law that we want to choose. For this to happen the concept in question needs to be in the public consciousness. It is therefore essential that fundamental wrongs however long they have stood should be exposed and debated in as wide an arena as possible.

The legal system will be bound by the resulting legislation, of course. But as allegedly impartial professionals it is incumbent on the lawyers to comment on the nature of justice, and if enough of them did so and repeated themselves often enough in the case of Rent, as a few have, then they themselves would spark off the necessary awareness in society. We can blame ourselves for being stupid and ignorant. I blame the legal profession for seeing the wrong and keeping quiet.

Unhappily, in recent times judges have been allowed to define their own legislation by re-defining terms in existing legislation that were never intended in the original legislation. This tendency has been most prevalent when the opposition in parliament was weakest. Even if parliament itself is in danger of being side-lined by governments with large majorities, a democracy should not tolerate the judiciary making or re-defining legislation. The most they can do is make judgements that clearly indicate that new legislation is, in their view, required. It is essential in a democracy that the functioning of the legislature - parliament - and the judiciary are kept separate. These forays into law-making show how powerful the profession can be and sets itself up to be. If they can, wrongly, seek to usurp the role of parliament, they have the clout to, quite properly, draw attention to injustice, and put an idea that promotes justice into the public consciousness.

Crime

Civil disputes are made more likely and more difficult to resolve by our poor legal system. I will return to them. First I shall address the question of criminal activity.

It seems evident to me that people denied freedom and repressed by being unable to work will turn to crime and abuse themselves with drugs as well. These traits are a response to boredom and low income, and secondly, the need to finance the ordinary needs of life and the drug habit.

As good citizens ourselves we want as few desperate down and outs as possible in our communities. Many of us especially the elderly, the weak, and women feel vulnerable and unable to enjoy the freedom to go about unmolested. The reaction of the good and the great and the legal system is to convict and to lock away. "Tough on crime; tough on the causes of crime" was a slogan in Mr Blair's 1997 election propaganda. It has been quoted back to him many times since.

He didn't say then and hasn't said since what he thinks are the causes of crime. I have, and I will say it again here. It is poverty. Poor living standards. Poor education. Poor health. Poor prospects. Poor justice. Mr Blair knows, or if he doesn't he ought to know, as should any politician, that we as a nation - as a community - deliberately deny people young and old access to employment. New Labour talks of equal opportunity. They know that policies they sanction fail to collect Rent, and then have to tax employment and initiative to raise revenue for government. And on top of that revenue, more revenue to hand out welfare benefits. Meanwhile the desperate ones are on drugs and committing crimes to pay for the drugs. A vicious spiral downwards if ever there was one.

All those unemployed people would have equal access to opportunity, to work, if Rents were collected. It would have been much better for them if they had had a better education, but with what they have they could soon be back in business under a proper system.

And what of the drugs? Stop the demand. The supply will then dry up. There is no profit in pushing what people don't want and certainly don't need. Alcohol is relatively cheap, widely used and regrettably a minority misuse it. But here again it is the misfits who misuse it. Informed citizens in charge of their own lives do not by and large abuse themselves. There may be certain individuals who have a genetic make-up that makes them susceptible to alcohol; and maybe other individuals to other chemicals. With help from those such as Alcoholics Anonymous they have to learn to avoid or limit their exposure.

Set the people free to look after themselves and they will. Drugs will not be used to any large extent. Crime related to drugs will cease.

There will always be some crime, of course. For the punishment of criminals we could do no better than take a leaf out of our own history. We sent thousands to Australia. And what happened? They eventually flourished and set up a whole new worthwhile community. We will not see again petty sheep thieves in droves being transported as there were then. But we would have a fewer number of real criminals in a just society.

There is no vacant Australia, but there are many isles in the British Isles. Small colonies of those detained should learn how to fend for themselves and be self-sufficient on a suitably remote small island. They will of course learn from the ground upwards how a new community generates its own Rent! It is in my view probable that they will come back from some small island very well adjusted indeed.

Civil Disputes

If any lawyer reads this chapter I am sure he or she will have much to say on what I have written so far. But I want to suggest a further reform to our learned friends.

Civil disputes are poorly addressed by the current legal system. None but the very rich, large corporations, and the very poor can even get a hearing in court. It is just too cumbersome and too expensive.

The flavour of this chapter has been that we as citizens should decide what we are prepared to consent to. We should not have an out of date legal system handed down to us from a clique of well paid lawyers who have a vested interest in keeping things the way they are.

The platform on which the current legal system works is adversarial battle. In some industries and some parts of the system so-called arbitration is an alternative. But this too is expensive, cumbersome and adversarial.

Other countries have better ways. One in particular commends itself to me that would reduce the time in courts to a minimum. It would also be certain to stop most disputes ever coming to court, because they would in most cases resolve themselves.

Contract law would insist that all contracts had an arbitration clause in them. In the case of a dispute the parties would be free to seek arbitration, but only after each side had put forward a compromise solution that they would find acceptable. The early stages of this process would be between the parties, usually verbally, but within a defined reasonable time, if the exchanges so far had not resolved the dispute, a written compromise would have to be submitted from each side to the other. Both would then be free to accept the others proposal if they wanted to. But both would also have the right to put the two compromise solutions to an independent arbitrator or court. But he (or the court) would have no freedom except to find in favour of one of the two solutions, in its entirety.

No modifications, no compromise. It will quickly be seen that in formulating their own compromises each side will need to be as reasonable as possible so that their solution is chosen. The process would mean that normally the parties would find a solution between themselves.

The whole tenor of the courtroom would change. And yes, there would be less for the lawyers to do. So we would need less of them, and more of our talented well-educated people could do things that we really do need in a community.

CHAPTER 18

Free Trade

If you live in a quiet suburb, or a rural village, there may be few if any retail traders. You may have seen a steady decline in the number of village shops, post offices, pubs and garages. There are real concerns that the decline of these trades, which were such a rich part of small communities, impoverishes all our lives when they are gone. There have been brave communities who have 'taken over' their village shop and run it as a kind of cooperative. But they are few and far between.

There is an argument that suggests we should all patronize our local retailers, and indeed other local industry on the grounds that if they thrive, the community will thrive by the trickle-down effect. This, so the argument runs, means that wages of the employees of that small enterprise are spent locally thereby encouraging other businesses to start. The profit of the business is also spent by the owner with the same effect.

This indeed is the nature of the development of small isolated communities. But no community is an island. Not even the true islands anymore! So are we being sentimental in trying to keep these small businesses open when they are so clearly struggling? Should we at least buy from them, "other things being equal"? Should we measure the benefits to us in having a retailer near to hand against the prices offered? The prices are almost certainly higher than those in the large supermarket 10 or 20 miles away.

The range of goods is also more limited. Yet if we are car-less we need them. If we run out of a daily necessity they are near while the alternative is distant in miles and time - even if we can use the car.

If we let the businesses close they will never come back. That is true because the established trader will probably hang on long after his profit and loss account tells him to stop. And no new trader having the same parameters would risk his capital.

All this is another way of saying the market dictates what is and is not possible. Enough people without cars who therefore have to rely on a local shop will dictate that the shop is viable. A distance of 30 not 20 miles to the supermarket may be enough too. If there is a mountain pass, or sea passage to cross, again the market will dictate that the local trader is viable, even if the community is very small. The market in the end will decide what is viable.

We have seen the world 'shrinking' in our own life times. We find journeys we did rarely which took hours or days are now easily accomplished in a fraction of the time. So it is for commerce. Goods are more mobile as communications have been developed. Because we have seen a gradual but relentless change we have become used to the idea that progress means these changes in local facilities will happen. We regret the loss of some facilities while approving of and fully using the new methods ourselves. While regretting the loss we may think it is an inevitable and fair trade-off. We are perhaps also conscious of the loss of jobs in those activities leading to a downward spiral of job losses, people moving away, resulting in a smaller community, which heralds more closures, followed by more job losses, and so on.

But we need to answer the question posed already - should we support the small trader if other things are equal? The answer is almost certainly yes. Why not, if prices are as favourable? Or if the benefits and disadvantages weighed together in a subjective way by each of us is neutral, or better.

And if enough of us come to that conclusion, and if there are enough of us around, then the trader will flourish. And others may start up because he is flourishing.

We also need to examine our acceptance, conditioned by many years of decline, of the inevitability of the balance always swinging further and further towards the supermarkets miles away.

I point again to the lack of fair competition in these trades familiar to all of us as a result of the failure of us - failure of the community - to collect the Rent where it falls due. In all the examples cited above, there is a disadvantage to the small trader who is hammered by overheads, and an advantage to the new out-of-town retailer who should pay a realistic Rent, but does not. That realistic Rent will be quite small at first; it is after all an out of town location. It will however be many times the previous probably agricultural Rent as a result of the planning permission being granted. But the market will soon decide what the Rent should be. If, as on most peripheries of old market towns, there has sprung up a variety of new large retail outlets, the Rents will be high. At the same time the lessening of trade in the quieter villages and corner shops in predominantly residential areas will ensure a lessening of Rent for those small traders. So too will the Rents in the centre of the town fall as the retail sheds on the outskirts command higher Rents.

Thus we can see that at last there will be a level playing field; one which is constantly adjusting to changing local conditions. And changing locally as more distant conditions change too.

It is possible perhaps there will still come a time when the community really is too small to support a particular kind of trader, even if he has a nil Rent because he is now operating on a marginal site. But that will not happen so inevitably as it does now. As we have seen success of one retailer encourages another, and both employ staff who will spend in the community. Furthermore with the wealth of the nation developing as with human initiative it will tend to do, the community which was once small will now not only be larger but will also have grander tastes.

This trend too will be encouraged by the removal of the tendency to congestion. As I explained in Chapter 9 if Rent is collected cities such as London and the surrounding counties will not be as congested - and would never have grown to be congested, while market towns and rural communities will be growing.

However, I do not want to give the impression that the whole of rural Britain will become an amorphous semi-suburbia. The population is static, and the community should have, as a high priority on the public agenda, proper consideration of planning.

What will have been avoided, and should have been avoided throughout the last hundred years at least, is the concentration of all activity in congested cities and the decline of thriving rural communities.

Now this chapter is headed free trade. This is normally a debate about trade between different countries. I have chosen to draw attention to trade within a nation because the questions are more easily understood and are parallel. The debate about international free trade is whether it is a good thing or not. The alternative is protectionist tariffs. These are often coupled with unfair practices such as making importers meet impossible criteria, delays in approvals of specifications etc. Japan was and is an example of such a country to which it is difficult to export.

We cannot as one country compel another to allow our goods into their territory. The question is should we allow their goods into our country.

The reason I drew attention to the imbalance between small communities, which seem to become more and more impoverished, and larger and growing communities which seem to expand in an unwieldy fashion, is that the inter-nation trade is no different. For residents of the small community read traders in the small nation. (It is traders who are the buyers in international trade just as we as consumers are buyers in our local community.) For supermarket read the low cost producers and exporters of a larger thriving economy. A good example of this was again Japan in the 1970s and 1980s. Their cars were sought after in Britain and Europe, but imports were limited to protect UK and European car manufacturers. For small shopkeeper in a small community read manufacturer in a small weak nation.

There is no chance of legislation directly interfering in the trade between communities in the UK. Nor should there be. (Though we have seen that the non-collection of Rent is a distortion.) Nor should there be between countries. The trading between nations is of benefit to the traders otherwise they - as the makers of the market - would not do it. It is also of benefit to all of the consumers in both the countries. They must be happy with their purchases otherwise traders wont be able to sell their goods, at a profit, to the consumers. So whom are governments that raise tariff barriers, and other hurdles to imports, trying to protect? Not the international traders, not the population as a whole as consumers. Not the jobs of the people in, say, car manufacturing.

No, the only people that gain by protection of any sort are the producers in the home market. They are in international terms the ones analogous to our small shopkeeper. These producers are the ones who are protected anyway by usually paying no Rent to the community, and the more tariffs protect 'their' market the more the value of Rent due, but uncollected, profits them. The protective tariff or practice means higher prices. But not higher wages, because wages are set by the market as a whole and will fall to the least that the man or woman available for work will be prepared to accept.

So the protective tariff raises the return to the owner of factories that produce the protected goods. But since the market price for the goods has been raised by the tariff (or other barrier) this is at the expense of all the other members of the community, who would otherwise buy the product cheaper.

In the purely national situation it is as though the small shopkeeper has a protective barrier around him enabling him to charge high prices: a barrier that would stop the public from shopping elsewhere. Clearly it would be unworkable in a domestic economy.

If Rent were properly collected in the nation, as a whole, there would be no call for protective tariffs because the owners could not themselves profit from the tariff. (Protecting an industry increases its profitability that in turn increases the Rent where it is located.)

I have explored the subject of trade within the community or nation and between nations. In both cases we can see harm being done by the failure to collect Rent. We see the over use of parts of our own country alongside a spiral of decline in other parts. While we do not expect to see protective tariffs between one part of a nation and another part, which would be unworkable, we can see that if that were to happen this would only raise prices generally. Similarly, we see raised prices if free trade is not allowed between nations. These higher prices mean fewer goods for all consumers for their wages. We have also seen that no tariffs would be imposed if Rents were collected because no one in the community would be in a position to benefit.

However, old habits die hard, and governments themselves, without the lobbying of producers, might impose tariffs to increase revenue that is then spent in the name of the community on projects that may or may not be useful, or desirable. As we have seen already, only in dire circumstances should a government be unable to fulfil its duties with the Rent collected. And it should be only the Rent collected that government spends. Any other imposition in the form of taxes will be taking money from wages so lowering the standard of living of all the community. Or, if the imposition is a tariff it will raise prices, so also reducing the standard of living of the community.

There is however, a difficulty. Nations are all different. Some are more democratic than others. Each will have a government of the left or right and the government may change from time to time. None in the world now collects Rent properly, and all have a taxation system of some kind. Many use taxes to subsidise exports.

We need to step back and see the implications of this in a free trade world. Before doing so let it be clear that if all nations entering the free trade arena collected Rent there would be no problem, and it is the function of government at international forums to present any non-collection of Rent in other nations as a problem, and lobby for change. A change that in any case would be in the interests of the citizens of all nations.

But should we when we become a Rent-collecting nation allow imports from rogue nations that subsidize goods coming to the UK and exploit their populace by allowing low wages that translate into low prices of commodities and manufactured goods coming into the UK? Cheap goods from other countries entering our country - assuming this country is now under a regime collecting Rent and having no other taxation - are no problem to the economy as such if the commodity or goods are not produced in the UK. Coffee, for example, would simply be cheap and the citizens of the UK would have to spend less of their money on it. We then have to examine whether the workers producing coffee in the country of origin are being exploited. If Rent is being collected there, this cannot be so. But if it is not, there is every likelihood that they will be being exploited to some extent. And in many well documented cases to a large extent. Should we as the end users be concerned? The answer on a personal basis is a personal answer. In my case the answer is yes, and I should not buy products where I know that exploitation occurs. My view is that this is the only sanction. This personal freedom of choice should be facilitated by information being provided, and the media should be vocal in alerting consumers to conditions in coffee growing countries, if that is a problem, and to similar exploitation where other produce is grown or goods made. But could governments help? It is doubtful in my view. The country of origin is sometimes impossible to trace, especially if it is in the interest of traders to obscure it. The only way governments could help would be to inhibit imports by some tariff barrier, and this would only help if the trade were actually stopped completely. Even that might be worse. For example, the coffee-pickers would have either no work or have to find even less congenial work. This is an important question, and one that causes much vocal campaigning against free trade. There is really only one answer. That is to use every effort at an international statesmanship level to achieve changes in foreign countries. Clearly that is not easy. There will be the temptation of governments to think up sanctions of some kind that they can impose. But at the end of the day none are likely to be anything other than irritations. The irritations may lead to deeper dialogue, and that dialogue may eventually lead to Rent being collected in all countries with which we trade. That is a long way off. Let us put our house in order first and collect Rent in the UK!

Coffee is not produced in the UK. Cars were, and are still produced, under foreign ownership. Other agricultural commodities are grown here. Many electronic goods come from the Far East. There, in some parts, labour is virtually slave labour. As producers in the home market have always done when threatened by cheap imports, they will lobby for tariffs. Should the government give-in? Certainly not if the only effect is to increase the uncollected Rent for the owners of the UK producer. But what if Rent is being fully collected in the UK, and not in, say, Far Eastern countries exporting cheap goods to the UK and undercutting prices so much that UK producers go out of production? Like the coffee question, the media should be alerting the consumer to the moral position. We can choose not to buy that TV, computer or CD player from places where labour is exploited. Again governments can raise the question of Rent in international forums. But in the meantime, will UK producers go out of business? History dictates that the answer is yes, but that was when Rent was not collected in the UK. The answer might still be yes if Rent was collected. Taken to extreme, many commodity goods, and manufactured goods that are easily transported and function as well in the home market as anywhere else, would cease to be produced in the UK. Quotas, subsidies, and tariffs have all been tried. At the end of the day, and at the end of the twentieth century, we can conclude that none of them worked anyway. Certainly they addressed the problem in the wrong way. It would have taken longer, perhaps much longer, but the way to achieve a level playing field is to set the conditions of Rent collection in all countries, not to fall for the easy option of artificial barriers which can be imposed quickly, but do not achieve their objective in the long run.

Globalisation, the modern word for free trade, is seen by the multinational corporations as good for everyone. They think in terms of world coverage of markets for their product, and seek to eliminate all artificial barriers. From what I have said already, the picture they paint is not as benign as they would have us believe. They are powerful forces, often more powerful than governments. Let them push for and agree Rent collection in all countries they operate in or buy raw materials from. If we see that happening we will have less problem with global free trade. Until they do we should be very wary of their motives. In fact the multinationals want to go further than free trade. They want to set conditions in international law that will make their operations, and freedom to operate, take precedence over the interests of democratic governments. Giving up the control over their own affairs is 'sold' to the smaller nations, and poorer nations, as being in their interest because it will - they are told - lead to more trade and therefore - they are told (wrongly) - better standards of living for their populace. But as will be clear from earlier chapters the benefits of increased activity will accrue not to the working population but to the holders of property and the most benefit will be accruing to the holders in the centres of activity. So it will be the already rich in the Western countries who benefit most if, under the present system, all the world were open to trade for the largest corporations.

The opponents of free trade and globalisation of trade crudely identify some of the problems. They do not see the root causes. Demonstrators at Seattle and other WTO gatherings have been criticised for lambasting the very process - trade - that has given them in the West a high standard of living. But we should instead of criticising, applaud their concern for the universal well-being of all humanity. (However, not all are demonstrating because they are altruistic. Some are on the streets in an attempt to highlight their vulnerability to the import of cheap goods flooding into the USA and other high labour countries as a result of free trade allowing the import of goods from very cheap labour markets. We should note their concern, and tell them why such a state of affairs exists.)

While applauding those who have concerns for the whole world community we can at the same time educate them to speak with rational arguments. That dialogue cannot begin without the understanding of the part Rent plays in the welfare of the participating nations. It should be clear that nations cannot trade fairly with each other unless both countries assess and collect Rent. Since none do, free trade today is inherently unfair, and has led to the ever greater enrichment of the USA and other dominant countries home to the multinational operators, and the ever greater exploitation of the primary producing nations with their cheap labour and mounting debts. Yet, as I have explained above free trade is in itself good for the economies of all nations and protectionism disadvantages the mass of the population. It can only be concluded that we must recognise that Rent is to be collected and only by this method can we find the elusive level playing field.

CHAPTER 19

Agriculture - Is it a Special Case?

Agriculture in the UK has been exempt from business rates for decades perhaps on the basis that the country needs to feed itself, and its costs should be kept to a minimum so that food prices will be kept as low as possible. Food production was crucial in times of war. Every spare allotment and corner of a garden was cultivated to produce food of some kind. After the Second World War, agriculture was also grant-aided to improve the infrastructure of agriculture by targeting such items as drainage, and modern buildings more suited to new agricultural methods than the buildings suited to pre-mechanised agriculture before the war.

Certainly in times of war it is crucial to have food supplies, and it makes sense not to risk loss of shipments on the high seas more than is essential. To grow as much as possible at home is therefore good strategy from a military point of view.

Luckily most countries are not at war most of the time, though unfortunately there are wars somewhere in the world practically all of the time. It can be seen from Chapter 32 that these wars are very often if not always caused by failure to adhere to the principles put forward in this book.

But should governments follow a military strategy for food production in times of peace, perhaps on the old adage: 'if you seek peace prepare for war'?

And anyway what is this strategy that governments pursue in times of war? Encouraging agricultural production, by persuasion and informing potential producers of the situation is clearly beneficial. To exempt them from burdens that might otherwise be imposed is less likely to be useful. To continue after the war, to "direct" entrepreneurs to develop new buildings and better methods is unlikely to benefit society as a whole. I use the word entrepreneurs in this context rather than farmers, because it was often building-firms and other specialist trades who actually became aware of the grants, and sold the ideas to the farmers.

No, the answer to all these questions is that agriculture should be no exception. The community will see from the prices paid for farms that there is a Rent to be collected from the land in the same way as land put to use for any other purpose. But I will put in a reminder here that the local 'rates' if they were chargeable would not have been the same thing at all. They would have penalized farmers for making improvements to drainage or putting up modern buildings. Whereas Rent will only apply to land that someone is prepared to pay a premium for if there is no Rent being collected. The premium being the difference between the price paid and the current market value of any improvements to the land.

In times of war farmers and potential farmers will see that there is likely to be a shortage of basic foods, and will not only try to maximize the production of those basic necessities, but will also give preference to growing these rather than luxury crops. As imports of all kinds become difficult the prices of food will harden, and the farmers will seek to acquire more land from those retiring. The prices paid for land will also rise temporarily, but the community will react by adjusting Rents. However, hand in hand with this change farmers will also use their skills to produce more on any given farm by investing in new equipment, buildings and techniques. These improvements will of course not change the Rent collected.

The role of government in such times is to let the market develop. It surely will. It is understandable that in a rapidly changing market place such as in war-time, governments feel the need to intervene. But the best they can do is inform. The ministry of agriculture for example could indicate from past records how much wheat had been imported in previous years, and how much they expect will be needed from home production in the coming year.

Now think about the peace years. These are really no different, though the pace of change is normally likely to be slower. The government need not interfere at all. It is doubtful whether a Ministry of Agriculture is needed at all. Indeed wholly government bodies such as ADAS (Agricultural Development and Advisory Service) have been privatised and there are numerous independent advisory services that will provide information for farmers. Whether or not a small MAFF (now absorbed into DEFRA) is a necessary part of government, it is certain that agriculture will flourish in the UK, and in most if not all parts of the world where the climate is suitable.

Climate of course plays a large part in the success or failure of agricultural production. But as with all production there will be marginal places where wheat, for example, can be grown. In any less favourable conditions no one will bother to try. The Rent due to the community for such marginal places will be zero. And it may be that even the best part of the UK is such a marginal place for wheat production. Though I am not suggesting that that is the case. But it may be. Only the market will determine that. And the same is true for other agricultural production.

Even the farm that is unsuitable for wheat production to the point where no one will bother to try is very probably suitable for other crops. Treating grass as a crop, hay can be made, or direct grazing by livestock will take place. In all cases the market will decide, and the Rent to be collected will be decided by the market. Yes, by the market: the only function of the collecting authority is to correctly interpret the market.

I should note here that the marginal land where no Rent is payable will be unimproved. From this it follows logically that the land changing hands in the market all the time and regularly in use for agricultural production will have a price based on its improvements. In the same way that land which has been built on has improvements - the building. Neither the building nor the improvements to agricultural land will command a Rent because they are not natural features. In the case of improved land the improvements will be drainage; fences and hedges; freedom from weeds, gorse, brambles and other scrub vegetation which would quickly take over neglected land; clearance of rocks and stones to enable cultivation. These and other factors are as relevant to take into account when a price is fixed in the market place, as a building would be. In neither case should they be confused with Rent due on the unimproved land.

With a Rent being collected on all but the marginal land in production, there will surely be some land held out of production because the market place has been satisfied by home production on the good land and from imports. Depending on the demand for land for other uses, such as housing, it is this land that should be released from agriculture. The planning system needs to react intelligently to what the market place is telling it. Planning as a whole and a further development of alternative land use was discussed in Chapter 8.

It will be evident that the capital value of agricultural land will be lower that it is now, and will only reflect the improvements that have been made to the land. This has the obvious benefit that new entrants to agriculture will be able to start up. Traditionally the well-trained young man newly out of agricultural college has either had to inherit or marry into a landed family to get established. This will no longer be the case, and the quality of entrants into agriculture will therefore be better as the field is opened up to many more people.

Because it has been fiercely debated for many decades, I have to explore the argument that says that unless agriculture is treated as a special case it would cease altogether in some parts of the world, even some parts of the UK where is has previously been successfully practised. The argument, which is exemplified by the Corn Laws, and the debate over their repeal in the 1840s, runs that to encourage home production and stop unfair competition from other countries tariffs or other methods of protection have to be put in place. This, it is argued, will keep the price higher than it would otherwise be and will allow production to continue. But first I must mention some elements that confuse the debate.

The concerns expressed about foreign competition are exacerbated by other factors. For example, in recent years the introduction of genetically modified (GM) foods has happened in the USA and pressure is being brought on Europe to allow these to be both imported and to be grown here. However, the GM debate is really a quite separate issue. As a community we are entitled to police what happens in our community that might affect the whole environment. We should have a mechanism for coming to a conclusion about what is unsafe for the environment as a whole in the same way as we have strict limits on radioactivity loose in the environment. But apart from that it must be for the individual to choose what he or she wishes to eat. To be informed about what we do eat, we should be demanding in only buying properly labelled foods.

GM food is one example. BSE which caused most of the world to stop eating UK beef by virtue of a EU ban was another - in reverse. This of course was a nonsense. If the beef was unsafe to eat and came into the extremely dangerous category like radioactivity mentioned above, then the EU should have banned the UK population from eating it too. Clearly the risk was not in that category. The EU was therefore morally wrong to ban its export. Buyers in other countries should have been free to make their own individual buying decisions.

Other nasty practices can be highlighted. Examples of these can be what goes into the food, as adulteration of many kinds; how the plants are treated by chemicals - some of which are banned in some countries while allowed in others; and how animals are treated from a food, chemical or welfare point of view. The examples are legion. It is the purpose of a free press and other channels to inform the public, and the public should decide for themselves what is right for them.

All these things may impinge on the production cost of any one food commodity. It has been pointed out many times that opinions about food safety lead the public to say they will not buy such and such on health or animal welfare grounds, yet when the same people are presented with lower prices compared with the good product, many will in fact buy the cheaper product.

This may be so. It is likely to be more so when the people buying are under financial pressure. If they have to feed a family on a modest weekly budget, they may overrule their own scruples. But a well-paid population will be less under such constraints. A reminder here that the wages of the bulk of the population are wrongly depressed may be useful, and I refer back to Chapter 12 to see how this is so and why it should not be so.

What we buy, and particularly what we buy daily or weekly are in the aggregate of all those buying decisions important in making up the overall economic pattern. By being financially independent and well informed we can expect the aggregate decision of all the community to reject the clearly inadequate. This should apply to all purchases not just to food. But the food we eat is a major part of the world's trade, and agriculture is a major part of the wealth creation process in most countries, even the developed countries of Europe and North America.

Given a discerning body of consumers as outlined above, who have rejected the worst, we still come back to the question that has worried our nineteenth century forebears, and still is part of the thinking of people today. Should we buy cheap - good - food from foreign lands rather than grow it ourselves. The answer is yes. We have no hesitation in buying oranges because they do not grow easily here. Then take tomatoes. We import plenty from sunny parts of Europe, and we grow plenty under glass in this country. As home gardeners we can even grow some in the open. When we look at each plant food or animal food we can see that there is a spectrum of possibility. Some things we have to import if we want them, some can be partially home grown and some it would be foolish to import, at least in the growing season here. Examples of the last are low value/high bulk vegetables that have a short life and are easily damaged in transit. The less they are handled the better so a short journey from field to shop is desirable. Because they are bulky and low value, transport would be a major part of the cost so they are uneconomic to fly in.

We cannot be certain until we have a free un-subsidised market what the marketplace will decide for each type of foodstuff. But decide it will and decide it should. To illustrate the points most clearly, let me continue to consider only one commodity, wheat. Let us suppose wheat is no longer grown in the UK because it can be imported so much cheaper from North America or elsewhere. Then there will be that much less pressure on the availability of land in the UK. More land can be devoted to growing and exporting what we can do best. But if some land goes out of agricultural production, the naturally better land will be now at the margin and paying no Rent, so the cost of our agricultural produce will fall, and both home prices and exports will be cheaper.

As we have already noted in Chapter 18 we would expect other countries to apply the same economic laws in much the same way. And because they do so, their wheat growing areas will command a high Rent because they are naturally more favourable. This increases the production costs a little in that favourable area. What is happening is that the favourable areas will be used to their full potential, but the Rent collected will tend to equate these favourable areas with the less favourable so that these too are called into use when the total demand is sufficiently large. When this happens we should expect wheat growing areas to be spread around the globe, and not expect it to be concentrated in just one huge area. On the other hand we would not expect wheat to be grown where the climate is very hostile nor where it cannot be grown using the best of modern machinery and practices. What is true of wheat will be true for all other crops; though of course each will have its own criteria.

What if other countries do not recognize the universal law of Rent and do not collect Rent from their farmers? It will make some difference to competitive prices but not as much as you may at first think. What happens when Rent is not collected? Do producers have an advantage? Their land is either rented from a landowner or the farmer himself has bought it. If no Rent is collected, the landowner will demand a "rent" from the farmer. If the farmer has had to buy land himself he will pay in a capital sum many times the annual Rent. If borrowing from a bank is involved his overall costs will likely be higher than the true Rent.

So there may seem to be no advantage to producers in countries who are not collecting true Rent. But there will unfortunately be an advantage remaining to them. They will as a community, by failing to collect Rent, allow the wages of workers, particularly unskilled workers, to be much lower than they should be. Large scale agriculture these days uses very little labour, so even this is not a crucial factor in the wheat from North America example. (Even there the fact that the general level of wages has been depressed will make the machinery used cheaper to make and to buy, and to use, so lowering the price of agricultural produce). But there may be other crops in other countries that are produced with a large input of unskilled cheap labour.

Consideration of the plight of such people has been considered in Chapter 18. And it is a matter for churches and world government bodies to address these wrongs. To be more precise it is for all humanity - all of us - to address these matters. But the churches are a medium through which to express our concerns, and they in turn can bring pressure to bear on governments meeting at world summits, congresses or otherwise. We can also make our views known to politicians through other democratic channels.

Agriculture has been plagued by government intervention. We should examine two other common occurrences: Intervention buying, and boom and bust cycles of production.

Intervention buying has been justified in the EU and elsewhere on the basis that farmers need a minimum price below which they will not be forced to sell their produce. In other words a form of protection. As we have seen this is unnecessary, expensive, leads to mountains of food being stored and benefits neither the farmer nor the consumer. It can be argued that the storage of commodities, particularly grain is beneficial because it will smooth out the price from one harvest to the next. But the need for this is made more acute by protectionism that inhibits international trade. If the EU tries to match European production to European demand, then there will be twelve months between each new harvest. If however, there is free trade throughout the world - and it is the EU that stops this - then harvests in the southern hemisphere will counterbalance the winter months in the northern hemisphere. But of course the grain will in any case be stored somewhere by someone. It has to be. It cannot be all consumed at once. This storage function is much best carried out by the farmer, the wholesalers, the importers and exporters, or any one or any combination of these business people. Prices will fluctuate, but less so in a truly world market. There is of course a 'futures' market in all commodities and these go a long way to evening out the price fluctuations. There is in fact little chance that farmers will suddenly find the market has changed so much so rapidly that investment in grain production, or milk, or viticulture - all of these require large capital inputs - that they are forced out of production so wasting the investment made. Markets will change over a longer period but this will allow changes by degrees and more naturally, as machinery wears out, cows become too old to milk, or vines need to be replaced.

However, there are shorter production cycles, such as pigs. These are notoriously boom and bust cycles because it is relatively quick to establish production, and as prices rise more farmers are tempted into the market. As over-production looms, prices fall, and the less viable farming operations go bust and stop production. But again free trade in pig products is the best guard against this. And again an informed public should not be willing to buy inferior products from farmers who cut corners and produce cheaply but badly; whether that is in the home market or abroad. There will always be changing conditions in some markets that lead to boom and bust, but the best response would be adjustment of Rents downwards when times are hard, and upwards when they are good. As should happen in a well adjusted community. But if the cycles are very short this may not be possible, in which case the farmer himself must take a view over the short cycle, that in the round he can make a profit. Pigs have never been subsidised in the UK, yet farmers still rear pigs. The same applies to all markets for all agricultural produce. If the ease of entry is low, there will be larger price fluctuations; if it is more costly there will be smoother fluctuations. In both cases the bigger the market the more the market will be smoothed out.

It is true that the consumers do have to pay an average price that compensates the producer of pigs, say, for the risk he takes and the fact that some investment in the cycle will be wasted by bankruptcy of some producers. But the alternatives are all more expensive for the community as a whole. For example if the community has to find ways of storing pig meat - expensive cold stores. Prices generally for pig meat will be that much higher if intervention buying is introduced as a true cost of the whole operation. And the distortion in the market will have some knock on effects in other markets.

My conclusion is therefore that no industry, not even the most basic one of agriculture should escape the universal law of economics. Rent should be collected from all titleholders whatever their occupation. In peacetime and in wartime, the community will be best served by treating agriculture in this way. To make an exception would be to create a distortion that would have repercussions that would injure the community as a whole just as the present legislation has created injurious conditions in so many walks of life. And we have all become the poorer as a result - materially, morally and spiritually.

I have answered the question I posed, namely should agriculture be a special case in being exempted from the principle that Rent be collected where it is created by the community. There are, however, other important questions that arise in the agricultural sphere. One is the question of subsidy. Subsidies are such an entrenched way of interfering in the agricultural market that the consideration of them in the world today, and in the world if Rent were collected, must be considered.

Protection has been mentioned, and the method used the imposition of tariffs to raise the price level in the home market. Another method of protecting home-producers is to provide subsidies. These can be increased prices for the produce over and above what the market will pay, or payments to producers per acre, per animal, or on the basis of some other physical criterion.

It can quickly be seen that this is a cost on the consumer, either in higher prices, or cost on the taxpayer, who is also a consumer. There are extra costs in administration, so the public pays twice for maintaining agricultural production.

Now it is clear from what has already been said that costs of production are inflated by Rent not being collected, resulting in capitalized Rent creating an unreal value associated with holding land, and on which the holder will seek to make a return. A result of this is that costs are higher than they would otherwise be, and production might cease unless it is subsidized, particularly in less favourable areas.

Collect the Rent due, which will probably be quite small in terms of overall production costs, and the market will set its own price for each type of produce. Rents will fall if the total return to the farmers is low, and rise if they are high. The market will therefore dictate that farming is an efficient and modern industry. There will be no incentive to hold land for non-agricultural reasons, and no likelihood that small farmers will hang on when the market dictates that large scale operation is necessary.

I can contemplate the land being owned by non-farmers. There have always been people with wealth accumulated from other activities who wish to buy an estate, and live a country life of open vistas, spacious houses, and country sports. Such buyers in the past and present have pushed up the value of estates, particularly in accessible areas. The high prices paid have then had a knock on effect on smaller and less desirable farm land. However, if Rent is collected the Rents due on houses may be high, but the Rent on the agricultural land actually used for agriculture only will be modest, because the wealthy estate owner probably will not farm himself, and will make available to the real farmers the land he doesn't require. The commercial arrangement between the parties will reflect the market prices for food production. This commercial rent may be lower that the Rent dictated by the higher prices paid for desirable estates, but in this case the wealthy are paying a quite proper Rent for their vistas and their sport. As noted already, the houses should be assessed separately. The Rents will be high.

The important point is that the agricultural land everywhere will be put to productive use. The cost of doing so will be dictated by the market for food.

Other countries may subsidise their food production and fail to collect Rent. This scenario has been examined in the arguments I raised about the best places to grow wheat in the world. If governments perceive the need to interfere, they should make representation at WTO meetings or other international bodies. In the meantime the Rents in the home country will have fallen - perhaps to nil. Indeed, the problem only arises if the imports have reduced the prices in the home market to levels at which production is unviable even when the Rent on land is nil. Until that point production can continue satisfactorily, and the effect on the home nation is that other nations are in effect making a gift of cheap food to us. Put this way it will be more readily appreciated at WTO-level discussions that each country should collect Rent so making a free market in agricultural products.

The other burning question of the day is the question of quality; "green-ness", organic husbandry, and animal welfare. These are major topics, of course, but well educated, well paid people with real choices rarely choose the cheapest. So low cost, which has driven the production of artificially grown food and horrendous animal conditions, should be less of a factor in a free society. As for the physical practicalities of producing enough food for 6 billion people without the use of not-so-green methods, it can be argued that just as living space is far from being in short supply, so growing space is also much more plentiful than we assume. Technology may need to concentrate on irrigation where drought is a problem - even desalination in appropriate places. Drainage and land reclamation in other areas will be appropriate. Plant development to grow good yields in harsher climatic conditions is another area where technology can play its part.

Much of the world cereal crop is fed to animals with very poor efficiency when measured against feeding human beings directly with those same or similar crops. There is of course enormous waste in the food chain as well, from on-farm spoilage, through the storage and distribution chain, and in the kitchens of home, restaurant and food processing factory. Dissemination of the economic activity – a benefit of Rent collection as I have already explained – will bring food production nearer to the consumer, lessening the opportunities for waste.

Policies formulated to provide cheap food to poor people have led to wrong policies in agricultural production. Discerning consumers will lead to less abusive agriculture.

CHAPTER 20

Europe

Let us remember that before the UK became a member of the European Economic Community (EEC) in 1975 we were members of The Commonwealth. While we still are members, our economic face is turned to Europe and America rather than our co-members, nowadays. As a true commonwealth of nations it was perhaps rudimentary. It had the UK as the leading industrialised head of The Commonwealth, and the other members were colonies or former colonies of the Empire. Nevertheless, there was a free trade structure, especially for agricultural produce.

Europe came from a different direction. The coal and steel federation, which preceded the EEC, was an attempt to create a protectionist block for the European producers against competition from elsewhere, particularly Britain and America.

Europe may now talk about free trade - the single market, and enlargement to bring in other east European nations - but it is primarily still a protectionist block. It does not want free trade with the rest of the world. It wants to protect its industries from competition with Asia and America, and elsewhere.

Having decided to be a protectionist block, it became desirable - in the minds of some of the builders of the European Union (EU) - to have standardisation of products. Or at any rate key products so that all nations could compete in the market place of Europe. First the EEC became simply the European Community (EC), and then the EU.

In reality it was not necessary to harmonise standards for products in Europe. The gains have been negligible, and the cost in terms of loss of variety and overbearing bureaucracy has been dear. All that we needed was free trade. The market place would have come to bear to standardise where it was sensible to do so, and keep variety where variety was a benefit. Taking an example outside of Europe, there were different methods of recording on video tape. The market place forced standardisation to the VHS system that is now universal.

It has largely been a myth that exporters of one country could not compete with another inside the EEC/EC/EU. It is true that protectionist regimes will try and use a standard as a reason for not allowing entry of goods into a market. Japan has done so to high degree, and still does so. But all the EU had to do to make a single market was to ensure that all member states recognised any standard that was valid in any other part of the EU.

So we have a situation in Europe today that attempts to protect its industries from competition, by the back door of setting product standards, and by the front door in keeping tariffs in place against products from other nations.

Free trade is an ideal. An attainable ideal if there is really a level playing field. But this is unlikely in the world as we see it at the moment. Free trade as opposed to protectionism has been a topic of political debate for well over a hundred years. And as transportation across the world has developed the questions are more relevant today than ever before.

For this reason the development of Europe whether as a fifteen-state EU or an enlarged EU is primarily a question of making free trade work. And it will not work unless we have liberty for all men and women to trade and to be rewarded for the fruits of their labour. Or alternatively it can be manipulated to work crudely at great cost to individual freedom by imposing ridiculous rules, burdening all the participants with a hugely expensive bureaucracy, and making arbitrary decisions about channelling funds to particular industries or particular areas.

The debates that have raged about Brussels interference are being opened up again as a result of the desire of the countries of Eastern Europe to join the EU. But they are being told they have to conform. Specialist local delicacies are to be outlawed if they join. The Czechs, for example, have a popular sausage-type fare steeped in vinegar that is likely to be banned. Much more fundamentally, the small and productive farms in that part of the world, which cannot at present be bought by foreigners, will have to be made available to all Europeans. While that might seem reasonable to us Western Europeans, the local population which is up to 40% agriculturally based are very wary of allowing richer Germans, for example, to buy up swathes of their country forcing the local population off the land and into urban employment. Now, if these developing countries started to collect Rent there would be no problem. The foreigners might wish to come in, but they would be competing on an equal footing. And while experienced Western farmers may wish to set up where there are new opportunities in Eastern Europe, and in so doing would help bring new expertise to the area, there would be no place for absentee landlords holding large swathes of land run by local management companies or individuals. The Rent collected annually would ensure that the well equipped farmer, whether with a local background or from elsewhere would be most efficient on whatever scale is appropriate to the type of agriculture, the terrain, and the market for the produce.

What I have just described would be the benign scene if Rent were already being collected properly throughout Europe, or throughout the world. But it has to be said that the Eastern Europeans are in a bind. They could and should collect Rent as the source of their governments' - the communities' - revenue, but if they do so and allow foreigners equal access to their territories they will still find that the rich Westerners are at an advantage to themselves. Not all Westerners, of course, most are severely disadvantaged as we have seen. But there will be enough over-privileged foreigners benefiting from the privatisation of Rent to cause disruption in the smaller and less developed industries. Not only in agriculture, but many other industries also. So what can the Czechs, the Poles, the Hungarians and others do? They want to have access to the EU for its markets, and if they are honest for the rapid expansion of their economies from inflows of capital, grants and expertise. It may look tempting. It would almost certainly be a mistake at this point in time.

What they should be thinking is that they are a powerful and energetic populace of some size by themselves. They should set their own conditions outside the EU, and should make Rent collection the fundamental basis of their economy. Setting the people free in that way will lead to a powerfully expanding economy, where finance will always be available - even if from foreign banks. They will have their own strong currencies because their economies will be strong. They will encourage expertise to come from other parts of the world because their economies will be growing strongly, and more soundly still as new activities are introduced. They will have an enviably mixed economy because their populations are not all located in a few large cities. And Rent collection will ensure that the populations develop infrastructure and activity throughout the territories.

They will be well advised to cooperate with each other in a truly free trade area, but for the time being anyway should keep barriers with the rest of the world. In time they will be able to set their terms for joining a larger free trade area, the EU. But their first condition for joining, perhaps in 2015, should be that the EU collects Rent as fairly and as efficiently as they will have done for the last decade or so.

And if they cannot negotiate that, why will they need to join the EU anyway. My expectation is that their own free trade area will be far more buoyant!

Free trade as we have seen already is only in the interests of nations - more particularly the people of a nation - if the conditions are such that people across the frontiers can compete on equal terms.

If wheat is grown in America and subsidised by transportation costs being met from state funds - as it is - and is then flooded onto the markets of the world without any tariff barriers the rest of the farmers in Europe and elsewhere are rightly to be aggrieved if they are forced out of production. Hence the calls for protectionism.

It may be that even without subsidy the prairies of America can produce wheat far cheaper than can be produced in Europe or other cereal growing nations. It is possible but unlikely. If it seems to be so to those agricultural experts who have studied the conditions in all parts of the world we need to ask them and the politicians what is so favourable about those prairies.

We will soon establish that if we as good farmers can set up a wheat growing enterprise in America more profitably than we can in say northern France or East Anglia, then that good farmer in America should be paying a Rent to use that land that is that much more productive than his equally good counterpart in France or England.

In other words when Rent is collected it cannot be cheaper to produce in any distant land, and then to transport a product, than it is to produce nearer the consumer and pay little or no transport costs. At best if the product is very expensive compared with the cost of transport the two end costs will be similar. Perhaps so similar that the difference in price is negligible. But also in the equation is the natural tendency of consumers and business buyers in many nations to want to support their own producers by buying the local product, if other things are equal. It is in their interest to do so. They have access to the people they are dealing with more easily, and most will have some sense of preferring to deal with their own countrymen.

We have come now to the point where we have to say the non-collection of Rent across the world is the root cause of imbalance in world trade. It is the reason why throughout the history of trading nations there have been calls for protectionism, and in the particular case of Europe manifested by the EU we have a complicated debate about the future of European nations. We have lost sight of why the EEC started. We have allowed it to be developed by elitist politicians who like the idea of a cosy centre-controlled economically powerful block. They have lost sight of the fact that their impositions foist on-costs on industry that weaken the industries that they think are being made able to compete. And the EU is not going to drop its tariff barriers with the rest of the world. Not without a fight anyway because otherwise it has no purpose.

Or does it have a purpose in the minds of those who have lost sight of the original objective? We have heard talk along the lines that, of course, the EU is not an economic but a political union. The Euro as the single currency is a step in this direction. Fortunately the UK and three other members did not join in 1999, and may never need to do so.

Why then do we need a political union if that is the objective? During recent years we have seen the splitting up of nations: Devolution of Scotland, and partly also Wales. They are not independent nations, but they seek to control their lives to a greater extent than before. More violently, war in the Balkan states has produced new nations. There are movements in Italy to split off the rich north and leave the so-called Mezzogiorno of the south to fend for itself. East and West Germany have not bedded down to be a unified state as intended. Spain has its splits or potential splits between not only the Basques, but also between Catalonia and the rest. France is actually allowing more autonomy to its regions than ever before. It seems no one wants a super state of federal Europe. Perhaps more precisely no one wants to be ruled by a remote government out of touch with local concerns. Nor one that takes away in the form of taxation and denies freedoms while giving nothing in return.

Regrettably things have developed so that at least some of these remote areas are getting something in return. They are getting large grants as regional aid from the EU. Aid that has been financed by contributions largely collected as VAT from member states. Some of these groups think that the EU will be their salvation. They can devolve from their former governments and get financial aid from Brussels. But a remoter paymaster replacing a merely remote master is unlikely to end in smiles all round.

Another reason the new Euro-elite think political union will be good for us is to stop us cutting each other's throats. Having had two European wars in less than forty years they can be forgiven for thinking thus. But their diagnosis was wrong and therefore their solution is misguided. And they have been leading us down the wrong path for fifty years.

Take any time in the last one hundred and fifty years. Take 1914 or 1939. All the time throughout the progression of industrialization in the Western world we have seen the wealth of nations increase; some more than others. Sometimes the increases have been tempered by recession. The successes of European nations were enhanced by their trade in less developed parts of the world and in the colonization of Asia, Africa and South America. It seemed to the politicians of the time that the way ahead for prosperity for all was acquiring colonies and developing trade with them, which usually meant exploitation of them for the mother nation. The cry of *lebensraum* in Germany was for more room to expand her trade, and not having a huge colonial empire her eyes fell on neighbours in Europe. At the same time industrial progress in Europe and America had led to a very wealthy ruling class and a suppressed wage-earning class. The ease with which the rulers were able to harness the manpower of the wage earners, especially for the 1914 war seems incredible to our more sophisticated wage earners today.

But is it really likely after fifty years of freedom from war in Europe we want to set about armed conflict with our neighbours again? A very large percentage of all Europeans have travelled widely through Europe and think of Europe as their own. Not as a collection of warring tribes. Yes, Yugoslavia did just that, and we need to bear that in mind when we see how the Euro-elite failed to assess the causes of conflict in the first half of the twentieth century, and have led us down a faulty and unnecessary path since 1950. The sections of Yugoslavia were bound together by a centre denying freedom to the different ethnic groups.

We have seen how the enclosure of land coupled with the failure of governments to collect Rent have led to the majority of populations depending on wages at a low level to sustain themselves, but only partially able to do so. We also have seen how the minority with title to land on which Rent is not collected become the wealthy class. We can see that as populations expand the available land that can be brought into production is exhausted. We should also remember that populations expand fast both when production of the community increases rapidly, and when poor people are feeling insecure. So population in Europe in the industrial revolution grew rapidly.

The simple solution to a shortage of land - or rather a perceived shortage of land - was to look for new pastures. The rest of the world was regrettably "waiting" to be exploited. The empires and potential empires of Europe were geared up to conquest, and though some were bloody, most colonisation was a matter of walking in with arms at the ready. Much of it was simply setting up trade.

The wars that followed were therefore squabbles between the elite classes of Europe who perceived that they had been disadvantaged in a world wide game of chess. The masses were led by the nose into war.

Now instead of thinking that the same thing could repeat itself in 1950, 1960 or later the rulers of Europe should have analysed the problem and concluded that the mass of the population would better create wealth for themselves if given the liberty to do so. And then they should have given them that liberty by collecting the Rent from all the people using the land in Europe, which was then in the hands of very few landowners - as it still is to a lesser extent. Then the development of Europe nation by nation separately would have been rapid, would have rivalled America and would have led to a people self-sufficient and content with themselves as well as with their neighbours. The nations could and should have remained separate nations, as indeed they still are, just. And we would have avoided all the costly impositions of Brussels' bureaucracy.

This could have happened one country at a time, or in concert in some kind of economic community. In the same way as we now perceive that a larger single market is likely to benefit trade it would have been best if the major nations of Europe co-operated to follow the same economic model of Rent collection.

We can see from our detailed examination of free trade that no block of nations can have free trade that will benefit the populace of those nations unless we do have agreement within those nations that Rent is collected by all the governments. We should therefore expect there to be calls for protectionism from vested interests where that is not the case. And we should expect those calls to come most, and most loudly, from the individuals, companies and nations who are the most disadvantaged. Because the nations - or any other block of territory which sets out to be one economic community - at the edge of Europe are the least favoured, when Rent is not collected, it will be the companies and individuals in the nations away from the centre who will call for protectionism, other things being equal. This natural consequence will be manipulated to disguise the true situation by the regional aid programmes; by an acceptance that the far flung places are less economically active. And we should expect to see inefficiency in the central nations who will succumb to the temptation to cushion their workforces with generous pension arrangements, a shorter working week and longer holidays.

We should not expect the EU to work without setting the fundamental conditions correctly first. The EU has been a fudge from the setting up of the Treaty of Rome, and it has been seen to be lacking to such an extent that the powerful elite keeps calling for more unification. They call for harmonization of products, of taxes and VAT rates. They think a common currency will be a benefit and stepping stone to the perfect model. But all will be in vain.

There could be in the next decade or so a united federal states of Europe, but it will come about at the behest of socialist and corporatist thinking people who do not have the interests of the people of the nations in their hearts or in their minds.

Europe as a united states with common currency would operate poorly because of the rigidities in the history of the many nations. Culture, language and lack of mobility of people in particular would make it too rigid to operate even as well as the USA. And the USA is no perfect model. It would therefore be propped up by socialist interventionism as it is already. For example, Ireland has flourished in the 1990s because they have been seen to be good Europeans and have had regional aid pumped into their economy. It must be seductive for them, particularly when they have a long history of being a depressed area because they are on the fringe of Europe and the fringe of the British isles.

We need to come back to the example of the prairies of the USA being the wheat provider of the whole world. If it is true that under the current economic conditions wheat can be grown more cheaply there than virtually anywhere else in the world, then what are the reasons? Large areas uninterrupted by obstacles help. There are economies of scale so that with little labour input large machines can cultivate and harvest very efficiently. Also the climate is suitable. Again, wheat can be stored without much deterioration, so can be transported slowly and cheaply by ship. Nevertheless grain is a low cost commodity so transport costs are by no means negligible. But now change the economic system so that in the USA Rent is collected. By definition Rent will equalize the cost of production with other agricultural areas. Now we are supposing that America will adopt the same economic rules as the rest of the world. Or perhaps I should say the rest of the world will adopt the same rules as America may one day adopt. I say this because America so often in its short history has been the leader in ideas. And Americans have at least some understanding of the concept of Economic Rent and the effects of its non-collection.

But never mind who adopts it first, the collection of a proper Rent is a *sine qua non* for free trade. If it is not collected and not properly administered in each part of the world then we should not expect to have world free trade, and the peoples of each nation would be better served by not having free trade. The WTO, the World Trade Organization, should be the forum where these harmonisations should be discussed and implemented by agreement. Until that it is on the agenda the WTO will only be a debating ground for vested interests from different nations. And we in Europe should use every ounce of influence with world economic blocs - which do not intend to really have freedom in all trades - to insist on the fundamental necessity of Rent collection so that then free trade can operate successfully. Freedom that can only come from recognising the importance of Rent and putting in place a system that assesses it and collects it.

It follows from that, that if Rents were collected in a similar way across the world or across several economic blocs there would need to be a component of that Rent collected that finds its way into the international system. In a similar way to the national government meeting its obligation to collect Rent and use it for the benefit of the people of the nation in ways that I have discussed, so a component should be made available to all the people of the world for proper governmental functions on a world scale. Financing the UN, and its peace-keeping role would be one such function, just as nations have a duty to protect themselves by having armed services, and internally by having police.

It will now be clear what the real role of the EU should be. While it can be argued that nations the size of France, Germany, Italy and Britain are large enough in themselves to be economically viable meaning that they have a full range of industries and commerce to satisfy the needs of their own people, it can also be argued that a larger single market and mobility of people within that market makes for a better quality of life for all Europeans. The EU would be redundant if there were worldwide free trade and worldwide mobility of populations. The latter is certainly a long way off, so the fact that the EU allows virtually free movement of all fifteen member nations' citizens is perhaps the single most beneficial feature of the EU at the present time.

I have explained earlier that the role of government should be confined to a few essential roles. The need for a federal government of the EU is therefore clearly unnecessary. It would also be costly, and damaging to the nations and peoples of Europe. But what is required is a treaty between all the nations that they will collect Rent using common principles, though not centrally. Each nation would finance its own government with the Rent collected and would apportion some of the revenue to finance the UN and other essential world bodies. The EEC started with a treaty, the Treaty of Rome. And treaties are all that are required for sovereign nations to cooperate. The EU parliament and commission would be disbanded.

CHAPTER 21

German Unification

This was Chancellor Kohl's act of faith. He promised the West Germans it would be without pain. He knew and they knew that that was to prove to be a lie.

The first problem was with the East German currency. This had little buying power, but Kohl converted it into West German Deutch marks, and gave the East Germans buying power. As individuals they had small bank balances. The ones with borrowing must have had a problem.

Companies in the East were virtually bankrupt, and were certainly under-equipped compared with the equivalent operations in the West. The result was take-over of anything worth having by Western companies. And closure with job losses of anything that was economically unviable.

All of this amounted to pain for the East. The pain for the West resulted from having to finance the social costs - mostly unemployment - that integration of the East involved. Taxes rose and employers' costs rose. There should have been a thriving economy because there was so much to be done in the East. But the two halves kept themselves to themselves.

As we have seen, when Rent is not collected people and capital flow not to where there is decay and need for regeneration, but to the active and over populated areas.

Those that had not been numbed by years of communist rule and methodology - and it was mostly the young who had least experience of it - moved to the West to obtain employment where the wages were high and the living modern. The diehards stayed in the East and drew the dole.

They didn't see why they had to do anything to enjoy the lavish life-style of their Western neighbours.

None of this should have come as any great surprise to those who have observed distribution of populations and economic activity in other parts of the world. The UK, for a start, with its North-South split.

Had the West been a low cost and high productivity area it is conceivable that that culture would have permeated through to the East. But it would have taken time. In fact Western Germany was no such thing. It had become, as the rich man of Europe, used to the idle life. With a high percentage of Gross Domestic Product going in taxes there was a top heavy burden of unproductive people working in the civil service. And being at the centre of Europe, more or less, and certainly more in an economic sense, Western Germany had its fair share of uncollected Rent accruing to the businesses and manufacturers. Strong unionisation and predominantly socialist thinking at all levels of society led to very favourable wage rates, holiday entitlement, pensions, and other benefits. All this on the back of uncollected Rent.

It was a recipe for failure to do nothing except give the East equal rights in terms of their currency. The other pain for the West was regional aid payments which were made to parts of the East to try and kick start the economy there. These added to the German tax bill, and the richer Westerners were the ones paying the taxes and social security levies.

Had a proper recognition of the reasons for West Germany's prosperity been forthcoming at this crucial time of the politically desirable unification the integration could have proceeded smoothly and all of Europe, indeed all the Western world, would have marvelled not only at the success of integration, but also at the social justice of an important industrialized country. This would have meant, of course, recognizing the role of Rent in driving the economy. The Rents would have been collected in the West, yes, and little if any in the East. This may sound like an equal amount of pain for the West as that described above. But the crucial difference would have been the certainty that Western capital would have been drawn to the East, and the certainty that labour of all talents and all ages would have been employed in the East. Employed, self employed and employing each other, they would have had enormous opportunity to fulfil the desires and needs of the now free East Germany. They would have been no lack of capital from the West or from real bankers in both West and East. Real economic growth would have increased year on year, just as it did in Europe as a whole after the 1939-1945 war.

It has been observed that if the masters of early civilisations wanted to subjugate a population and to build wealth for the masters, as for example the Romans, the masters have to enslave the population and make them work by coercion. In a similar way the peoples of the Eastern Bloc, before the fall of the Iron Curtain, were enslaved. They had no chance to go anywhere else or live under a different system. It has also been observed that when all land is enclosed and under private ownership there is no need to enslave the ordinary man or woman as worker. He too has nowhere to go and cannot work under any other system. In fact he or she has to offer themselves to the owners of the enclosed land and all the owners of business, and has to accept whatever the 'new masters' now dictate. This will as we have seen be a very small wage indeed unless a state subsidy steps in with an unemployment dole payment.

It can be concluded then that the poor down trodden East Germans were merely offered one kind of slavery - the Soviet way - for another - the Western way.

CHAPTER 22

Currencies

It may seem strange to ask why each country has its own currency. The obvious answer is of course history. That is the way the dollar, the pound, the yen, the franc, the mark, and all the other currencies both major and minor grew up. The exception now is the Euro, born on January 1st 1999. And perhaps this is the reason why the functions of currencies need to be examined.

Historically, money itself is a complex subject, which needs to be understood. We can summarise the existence of money as tokens of exchange. Many items have been used as tokens, some in special circumstances, some for long periods of time. Precious metals such as gold and silver have played a part over the centuries because they have the virtue of being stable (chemically), compact (a high ratio of value to volume) and universally traded.

With the advent of specialist handlers of money, namely banks, each issued its own money, but always with the promise to pay the holder of their notes in gold or in the units of the national currency. Units of currency have normally, but not in recent years, been convertible into gold.

Broader considerations of money and the social consequences of its use and misuse are discussed in a following chapter. I want to concentrate now on the interrelation of different currencies and the functions served by them.

All the currencies mentioned above, with the exception of the Euro are specific to sovereign nations. As I have noted this is the result of historical development, but it is no accident. In the less fluid world of earlier times, the currency of each nation only came into contact with another in the border areas. Even trade across the oceans was only loosely instrumental in comparing currencies, because trade was often conducted in terms of gold. Therefore the currencies of each nation could be controlled as more or less islands of independent money.

With the great increase in international trade in recent times, all currencies are forced to be compared with each other, or more usually with one of the dominant currencies such as the US dollar.

As independent units of circulation the currencies could function inside each nation even when the currency itself was being debased. In the 1960s Harold Wilson, the then Prime Minister, was infamous for his comment that the pound in the peoples' pockets had not been devalued following the government's large devaluation of the pound. This was in the days of fixed exchange rates. What is important here is to recall that in many cases currencies have been debased.

Until the last quarter of the twentieth century currencies in Europe were confined to each nation. It was not possible to exchange pounds for other currencies, except for small amounts for personal use, without Bank of England approval. There were therefore major barriers to investment in other countries.

Nowadays most of the Western world's currencies can be freely exchanged with each other, and many of the minor currencies have no restrictions either. But economies in crises, such as Russia at the present time, are unable to trade their currencies because no other party will accept them. Trade into and out of Russia, such as it is, has to be conducted in dollars or some other country's 'hard' currency. We see then the development of 'hard' and 'soft' currencies. The latter being only used inside a relatively isolated economy. It is clear therefore that a hard currency is a *sine qua non* of international trade. By hard we mean one that will be trusted; and it is trusted because it is sound, or not being debased. A dollar or pound will buy goods on the world markets to the same value today as it would last year and will next year. That is the ideal. It is not always exactly so, but it is sufficiently stable to be traded. To the extent that it is not absolutely true, each currency will be traded with a discount or a premium (to the current exchange rate) if a contract is made for exchange at a future date instead of at today's date. But, of course, if the behaviour of a currency is erratic it will be virtually impossible for a future market to be made in its exchange.

In today's imperfect world, since the government, directly or indirectly, controls the stability or otherwise of a currency, it is essential that currencies are national units. The direct link between the value of any unit of currency and the actions of the issuing authority of the currency inside a nation cannot be divorced. The attempt to forge together eleven countries of the Euro-zone as if they were under the control of one government is therefore either an extremely brave or an extremely foolish manoeuvre. What is certain is that the eleven governments cannot act independently anymore, which is the secret agenda of those who advocate a pan-European currency. As I will explain in the next chapter, governments are poor at keeping their currencies stable, and essentially only have two methods of doing so. One is higher or lower interest rates. The other is higher or lower taxes. For me, the second option is closed anyway, because all taxes are unfair imposts on human endeavour. Nevertheless, looking at a government's options as they are today, we see in the 'Eurozone' that the eleven governments only have this option to control their activity and hence their currency, because the control of interest rates has been removed from all the national government's control.

Take as an example Italy. If their tax regime is harsh industry will be discouraged from borrowing to invest. Banks will be lending at a low interest rates, set by the European Central Bank (ECB), but still compared with France or Germany, business will avoid Italy because of the tax regime. An independent nation would at this point lower interest rates. Inside the Euro that cannot happen, so the Italian government cannot lower interest rates. They are fixed Europe-wide for the eleven countries. Something has to give. Workers may migrate to other countries, but language will be a barrier. (The Italian workers can only go to other EU countries of course.) But if they did do so, Italy would gradually become depopulated; indeed as the South of Italy has anyway for reasons wholly concerned with Rent not being collected. Two other courses of action are possible. The Italian government could lower taxes, but how then will they fund the public services they have certainly committed themselves to? Or, the EU could stimulate demand in Italy by making regional grants. If the former action were taken, and services were not cut, then the government would run a deficit, which has the effect of debasing the currency. But Italy now only has the Euro, so the other ten will not allow Italy to do that. For this reason there is a clause in the Maastricht treaty prohibiting member nations from running a budget deficit of any significance. It is possible that all the eleven nations will want to debase the Euro to stimulate exports, but they are unlikely to all be running the same level of budget deficit in each nation. So finally we have to conclude Italy has no room for manoeuvre. She either sees decline, or accepts grant aid from Brussels. She is therefore no more than a region of the European superstate. The whole of Europe has become analogous to the situation I referred to briefly when I said the South of Italy over many years has become depopulated. In that case the national governments - often very short-lived, weak, corrupt and ineffective, had no mechanism to stimulate economic activity in the South without over-heating the economy in the North. We have the same problem in Britain. Now the Eurozone is setting conditions just like that and over a much larger geographical area.

We saw in Chapter 8 how when Rent is not collected, congestion grows and intensifies round the centre of activity. In the European example this will be the centrally situated countries of Germany and France who in most ways control the whole EU project. Italy will be disadvantaged being one of the more peripheral nations. And unless the regional aid compensates dramatically she will become more and more disadvantaged.

Relying on a central bureaucracy in Brussels to target investment in all the peripheral parts of the EU is a recipe for disaster. The funds will go in fraud. An army of officials will be needed to administer the schemes. Investment will go into projects that the market might never have allowed, and will therefore fail. Yet this is exactly what is proposed. This is accepted by those in favour of a Euro for all EU countries as the necessary method of making it all work.

We must return from Europe and its experiment with the Euro to the purpose of currencies. I have, by showing what happens when nations do not have their own currencies, almost explained the function of a currency. But for the sake of clarity, let me use the same example of Italy before the Euro was born.

Italy had a reputation for being an overwhelming bureaucratic state. Many sinecure posts in local and national government meant that public services were poor, and expensive. As a result Italy did not have a balanced budget, and continually ran a deficit. So the lira was constantly being debased. Interest rates were high to encourage or compensate holders of the currency. High interest rates meant the cost of the government's budget deficit was made higher, leading to greater funding problems the following year. At various times the nations of the world have tried to lock currencies together in fixed exchange rates. They have always failed because governments have acted like Italy. But some more so than others. So Italy saw and needed to see its lira fall against other currencies.

Currencies can, of course, appreciate against others, or a whole range of key world currencies. This can be the result of some particular advantage or discovery or method in a nation. An example was given in Chapter 13. But it is usually the actions or failures of governments that make enough difference. Either way, appreciating or depreciating, currencies are the safety valve that allows trade to continue across national boundaries. That is not to say that some commodities cannot be traded in a foreign currency. Many are traded in US dollars. But the wealth generated from that trade needs to be translated back into national currencies so that the minutiae of everyday transactions can take place. Salaries need to be paid; government revenue collected; public services funded; goods and services bought locally by residents; money for investment borrowed from banks; loans made to buy houses. If that did not happen and, say, the UK tried to use only US dollars to make all those transactions the same constraints would be reached as we saw in the example of Italy inside the Eurozone. But without any supra-national government offering compensating regional aid.

At the moment there is a rather odd phenomenon happening in Ireland. Contrary to what one might expect as a peripheral part of Europe, its economy is booming. But it is not a happy situation and cannot last. What appears to have happened after it adopted the Euro in 1999 is that the sudden drop in interest rates compared with what had gone before triggered an inflationary boom. When Ireland controlled its own affairs it had set interest rates relatively high but at a rate consistent with its tax rates, and other fiscal conditions. The new lower rates encouraged new activity, but as is clear from earlier chapters such new activity will lead to higher Rent, which will be capitalized as higher property values, and higher share prices. And there is nothing the government can do about it. The only result can be that at some point the new higher cost of assets will lead to higher industry costs, which will then make the products of industry in Ireland more expensive than in other parts of Europe and the world economy. The result then will be a decline in activity and probably a severe recession for all the reasons we discussed in the case of Italy. Again the Irish government will be unable to change the interest rate to encourage new activity. We have to conclude then that the rapid boom in asset prices is a temporary result of the introduction of the Euro and its low interest rates into an economy that did not need those conditions.

There are some strange developments in other parts of the world. In September 2000 Ecuador finally adopted the US dollar in place of its own currency - the sucre. Dual pricing had been commonplace leading up to the change and for much longer major transactions had been conducted in dollars. 'Dollarisation' has been a hot topic throughout South America, and from Mexico to Argentina it is discussed as a possibility. The catalyst for change in Ecuador was the appalling fate of the sucre, which like many small South American currencies has been debased rapidly - sometimes as much as 25% in a week! The practicalities of achieving this switch are formidable, and the previous time it was suggested in 1998, the president was forced to resign. No one consulted the people this time. Holders of sucres have to be given dollars, of course, and it is not clear where those dollars are to come from, but we can only assume they are paper entries in bank accounts, for the most part. Nevertheless the banks will need some dollars to circulate in the real world. They will buy them from the central bank, which has to import them from the USA, paid for presumably with a book entry in the national ledger. The US authorities will have to print an appropriate amount.

How can we expect all this to bed down? Interest rates will be set in the USA, and although there will be variations for small transactions as there are in any economy, the local rates will have to tend towards the US rate, because otherwise major players could by arbitrage exploit the difference. America is said to be sanguine about the move and hopes to sell American goods more easily to Ecuador. Yes, if they can afford to buy them! But what is unlikely to happen is that there will be a rush to make similar goods locally. What is likely is that commodities, agricultural and mineral, and oil (its biggest export) will flow to the USA produced cheaply with wages remaining low in Ecuador. Very probably much of the ownership of the major extraction industries is in the hands of the foreign corporations anyway. Foreign will mean largely American in that part of the world. The uncollected Rent that should accrue to the local people will be creamed off by the USA. Ecuador is, I predict, likely to have traded one kind of nightmare (hyper-inflation and stagnation) for another (perpetual recession). Those corporations involved in the extraction industries will employ as few people as possible, and the unemployed will be scratching a ghastly existence on the slum periphery of Quito and the other major cities. You may well ask why with a pool of low cost labour available locally entrepreneurs will not set up new industries to provide the needs of the local population. And of course, some will. But they will have an up hill struggle. As we have seen the North-South divides in the UK and Italy, so with any other area using the same currency. Ecuador will be a far flung outpost, economically speaking, of the USA - but with no regional aid from that or any federal government. The result is always stagnation at the periphery.

To summarise, in a world where all trade balanced between nations, and where no government ran a budget deficit, or surplus, all currencies of each nation would always be exchanged and exchangeable for another currency at the same exchange rate. Because that situation is not so, and is never likely to be so, money used in one nation has to be freely exchanged in the market place for money used in another, and the exchange rate will vary perhaps a little, perhaps a lot. It is a dream of multinational corporations to use only one currency so that they eliminate the risk and cost of changing money. Some corporations are so large as to think their own 'economy' is more important than national economies. That large they are too large anyway for the healthy operation of a world economy based on competition. We should all be wary of them and any plans to eliminate national currencies they might promote for their own ends. Governments need to be as directly accountable to their electorates as possible and governments need to be able to control their currencies. Put another way, nations should not be manipulated from outside by any non-governmental body controlling the currency, whether that be a multinational corporation or a non-elected federal government. We, the electorate, need to be able to blame our elected government if our international trade, and therefore the wealth of our nation, is in ruins. And change the government for one that will manage our affairs better.

CHAPTER 23

The Euro - European Monetary Union (EMU)

The last chapter discussed currencies in general and mentioned the Euro in particular, but the subject of EMU is such a major topical issue and of such immense long term significance that no book of this type would be complete without a close look at the subject.

Regrettably most of the debate in all political parties and all parts of Europe will be conducted without the fundamental understanding of Rent. It will be clear from other chapters in this book that the control of economies in any part of the world becomes difficult if not impossible when Rent is not collected by national governments. Some of the symptoms of the malaise of economies may be the reasons why the politicians at the centre of the European debate wish to see change. But without a proper diagnosis of the problems they will certainly come up with the wrong solutions.

Even conducting the debate without understanding the role Rent plays in economies all the arguments are in favour of eschewing monetary union.

National control of interest rates is essential in the localized economy. As we have seen a proper and appropriate rate will be set when Rent is collected. When it is not the MPC or similar bodies in other countries have a fine balancing act to perform in setting an appropriate rate. And that rate will be wrong for different parts of even quite a small population, say the fifty five million in the UK, and will lead to stagnation in the North and hyperactivity in the South at the same time. A larger population using the same interest rate over a vast geographical area will multiply these problems. Of course if Rent were collected throughout

Europe and we had a European government and no national governments, then one currency would work. But if that were the case then we would not have the economic problems that made the politicians dream up political and monetary union in the first place! And there is very little evidence to suggest that a population of two hundred million or more will be better governed by one central government than smaller populations of around fifty million or less in natural, and cultural boundaries. The opposite is in fact more likely. The closer government is to their people, the better chance of democracy actually working.

Any body setting an interest rate - delicately twitching the economic levers - will have to compromise when doing so with the needs of the over-active region and the needs of the nearly-stagnating region. The result is inevitably wrong for both! The result is that the former gets closer to runaway inflation, and the latter struggles to avoid recession. So much for one interest rate being good for all fifteen (soon to be more) European nations.

The advocates of EMU insisted that before the launch of the Euro on January 1st 1999 all the members converged in economic terms. Much pain was caused in most nations to meet the criteria. Now they will all diverge again unless there is massive interference in each of the differing economies. Only migration of labour, government stimulus by some method, or regional grant aid can stop the inevitable.

But in Europe while many speak English there are many who have only their native tongue and English is far from being the lingua franca of Europe at all levels of society. Adding some new entrants from Eastern Europe will only make the mobility of labour throughout the region less likely.

Government stimulus on a national scale is unlikely to be possible either. Not only do the Eurocrats want to harmonize everything but the Keynesian method of stimulation using massive borrowing to finance public projects wont be popular either. For one thing the Maastrict treaty prohibits more than 3% of GDP as government borrowing, and secondly, such Keynesian stimuli do not work. As long ago as Callaghan's premiership it was recognized, by him, that the government could not spend its way out of trouble. And when we were locked into the ERM, the government spent up to 8% of GDP without curing any of the stagnation problems.

The other method of government stimulation is by setting 'competitive' rates of taxation, but clearly the high Rent parts of the economy can set more competitive rates than the others, because active economies provide in aggregate higher tax revenues even at low rates than disadvantaged areas. So it is unlikely that this method is going to get all parts converging again. And anyway the Eurocrats are interfering again and trying to stop countries like the UK setting 'unfairly competitive' rates. That will be another nail in the coffin of sovereign governments. Whatever will an elected government be able to do when it cannot set interest rates and cannot set tax rates?

Remember my comments are made in the context of economies not collecting Rent. How easily all these dilemmas fall away when Rent is collected, and there are no taxes, and interest rates set themselves by having a free and proper banking system (see Chapter 25). So while the above question will strike a chord with many in today's society, I say that government should not be doing those things anyway!

Very few of the above matters have been debated in any meaningful way by the advocates of EMU. What they have come up with are mere trifles when they are examined closely. For example the cost of currency conversion. While the spread of rates of exchange (the difference between the buying rate and the selling rate) may seem significant for the tourist in the ports and airports on the way to holiday destinations, the total expenditure of changing money is an insignificant cost compared with the total cost of the holiday. And it is even less significant for the business traveller. But the real concerns lie with the need for industry to sell and buy in different currencies. However, it is estimated that the costs to industry are a mere 0.15% of GDP. And unpredictability is taken care of by buying and selling forward to cover relevant trading.

Being part of a larger currency unit is often cited as a reason for joining. And by implication being only a small currency in a world dominated by the dollar, the yen and the euro would lead to unstable currency exchange rates and speculation against the pound. But the evidence is not there to support these assertions. The euro itself has dropped 30% against the dollar - while the pound has been relatively stable. The yen is up and down frequently even though the yen is the second largest currency unit. Smaller currencies such as the Swiss franc are more stable. The truth is that the underlying management of the economy is the important factor that determines the strength or weakness of each currency. Speculators only have a field day when the markets perceive an exchange rate that is not in harmony with the fundamentals of the economy.

"Entry of the UK into EMU is the price we have to pay for being influential in Europe." If it is that kind of club we don't want to be part of it! No, we will have influence anyway being the fourth or fifth largest economy in the world, and what is more being independent we will have our own voice in international finance forums. The UK can be a good member of the EU but we need to be sure what the EU is. It could become a super-nation state with no national governments in two, five, ten, or twenty years time. History shows that that would be a mistake. If that is the direction the EU is going, and the EMU project is a stepping-stone towards it we ought to know now so that we can make a rational choice. We would be foolish to belong to such a union. So there is no need to join EMU just to gain entry to a club we would not wish to belong to anyway.

CHAPTER 24

Money

Money is not a subject talked about. It is either in bad taste or boring, or both. But, it is necessary to understand why we are stuck with the kind of money we have today. Implying we are lumbered with a system means we could do better. Yes we could. There are many lengthy books on the subject of money and most will cover the history of its development, but very briefly I will outline the history here. It is necessary to know how things developed to understand the problems.

Exchange of goods doesn't have to involve money. Early traders bartered one useful material or animal for something equally useful, but these kinds of exchange are cumbersome, and even though you may wish to receive ten fish in exchange for something, you may not be able to eat ten fish before they go smelly. Tokens of value were therefore a reasonable development. In an agricultural community the goods that stored well might have acted as tokens. In other words grain, which stored well, might have been accepted in exchange for other produce, even if it was then sold again to buy something else. Grain is bulky, and does deteriorate with time, and does certainly get eaten by vermin, and needs a large building to keep it dry. All these were problems for farmers but especially so for the non-farmers. Nevertheless grain has been used as money as far back as ancient Egyptian times.

Traders who covered more than a local area, in particular, needed small valuable tokens, and the precious metals, gold and silver, were used in many parts of the world. Strangely other items of many kinds, which locally were perceived to have a high value, were also used as tokens.

Examples were sea shells, beads, whale's teeth, cattle, cigarettes, and whisky. Even gold has had to be given its preciousness by humans perceiving it to be valuable. And it became sought after because of its colour, workability and permanence. So it had a decorative use in primitive societies and maintains its usefulness for decorative purposes today. Today it also has industrial uses, of course. And, as it was used in the exalted courts and religious ceremonies, for example in Egypt and in the Inca culture, it became fashionable to have and to hold it if a rich man aspired to be exalted himself. This created a demand that was difficult to supply, especially as its sources became harder and harder to find. Even in early Egyptian times the natural sources were supplemented by tomb raiders stealing the gold of the dead pharaohs. Much later the Spanish conquistadors pillaged the Incas of all their gold.

Like all commodities its price will be determined by supply and demand. It is relatively rare, though it was common in some places. Millennia ago all the easy places to find it have been worked out, and its mining is difficult and costly. Because it was easily available in some places - Mali in the fourteenth century for example - it must have had a lower price in that region than in other parts of the world. But being relatively easy to transport, it would have a price not very different even in distant lands if we assume a perfectly operating market.

Merchants with gold on their hands that they had received in exchanges of various sorts needed somewhere to store gold. This would have been done in caches of their own, initially, but once gold was seen as a valuable token of exchange it was liable to be stolen. Security became a problem. Traders, particularly those that travelled themselves, needed someone to look after their gold in their absence. They therefore deposited their gold in the care of another trusted person. He stored it in secure premises on shelves, or banques, and hence the name 'bank' was introduced.

The bankers, who in the early days were goldsmiths, needed to operate a business to provide the service of keeping the gold secure. Obviously they charged a fee for storage. But that was just the beginning of their business. As wealthy men themselves they were known to be able to lend gold to people who needed to borrow to finance some trade, project or building. One can imagine such men having in their strong-room, gold belonging to themselves, and to many others. Only they knew which was which. A credit-worthy gentleman well known to them who needed to finance a new house, for example, would be able to borrow gold to pay the wages of the builders. A merchant would be able to borrow gold to finance the purchase of goods to ship to, say, China so that he could trade goods in China for Chinese goods that he shipped back to England to sell. The object being of course to make a profit on the whole expedition. It could be expected then that the merchant would repay the gold to the banker, and deposit some extra: the profit the merchant had made on the round trip. The profit would be calculated only after paying some extra gold to the banker as "interest" - or a fee for the lending of the initial gold.

Now the banker, wishing to make a profit out of his business would be keen to lend as much as he could to others, to earn as much "interest" as possible.

Whatever the ethics of doing so it became standard practice that he would lend the gold stored on the shelves whether it belonged to others or to the banker himself. It was only his concern that he could provide the service he was asked to provide. Namely, storage of gold for some and lending of gold to others. He did have to ensure that he could do this either on specific dates when customers were due to collect their gold or on demand if that was the arrangement. He was therefore careful not to lend more than he could be reasonably sure of having available. But if for some reason he was short on a particular date or for a few weeks, he himself as a credit-worthy man could borrow from another bank, in another city, perhaps.

Now this story was possibly accurate for a short period of time when gold was the only acceptable means of payment for trade. However, gold even if compact, is heavy and transport is difficult, and at risk from attacks of highwaymen. Obviously each depositor of gold was given a receipt for his deposit. Such a receipt would itself be recognized by others as being valuable. A trader might for example be able to purchase commodities from producers for shipment abroad or even locally by endorsing the receipt from the banker. The endorsement would state in words written on the back that the gold deposited by Mr A was now to be given to Mr B on demand (or on the due date). Mr B too could use this receipt as a token of exchange. He could endorse it to Mr C. It can be seen that the gold changes ownership, but the gold never moves.

I noted earlier that the banker needed to be careful not to run out of his stock of gold. Now, he need be less careful. His receipts, or notes, are in circulation as currency. A, B and C are able to buy and sell from each other and carry on their trades without ever going to the banker and asking to take away the gold that A deposited in the first place. The banker will therefore be tempted to issue more gold to his other type of customer: those wishing to borrow. But here again why move the gold? The banker can issue a note saying that Mr X can draw from the Bank a quantity of gold. Mr X can also endorse this note in favour of Mr Y. Although these notes are not strictly speaking receipts both the piece of paper issued to Mr A and Mr X enable them or anyone else to whom the note has been endorsed to go to the Banker and ask for a certain quantity of gold. The format of the two therefore become identical so that no one knows whether they have a depositor's note or a borrower's note. These personal notes of bankers circulated in large denominations of money, but of course as Banks became more established it was convenient for all concerned to circulate standard notes for small amounts of gold, what we now call banknotes, rather than personalized notes for large amounts. But in the meantime the practice of referring to gold was replaced by referring to sovereigns (gold coins) and later to pounds. It has to be remembered that there was a strong if not absolute link between the value of gold and the value of a pound. Indeed while on the 'gold standard' this relationship was fixed (1821 till 1971 in various methods, and with some interruptions notably during World War I and World War II). Until the 1970s the bank's notes in circulation referred to the Bank 'promising to pay £5' on a five pound note. Nowadays, it is only the bank of England that issues banknotes. Formerly, all the regional private banks issued their own notes. It was not unknown for the notes to exceed the true backing of the banker, perhaps many times over. Such problems created by the small banks resulted in depositors who held notes to call for their gold or coin. Clearly if the banker had not been prudent the gold deposits would soon be exhausted, a "run on the bank" would be the result, ending in the bank failing. The depositors who had not arrived in time to get their money out lost all their savings.

There is the story of money in very brief outline. The key thing to appreciate is the issuing of notes to borrowers by the banks even though the gold they hold is not theirs to lend. And furthermore issuing of notes to borrowers in excess of all the gold they hold. It goes further, they also issue loans to borrowers in excess - much in excess - of all the deposits of anything they hold. In other words, the depositors don't have gold to deposit because they don't use gold; they only deposit notes which are seen to have value because they have been issued by a banking institution of some kind; and the banks continue to lend much more than even the sum of these 'paper' deposits.

Now, it can be seen that borrowers will trade using their loan, repay it and pay some interest and make a profit, that profit will also be deposited with the banks. This extra swells the total deposits with the bank. It can also be seen that money is nowadays simply tokens - paper tokens - which society accepts as a means of exchange. But clearly this system is fraught with danger. There is the obvious danger of counterfeit money. But there is the much larger danger that the banks issue too much new money by making too many new loans. Remember none of these loans are constrained by what the banks have taken in as deposits. Actually there are some rules. Not any individual or organization can set himself up as a bank. Banks are, in the UK, licensed to operate by the Bank of England, and have to abide by guidelines which lay down that they should have certain ratios of deposits to loans, and are obliged also to hold reserves of various instruments collectively known as Legal Reserves.

Nevertheless the banks do have a considerable freedom in making loans. And as I indicated in the case of the bank that held gold, the more they can trade by making loans the better for their profits. So also with the banks of today and paper money. They do have worries, of course; that their loans are made to sound customers. They want the loan to be repaid at some time, to receive interest regularly throughout the period of the loan, and to avoid defaulting customers.

But this freedom of issuing new loans is the danger in the system. If they issue new tokens (and every overdraft and loan arrangement of every kind is just as much a money token as new £20 notes) then there will be in aggregate more money in circulation than before, and unless the real wealth in terms of economic activity has grown by the same amount in percentage terms, there will be inflation. Again, whole books have been devoted to the subject of inflation. The dangers in particular are that savings are discouraged: they rapidly become worthless in high inflation economies; traders have to raise their prices regularly and rapidly to create enough cash flow to re-invest in new working capital: this ratchets the inflationary spiral upwards; workers demand higher wages to pay for the high prices: ratcheting the spiral again; and, the retired on fixed incomes cannot afford to live on a once adequate pension: so the government has to increase state pensions, and to do so has to raise taxation - which is unpopular, or borrow more money. The lenders to the government are the same financial institutions and bankers who create money. So another turn of the inflationary spiral is created.

Rapid inflation is a bad thing, particularly the nature of it which tends to spiral upwards ever accelerating. However, the current conventional wisdom says that a little inflation is a good thing; because it 'oils the wheels' of the economy.

Until 1997 the Chancellor of the Exchequer acting with the backing of the government had the task of setting conditions in such a way that the (almost) independent banks did not issue too much credit - new loans - and therefore did not cause inflation. Since 1997 the Bank of England acts to change interest rates, advised by a team of experts; the Monetary Policy Committee (MPC). The Chancellor and the government still have the tools of fiscal policy to affect activity in the economy, but the changes are both infrequent and have a delayed action. The MPC on the other hand can change rates monthly - more often if need be. Though here too the effect of interest rate changes takes time to affect the economic activity.

Inflation therefore can be controlled only in so far as the public and industry are choked off from borrowing. If you and I face high interest rates we will not borrow to spend and if we have money to save we will be encouraged to save it. If we don't spend industry will be slacker, and will need to borrow less for working capital and seeing less buoyant times will postpone or cancel new investment. The result of that is less people being employed. So the way to beat inflation, so the conventional wisdom goes, is to create unemployment. Governments do not actually say this, but recent decades have proved that this is the policy being pursued, by both Conservative and now New Labour governments. They may talk of full employment, which has long been a holy grail for Labour, but what they now mean is full employment up to the 'natural level of unemployment'. And what this means in fact to the majority of the workforce is someone else is there to do your job if demands for higher wages are made or if productivity is poor.

The money is paper tokens. The private banks, shepherded by the Bank of England but fairly autonomous, create new tokens (not just new notes, remember, but every new loan agreement or overdraft). Too much new money leads to inflation. Inflation is a bad thing because it causes disruption and real problems for everyone. Everyone except borrowers, and we cannot all be borrowers. If many people try and be borrowers the banks are pushed into lending more money and inflation gets worse. So the government and the MPC of the Bank of England create unemployment to stop inflation. The unemployed are usually the weakest members of the workforce, but the whole workforce is kept on tenterhooks in case they lose a good job. Is this the way to run an economy?

If the MPC, or whoever, gets it wrong we get either inflation or a recession. I noted some effects of the former. The latter is at best a waste of everyone's time and effort. At worst there are business failures, which may mean ruined lives. Also high unemployment, which for the less educated, the disadvantaged and the near-retirement-aged may mean permanently no work. Will they always get it right? They (the government then) did not in the early 1980's and the early 1990's to take two recent examples. Is this the way to run an economy?

Would it help if the banking rules were different? Books have been written suggesting the whole system is rotten, and should be cleaned up. Should banks only lend what is there to be lent? In other words, if A, B and C deposit enough the banks can lend to X, Y and Z just so much and no more. Would this mean that in 2000 the money in circulation would be the same as it was in 1900? Yet the population is much larger, and the activity in the economy is many times larger. The price of everyday items would therefore need to be many times lower than before. This is deflation: the prices of identical items falling month by month, year by year. All the symptoms of the inflationary spiral, but in reverse, can then be seen.

In the deflationary spiral savers want to save, but no one wants to borrow: the borrower has to repay the same number of tokens but they are much more valuable. The retired may feel good if they have a fixed pension: prices are falling. But everyone else is unhappy. Employers need to reduce wages year by year. This is difficult and the effect on employees is that they will tend to spend less, and borrow not at all if they can help it. The economy as a whole therefore slows. Businesses go bankrupt for lack of customers. Even less people want to borrow even though interest rates will now be near zero. All the symptoms of the 1930's would come back to haunt us. Japan has been living through ten years or more of such stagnation.

A fixed quantum of money doesn't sound very attractive either. In the next chapter I shall look at banking as it is and as it should be and show why and how the pitfalls of inflation and recession should be avoided.

CHAPTER 25

Banking

In the last chapter I have described money as it is: the product of a banking system, but also assuming the conditions as they are. But what if Rent is collected, as it should be? As I have explained in earlier chapters, labour - all working people - will be free to be their own master or to take employment from another person, or with a larger or smaller organization or company. Wages will be high: as high as the average skilled and properly set up person can earn for themselves - with or without others - on any site. If they choose to be employees in this economy, it will be the needs of the organization of which they are part that we will need to consider to establish the banking and monetary requirements.

But first look at the sole trader or maybe a small partnership. He, or it, will need a site. He will need tools and he will probably need some working capital. As a well 'paid' man he will probably not spend all he earns. He will be a saver. But the savings may go into providing more working capital to build up his business, and may also invest in new equipment to expand the business. In a rapidly growing enterprise he may see the desirability or need to find funds greater than his own savings. He could team up with others. He could go to the bank and get a loan. The bank will be forced to look carefully at his prospects. They do not want a bad debt. They cannot take the easy way out as they do now and say "let me take a mortgage on your house, then you can have loans up to that value, or 70% of that value". No, that will not be possible because the house is now less of an asset, and has in fact outgoings of its own - the Rent for the house. It still has some value, of course: the value of its construction.

But like all assets it depreciates with time. This will be no alternative to the banker. The banker is forced to look, as he should, to the prospects for the business. The banker may say no. If he says yes he in effect will be giving true credit: that is belief in the venture. He will lend the trader a sum. The trader will earn enough to pay the loan back over some years, pay the interest, and pay his own wages roughly equivalent to what he could earn elsewhere. If he could not he would not be in business himself, but would go and get good wages elsewhere.

The interplay between banker and large corporation will not be very different. We should remember that finance directors have the responsibility of maximising the profits of the company to the extent that is possible from arranging the financial structure of the company. Any company will expect to earn much more in percentage terms as return on capital employed than the company will pay out as either dividends or interest on bank loans. There will therefore always be a tendency for finance directors to borrow to fund part of the company's employed capital. Most of this borrowing will be on fixed terms. Some will be on overdraft.

From the bankers point of view they need these customers. This is where most of the loans of bankers will be. When Rent is collected, there will be very much less domestic mortgage work. The value of domestic - and indeed commercial - buildings will be lower. And as we noted before, the buildings are depreciating assets, needing constant repair and maintenance and also real outgoings as Rent. So, again, the banker looking at ABC Ltd's or XYZ Plc's borrowing requirements will need to be sure that the trade can support the level of borrowing. Genuine credit to be returned in loan repayments with interest over a period of time. Of course, as the company grows new loans for new expansion will probably be arranged.

Reckless bankers may be few and far between, but many have lent for speculative ventures in the nature of increased property values. The bankers weren't reckless because usually the ventures indeed saw increased property values. Such loans will not be made anymore. The cautious banker will only make loans to well run companies who succeed.

Bankers did catch a cold in the negative equity scenario of the late 1980s and early 1990s. That will not be happening anymore. Bankers will be cautious when lending against the security of a depreciating asset, and property prices will reflect only the building or re-building cost of the property. All buildings need some expenditure as repairs are needed, but the re-building cost is unlikely to fall because wages and material costs will not fall except in a severe recession. A severe recession is unlikely to be a feature of a Rent-orientated economy, as I will demonstrate.

I am pointing to the need for bankers to be, in their own self interest, proper providers of credit to business and to individuals. If credit is justified by the belief (credo, Latin for I believe) then the banker will be repaid and will suffer few if any bad debts. Furthermore his credit will have financed real wealth creation.

Suddenly we see what was so elusive before. The money supply is created by bankers. The danger was they created too many new loans, and triggered asset price inflation, giving themselves an ever-better security at the same time. Now they cannot. There is nothing to be gained and no comparable security. Because they are only financing what is to be new wealth creation, the relationship between new money and new wealth is preserved. Therefore there is no inflation. There is no inflation because inflation is the mismatch between the money supply and the volume of wealth. When they are increasing in step prices remain constant or only mildly fluctuating.

Now, the MPC can be disbanded. Interest rates will set themselves. Supply and demand will do that. I discussed the setting of interest rates in Chapter 13 It follows that what was wrong before was that bankers were making loans not for wealth creation but for other reasons. As I explained earlier bankers will want to lend as much as possible to make profits for themselves. In falling over themselves to do so they have lent and still do lend for non wealth creating purposes. The 1980s property boom was an example. It is now happening again in the late 1990s and early 2000s. I have highlighted in Chapter 13 the fact that interest rates can be too high for industry and still too low to stop asset inflation. Bankers wanted and today still want to make money lending to people who 'own' Rent - or rather 'own' capitalized Rent - in the shape of titles known as freeholds. If Rent is paid freeholders are simply titleholders, and the only capital value attaching to their title is the value of the buildings or other improvements. But no new wealth is created unless goods or service are created. Capitalized Rent is not wealth. So if money is created for that purpose more money is in circulation but no more wealth; hence inflation.

Banks create new loans because usually they have security from borrowers that ensures the bank is repaid. This is often a charge against a property if a personal loan or small business borrower is involved. Also share certificates of companies quoted on the stock exchange can be deposited by the borrower, providing collateral for the loan. What is happening here? Rather than sell the asset the individual is able to use new money to spend or re-invest in new assets. What follows? Either the new venture succeeds and new wealth is created so the loan can be repaid, or the venture fails and the bank does then sell the secured asset to recover the loan. We see then that although the money supply is temporarily increased it is matched eventually by the volume of wealth. The fact is that by asking for security the banker is not offering his belief, or credit, but is asking the individual to express his own belief.

If the loan was just to spend some money on a new car, say, then the whole loan transaction is not financing new wealth, but is a charge on future earning of the individual.

What if the banks are so keen to lend that they lend rashly to all and sundry with little security. The money supply will certainly increase in the short run. This may cause a change in the price of everyday goods. But again either the loans will all be good and will be repaid from future earnings, and future wealth creation, or the banks will suffer losses and have to write off the loans as bad debts. The banker or his shareholders will be the poorer, by the amount that the borrower has been the richer.

If the general level of prices has changed in the meantime, i.e. inflation has been induced, the bank itself is the poorer because it will be repaid in units of less value than it intended. It is true that the other holders of cash will also be poorer because their cash units are able to buy less, but they will at least have the interest on top. The banker can of course charge high rates of interest to borrowers to compensate for the risk of bad debts and the effects of inflation, but no bank has a monopoly, and each will compete to attract business keeping interest rates low. Looking at all these transactions first under the existing system, and then one where Rent is collected, when freeholds are merely titles and the value in them is purely the value (depreciating every year) of the buildings and improvements, we can contrast the roles of bankers.

Firstly the existing system: bankers will make imprudent loans if they have security. If activity in the economy creates more Rent, as it does, then the security of a freehold will encourage imprudent lending. This will cause inflation. The Rent in the community will be increased in real terms (fixed price terms) and more increased in monetary terms. The banks will therefore be repaid without problems and will be encouraged to lend again against new inflated freeholds. Each new loan will be inflationary. Even though new wealth will be created by active producers and traders, the bulk of the new money created will end up as inflated asset prices. If some agency allied to government is keeping unemployment artificially high, the Retail Price Index may in fact stay relatively stable while equity and freehold prices soar. Any other asset in short supply or fixed supply will similarly soar in value - fine paintings and *objets d'arts*, classic cars, vintage wines, to name a few.

By contrast, when titleholders to land pay the correct Rent, the title a titleholder holds has limited attraction as a security. Share certificates may be used, but what is crucial is the belief of the banker or the client in the future wealth creation. If that fails the loan fails and the amount of money in circulation is as it was before. If bankers are free with credit, either they will suffer the losses, or the market will demand a high price for loans, i.e. interest rates will be high compensating holders of cash for the loss of purchasing power. New activity will lead to greater wealth creation leading to higher Rents in the economy which will be collected by the government, and not manifest itself in higher property prices or higher share prices. Therefore there will be a natural ceiling on the willingness of bankers to lend. They will do so in line with the true wealth creating potential of their clients and the economy generally. Of course share prices will increase in real terms as those particular companies grow, but they will not increase so exuberantly as when share prices have an element of uncollected Rent in them. Nor will a prudent banker take as collateral shares with an inflated ratio of price to future earnings. If he is not prudent and holds such a share as collateral, and fails to look carefully at the venture, he will risk losing the loan and the chance of realising its repayment from a worthless share certificate.

The bankers of today and yesteryear created the inflation, yes, but the system allowed them to do so. We - all of us - are guilty in not insisting that our sovereign government sets the right conditions. If we, the democracy, do set the right conditions of Rent collection no MPC or government needs to squash inflation, there will be no need to keep a 'natural' level of unemployment. There will also be no danger of such a delicate manoeuvre going wrong and creating a recession. As we noted much earlier only major natural disasters can upset the healthy economy of a sovereign state. (If Rent is being collected, and there is no taxation.) The Black Death must have knocked the wealth of the survivors back decades. In the same way as the wealth of nations grows with population expansion and increased trade, so a major decline in population reduces trade, and reduces wealth. But a recession cannot just happen if the population is steady or rising, and men are free to create wealth. If they are free to do so men will do so. The Depression of the 1930s and other lesser recessions were allowed to happen partly because of the monetary policy, but primarily because men were not free to work. They did not have access to the land in return for a very small Rent. If they had had they would have 'pulled themselves up by the bootstraps'. It is axiomatic that finance is always available to back good people with good ideas. Recessions therefore are caused by the combination of labour being suppressed, and poor banking practices, practices that are only possible when labour is suppressed. As is explained in the next chapter speculation multiplies the problem

CHAPTER 26

Recessions and Stagnation

There are always cycles of activity in any industry, and in any economy. Consider the production, supply and demand for any product or service. First there either has to be a fundamental need for the end product, and examples are food, clothing and housing, or there has to be a desire from people to buy what is produced. In the latter case, an entrepreneur will first have to have had the notion that what he intends to provide will be bought. It may be something that is an elaboration of the food, clothing and housing categories such as delicatessen food, smarter clothing, furniture or furnishings to make for more attractive living. All of these things and many others are subject to fashions and what was desirable to our parents may be wholly undesirable to us. Other products and services offered for sale are very soon out of fashion again. Every entrepreneur takes a risk when deciding to put a product – or service – on the market.

There will therefore be longer or shorter cycles of activity in any range of products, and some of these cycles may be very short. Typically a product is promoted, perhaps in a limited way as a test market. It is then seen to be successful or not, and if successful production and availability are expanded. Competition may also be encouraged by other operators in similar fields copying the first promoter. As the market becomes familiar with the new product the demand may be increasing rapidly, and the supply will be increased to meet this demand. The economies of scale normally allow the much larger supply of products to be offered at significantly lower prices than the first supplies, and again if competitors enter the same market, competition will keep prices low.

There will then follow a period of rapid, sometimes frenetic, growth. At some point the market will become saturated. If the product or service was a whimsical phenomenon the market may collapse nearly as fast as it mushroomed. Where the new product or service has longer term merits the supply and demand will settle into a steady state, but always entrepreneurs, whether small operators, or large companies, will be looking to make modifications to enhance the product and revitalise demand.

It is apparent from this pattern of activity that the cycle for any one product or service is likely to be different from that for other products. But, there is a growth phase, steady state, and a decline period for all products and services. It only depends on the nature of the product itself whether the cycle of activity is long or short.

It is also observed that when communities are prosperous there will be a wider choice of products on the market. Each individual will feel able to afford variety and tastier, prettier, or grander purchases. As societies grow and prosper and trade more actively so we can expect to see, and do see, this process gathering pace. The not so fortunate feel able to afford that bit more, and emulate their better-off neighbours.

I have described how in any thriving economy there will be ups and downs of fortune in the activity of individual companies and persons depending on the cycle of the markets they operate in. Some will make very wrong decisions and go bust. But one man's disaster or one company's failure is another's opportunity. In a multifarious economy the small mishaps of such markets will be masked by the greater mass of successes. The trend will always be upward. New inventions and ideas will tend to enhance the prosperity of every member of the community.

Why then does this gently increasing prosperity come to an end? Often it is a dramatic end that then becomes a general decline in economic activity, and sometimes a prolonged period of stagnation. The demand for goods and services is still there. The ability of people and companies to supply is as strong as it ever was. To reiterate, wealth is created when labour combines with natural resources to create end products that are seen to be useful or desirable. In combining labour and materials, there is the need for tools, or capital, to work efficiently, and the provision of finance from shareholders or bankers to enable the process to establish itself. I have explained in earlier chapters that the role of bankers is to provide credit in the belief that the enterprise will succeed and be able not only to pay the banker in interest for the money borrowed, but also over the medium term to repay the borrowing.

Now, it is easy to see that once a decline in activity is perceived to be happening all members of the community involved in the economic activity will take a different view to the one they held in the times of gradually increasing prosperity. The individual may be working less overtime and have less to spend. The company may feel that sales are static or falling and postpone investment in new plant. The banker may be more cautious in assessing demands for credit and decline to lend where previously a decision would have been favourable. And it can readily be seen that each of these decisions is liable to multiply the effect on other members of the community. As activity slows, so each becomes even more cautious.

At times in history the government of the day has sought to halt the decline. Where governments control the interest rate prevalent in the economy they lower interest rates. It is intended that lower interest rates will encourage the entrepreneur to invest and the individual to borrow to make purchases that seemed beyond reach before.

At other times governments have increased their own spending. This is based on the theory that their spending will create demand for materials and capital goods from suppliers and that the government spending will call forth labour directly in the projects and indirectly in the suppliers. The kick-start given by such spending encourages others to reverse the despondency they felt before, and the pattern of gradually increasing prosperity returns. But clearly action by government is fraught with danger. Either, the spending has to be financed by taxation, in which case the taxation is a new or greater burden on individuals and companies who will then not feel at all confident to spend. Or, the government has to create new money in the form of borrowing. The issue of gilts – government bonds – will have two effects. To make the issue attractive the interest rate may have to be high, or higher than the then ruling rate of interest, so interest rates generally are forced higher with the same depressing effect on individuals and companies as higher taxation. And secondly, the demand created for goods and services from a depressed and unprepared economy can cause the suppliers so motivated to increase prices. In other words inflation is encouraged by the government entering the markets. And as has been noted in Chapter 25 inflation in due course leads to problems that will cause decline in economic activity.

These government actions are all palliatives. They have not answered the question why does the increasing prosperity come to an end? The population as individuals still have desires that are never satiated. Manufacturers always want to do more. Bankers can create unlimited credit if conditions are right. So why does the party end?

The answer of course is directly connected with Rent. As I explained in the early chapters, increasing prosperity leads to increased Rent. Increasing Rents lead to speculation. This is not just speculation in land based assets, though that is rife in a prosperous modern community. The Rent (not being collected by the government) is traded in many kinds of ways. I explained how industry is permeated by uncollected Rent and peopled by individuals, serving the owners, who are allowed to enjoy – and compete for – the Rent that the owners control. Stock markets, while serving a useful and indeed an essential function in provision of funding for industry are very largely trading in Rent, if it is not collected where it should be collected by the community. We see therefore increasing activity leading to increasing prosperity in the developed nations, in turn leading to increased Rent, which capitalised when uncollected, leads to speculation in both land based assets and industrial assets, namely share values. As noted earlier all assets are sucked into this spiral of speculation: property, shares, paintings, vintage wines, and many other assets that are deemed to be in short supply, and which may be more valuable in the near future.

Speculation, on the face of it, does not seem to matter. Gambling may be seen as a vice, but dealing in assets could be just seen as another market operating freely. Many people argue just that. But consider the opportunities open to investors. If you or I are at all entrepreneurial we look for the best opportunity open to us to invest our money. We may be in business and seeking to expand. We may also have interests in property and the stock market, as investments for retirement. In America most of the middle classes have more of their wealth invested in the stock market than they have invested in the house they live in. In deciding where to invest, the individual will look at the potential return. If asset prices are increasing at 10 or 20 percent per annum, seemingly without much risk, who is tempted to invest in a new enterprise that is risky? To compensate for the risk of a venture returns of much higher percentages per annum need to be on offer. And yet we are all wary of enterprises that seen to offer so much. It just seems too good to be true, and very often so it proves. Put another way there are few opportunities for business to make high returns, and the ones offering lower realistic returns are passed over for the safer good returns that are open to investors in assets.

Speculation of course does nothing to produce wealth. Nothing is produced from property or share certificates or pictures changing hands at ever inflating prices.

In the case of property, speculators are tempted to hold more than they can practically use. Serious developers will tend to build up 'land banks' in the certain knowledge that the cost of holding the land will be more than compensated for by the increase in value as years go by. Others will tend to hold land and land based assets out of use or under-utilised because there seems to be no cost and probably some gain in doing so. The speculation in these assets therefore tightens the market, making the entry cost for the ordinary person who needs to buy a place to live or a place to work more expensive, and in tightening of the market gives another twist to the inflation of that class of asset.

However, there comes a point when the assets are so expensive that businesses will not pay the price to expand and potential home owners cannot finance the borrowing to buy a place to live. This for business is the beginning of the recessionary phase of the cycle. And when this happens the spiral upwards falters. As that happens the speculators who have held assets they do not need perceive that the market is turning and seek to offload their assets if they can. But in all markets when demand is less than supply the price falls. This always catches some unprepared. The unwary will be exposed to borrowing. Banks will foreclose on customers who they courted only months earlier. Each disaster creates a new problem and like dominoes the whole edifice of speculation comes crumbling down.

A new era is born. But it takes time for confidence to be built up again. With lower entry costs activity starts again, and a new generation of entrepreneurs and home buyers start the macro economic cycle again. If the timescale between cycles has been long, it really is a new generation of people and the lessons learnt so painfully by their parents have to be re-learnt all over again.

Politicians who promise the end to boom-and-bust cycles are therefore in cloud cuckoo land. The handmaiden of the Chancellor of the Exchequer is the central bank. Partly now independent, the Bank of England with its Monetary Policy Committee is able to prolong the party. And there is nowadays much talk of 'soft landings' to avoid the painful crashes implied by the collapse in markets described above. But like any party the longer it goes on the worse the hangover. For well over a decade we have witnessed stagnation in Japan. The interest rates are virtually zero and yet activity is still depressed. Rather than revitalise their own wealth creating process, the Japanese investor has been drinking at the table provided by America. Outflows of Japanese savings have poured into American speculation, in the process weakening the yen, and keeping the dollar strong even when the American economy is running deficits that would normally weaken their currency. Even the weaker yen has not been enough to make the Japanese economy thrive again.

Hand in hand with the boom in America up until the end of 2000, the breakdown of trade barriers at the insistence of American-dominated organisations such as the WTO has enabled the problems that would have become evident in America to be 'exported'. In this way Rent, which is highest at the centre of activity, is allowed to continue to grow in America while other countries continue to be active, if poorly rewarded. This is the globalisation that on the face of it seems such a good idea – being based on the free trade principle – but in reality it is benefiting the haves and exploiting the have-nots.

There will be those who accept that speculation in land and land based assets has unfortunate consequences who are convinced that the market in shares is a sound and useful market, and does not create recessions, but is the victim of the recession once it has started. They will, however, readily agree that the collapse of equity markets exacerbate a recession once it has started. And the wider the spread of shareholders in the population the greater will be the impact. Looking at America again, the long boom in share values up till the end of 2000 enabled the middle classes to avoid saving. They came to expect their shareholdings to do their saving for them. The danger inherent in such a situation has been well documented and everything possible is being done to avoid a crash. Except to recognise the role that Rent plays, of course!

Looking more closely at the effects of speculation in share certificates, are there parallels with land based assets? Both are inflated as Rent is increased. Both are priced on the basis that Rent is capitalised if it is not collected by the community.

The increased share price of the individual publicly quoted company enables the company, if it so desires, to increase its cash resources by issuing more shares. And companies that are expanding will do this. The higher their share price the more money they can attract from investors for a given number of shares. They have the alternative of borrowing from banks, but finance directors will be conscious of getting the right balance between equity finance and bank borrowing.

A high share price will also enable companies wishing to expand by acquisition of competitors to do so more cheaply than if their share price is low. The target company may also have an inflated share price in which case there is no advantage, but strong well managed companies can be more active in take-overs when markets are buoyant.

To see clearly what is happening in the pricing of equity shares it is necessary to reiterate the relationship between Rent and wages which was raised in Chapter 12. The increase in activity in any community, and increasing prosperity, means that Rents are higher than at levels of lower activity. As Rent rises (and remains uncollected), wages are depressed. If we were able to look closely at the industrial and commercial life of a developed nation a hundred years ago or even a few decades ago, we would have seen a strong manufacturing, extraction (mining, minerals, and aggregates) and agricultural nation. Each part of the industrial activity would also be serviced by many secondary industries. Their activity would have depended on the strength or weakness of the primary industries. The explanation of the speculation in land based property would have adequately encompassed all commercial and industrial cycles, and the periodic recessions that were experienced would have been a mystery no longer.

In the much more sophisticated markets of today no longer confined to one nation, but dependent on international trade, it is necessary to examine further the role of Rent.

As elucidated in Chapter 12 Rent rises to very high levels in a prosperous community, and wages naturally fall to a very low level. The fact that the New Labour minimum wage was initially set at £3.60 per hour indicates just how low wages, even now, can be. But there is a vast trade in Rent at the same time. By which I mean that to service the owners, or controllers of Rent there has grown up numerous services, both direct and indirect. Directly, the managers and executives of large corporations command very high salaries that have nothing to do with the level of wages generally, and have everything to do with the management of Rent. Indirectly, every conceivable service springs up to service the wealthy and the well remunerated. The examples are so obvious and so numerous that it is only necessary to mention one or two. Trendy restaurants serving over-priced meals; exotic holidays and luxury flights to reach those destinations; 'designer' clothes and fancy gadgets and toys for adults and children alike might be mentioned. Not that there is anything sinful about any of these goods and services. I merely draw attention to the fact that by and large they grow up to service the individuals benefiting in one way or another from Rent. In a community where Rent was fully collected and wages were high these same services would spring up to provide for high wage earners. And I have already explained that high earnings would be the norm throughout the population.

The trading on stock markets around the world is another service that flourishes when these people command high levels of Rent. Not only are these people drawn into the markets, but also all the other traders and employees of those traders who have benefited from providing the services mentioned above also become involved.

Again there is nothing wrong with equity markets as such. They do, and should however economies are organised, provide a service to industry. But the shares traded are inflated by the existence of high Rents. Not only by virtue of the higher-than-should-be trading profits reported which have a high element of Rent in them, but also because the share values are chased higher by the individuals, and fund managers on their behalf – another service expanded by the whole phenomenon – who have benefited from increased Rent.

Speculation in these assets does not hold the means of production out of use as speculation in land based assets does. But it does vigorously compete for everybody's attention and resources. The greater the attractions of the equity markets the less the attractions of everything else. The cash reward for holding cash or fixed interest bonds is low when equity markets are buoyant. Even more pernicious is the comparison made by investors in new enterprises. Why take risks, which are often unquantifiable, when faced with easy rewards in the stock markets?

So speculation in industries' tokens of Rent, share certificates, which are nominally a part ownership of the company, but in practice are priced on future profits, and the profits are a reflection of the Rent that the company commands, is a secondary cause of recessions. Real wealth creation seems unattractive when easy money can be made in trading shares. But as that becomes the all-pervasive sentiment wealth creation slows. It slows not just in one industry or product or service, but in all industries, and as we have seen once that happens sentiment changes and holders of mere paper certificates bought at a high price seek to liquidate their holdings as fast as possible leading to a further loss of confidence.

CHAPTER 27

World Debt

During 1999 there was a Church-inspired movement to examine and do something about the imbalance in internation debt. Actually this movement had been building up for some years. This is almost wholly a first world and third world imbalance whereby the wealthy nations of the West have lent the third world countries large sums which the poorer nations have been unable to repay. The transactions are through the intermediaries of the World Bank and the International Monetary Fund (IMF). The rich nations effectively control these institutions because they have funded them in the first place.

The debts are perpetual in the sense that unless they are paid off, and the interest payments kept up, the debt is not cleared. And the nation cannot default on them in the same way as an individual or limited company can go bankrupt or become insolvent.

Because many of these debts have been outstanding for years and because the interest has not been paid, or only partly paid, the sums have grown, rather than been reduced.

Over many years the interest that has been paid has in total amounted to vast sums, often more than the principle sum in the first place, and yet the debtor nation is no nearer paying off its debt.

What policies have these nations had to pursue to try and meet the sums due - whether interest or capital repayment? Being largely agricultural economies, even though often under-capitalized they have followed programmes to grow crops which are saleable in the west so that they can earn foreign exchange with which to pay the banks. They have therefore less of their resources to feed their own populations. And in other ways they have had development of their own economies stifled so that priority is given to paying off international debts.

Also because all available foreign exchange has been used to pay foreign creditors there is little or no currency for importing essential capital goods to develop their agriculture and industry.

The Churches' movement under the name Jubilee 2000 has been successful in terms of raising awareness with the politicians of the richer nations, and some fine sentiments have been expressed. Whether these fine political speeches are worth anything we will have to wait and see. The aim has been to arrange the cancellation of debts in the spirit of the biblical Jubilee. Jubilee is the name given in the Bible to the periodic cancellation of all debt between individuals. Debt cancellation was a practice in biblical times every seven years - the sabbatical year. But at the end of the seventh sabbatical year, in the fiftieth year the relief was wider because not only were all debts cancelled but people who had lost their land were given it back again. Some sources imply that all transactions however valid in the previous forty-nine years were negated, in so far as land was concerned, with the intention that the original families reverted to where they were fifty year ago. However, it is thought that this was not strictly adhered to. And it would seem that such an upheaval would have been hugely disruptive.

Furthermore in the jubilee year those in forced servitude or slavery were set free.

It is easy to see the parallels with biblical times, when we see the poverty of the peoples of Africa and South America in virtual slavery to their economic masters: masters who, ultimately at the top of the chain, are the banks and governments of the rich Western nations.

The Jubilee 2000 movement seeks only to wipe out the international debt, but we should ask ourselves how the chronic indebtedness came about in the first place. And why have the developing nations had to rely on Western intervention to finance their development?

Even if Jubilee 2000 is successful in nominally wiping out debts owed by the poorer nations, will the strings attached to the cancellation of debt only make things worse? It has been proposed that the IMF and World Bank will insist on Western style rectitude in the economies of the poor nations. They must behave as if they were defaulting developed nations as Britain was forced to in the days of the 1970s Labour government. In particular they are to impose so called Structural Adjustment Programmes that will mean a limit on the pay of civil servants; limits on the public expenditure in those nations, and other conditions that are clearly aimed to make them models of financial rectitude, Western-style. But not a word about putting the structure of society to rights. No mention of land. No mention of access to land. No biblical Jubilee in the sense of setting the people free to create their own wealth, and returning the land to the people. Each of these countries is very predominantly agrarian. Even now India, which can be regarded as a second world rather than a third world country, has 70% or more of its population living in the country, centred on villages. It is far easier for a nation to pull itself up by the boot-straps if it is agrarian, than if it is industrialized and failing. That is because the people are still in the right places and have the necessary skills. All that is needed is to set the conditions.

And a real Jubilee for the third world countries would say to them:

"Your debts are waived, but you must allow your people to earn their own living. Don't make them labourers for your elite. Don't enclose your land. Make it available to anyone who will work it. Yes they are free to do what they like with it. They can buy and sell it in the sense that they can have a title to it, but they will pay annually a Rent to the government. Because they do so the price of land will be low, and you the government will make available interest free or very low interest loans through a National Land Bank, with the sole purpose of enabling people to acquire a title to land.

"Furthermore, you, the government, will not interfere with the commercial life of the nation. You will spend the Rent collected in maintaining democracy and law and order in the land.

"You will also only allow help from other nations and foreign commercial banks on the basis of them helping to set up projects of an infrastructure nature by way of either outright gifts of aid which are complete and discrete projects. Or in the case of commercial banks on the basis that the money made available is equity in the enterprise. And all industry will of course pay a Rent to the government, which as the economy develops will be an increasing aggregate sum.

"Aid by way of supplies whether food or other materials will not be acceptable, because free supplies undermine the market for commodities in the economy, and put the local producers out of work. Should natural disasters strike so that famine threatens the very lives of the population, food can be gifted from abroad and accepted so long as the supplies of food, such as they are, are first provided by buying - or offering to buy - the local harvest production as and when it is harvested. Such intervention will be under the supervision of an international agency such as Oxfam, and must be kept in place for the shortest possible time so that normal commerce returns as soon as the famine is over."

We as members of a richer nation cannot be sure anything we, or our government, says will be adhered to in a struggling new nation. We should try and lay down real principles of sound economics if we have the chance, and to make their governments and their peoples listen, because we in return are freeing them from the yoke of indebtedness. We should ask what are the appropriate conditions in addition to those outlined above, and we should avoid making the mistakes that we have developed in Western societies, and which will take longer to put right.

Of course, we as citizens of Western rich countries should demand a Jubilee 2000 of our own and set our own people free. If we ask the real questions as outlined in this book, we could do just that. We will not find it easy. Not as easy as a developing nation. Our people are not used to being free (or self sufficient) and most of our people are in the wrong places doing the wrong jobs. But it can be addressed, it should be addressed and we have only ourselves to blame if we do not ask the right questions, the real questions; and find the real answers.

CHAPTER 28

Political Parties: Where Did They Go Wrong?

There are political parties of the Right and the Left, and shades in between. These are useful labels but unless we know what we mean by this shorthand they are meaningless. In the twentieth century in the UK there have been extremes of both Right and Left, and the poor economic performance of the country has often been attributed to the disruption of the swings in policy that have taken place as governments of one persuasion have been replaced by the other. Since the Liberals and other parties of the centre ground have not held office in most of the twentieth century, nor show any signs of doing so in the near future, we can concentrate on what has gone wrong with the Conservatives and the Labour - now New Labour - parties.

It can be argued that at least the existence of the Liberal and similar parties give a chance of coalitions that might be more benign than the two extreme parties. And they can make themselves heard in the public arena with a voice loud enough to be noticed, formulating alternative policies that may be sounder than the other two parties. Not that I am declaring that that has been the case.

Right at the start of the century the 'land question' was indeed hotly debated, and collection of true economic Rent was in a rudimentary form part of the Liberal party's manifesto. Their budget embodied in the Finance Act of 1909 contained proposals that would have implemented changes in this direction. It was infamously thrown out by the House of Lords and ever since that time the House of Lords has been denied any veto over Finance Acts. Their Lordships perceived a threat to their vested interests, since they were the beneficiaries of Rent uncollected by the community. Unfortunately, they could not see beyond their vested interests to the greater good of the nation as whole. Their privileged positions as land owners have been eroded in other ways in subsequent decades, and we eventually ended the century with the hereditary lords being thrown out of the House of Lords altogether with the exception of a few working lords nominated by them. This is not the place to debate the merits of a second chamber of government, nor how its members should be chosen. Suffice it to say there should be one, and the members should not be appointed by any method associated with the government of the day or the House of Commons.

The reason for raising the matter of the House of Lords is to show how a seminal idea was crushed by a vested interest, and how long it has taken for anyone to suggest that a second chamber composed of a better cross-section of the population might be more able to disinterestedly scrutinize legislation.

The current Liberal Democrat party is a poor shadow of the earlier Liberal party, and has no policy to collect Rent in its manifesto.

The other two parties have made the running in the twentieth century, and it appears that we have two parties of the Right at the present time with New Labour stealing many of the Conservatives policies. If socialism is now a dirty word for Labour, we should at least bury it understanding why is dominated much of the twentieth century, what was wrong with it, and why there are still elements in the party that think in a socialist way.

The Labour party was born out of the repression of labour in the nineteenth century. Massive strides in economic performance were made, particularly in the UK in the nineteenth century, yet as the wealth of the nation increased, the lot of the labouring classes improved not a whit, and the conditions of work, and of housing deteriorated for the many. Their answer was to organize themselves into unions, and with the collective bargaining that in many cases - though not all - the unions could command they managed to painfully improve wages and conditions in industry throughout the first part of the twentieth century. But at a terrible cost: the cost to themselves in having to go on strike, in the meantime living on strike pay or no pay; in having to contribute dues to the unions to fund strikes; and to fund the officials of the unions; and to fund the Labour party. And the cost to the nation as a whole in having surly labour constantly threatening to strike, and working unwillingly. The cost, too, of having deliberate over-manning so that each job was done by two or three men when one would have been enough. The burden of having to set up a 'welfare state' that needed high taxation to fund it and was poorly organized and managed so that it never did, and never will, provide the services it was set up to provide. History will enumerate many more follies of this period in our nation's past.

Organized labour cannot be criticised for organizing themselves into unions, nor for having a Labour party to represent them. But even with all the intellectual input that socialism attracted from university-educated brains the socialists always missed the point. They could not see why wages were depressed in the midst of growing wealth. It is fair to say they cannot see it now, even when they read clear explanations such as in the earlier parts of this book.

Is it because they see an enemy that has to be fought? The enemy they perceive is organized industry. An enemy that they think controls capital, and they wrongly think that capital employs labour. In fact it is labour - men and women of all sorts - who employ capital when they are given the freedom to do so.

The Conservatives are more of a mixed bag, and to generalize, the party is made up of the landed interests of the seventeenth and subsequent centuries, and the entrepreneurs of the industrial revolution onwards. Indeed the Conservative party has always prided itself for being a 'broad church'. While many wage earners have often voted Conservative, the party ethos springs from those who employ others. They have the self-satisfaction of feeling that they are the ones who create wealth. They see the opportunity, they raise the funds, they take the risk, and they employ others. It sounds as though they are the leaders they set themselves up to be. Yet few would deny that if *laissez faire* were allowed to be their sole creed, the conditions of the working class would be dire. It was in the nineteenth century, and it would still be if measures by legislation and by union bargaining had not tempered the 'capitalists'.

There have therefore been politicians and members of the party who have sought to use the welfare state to soften the raw effects of capitalism. They have been branded 'wets' in the Thatcher era, but there were many such thinkers before then. Indeed the welfare state started under a Conservative government.

The balanced ethos of the party members might be described as industry making as much profit as possible; taxation of profits and incomes at low rates, but high in aggregate when the economy is booming; therefore high revenue to spend on health, education, and the (few, hopefully) unemployed.

This recipe has led to some good standards of living for the many. The wealth of the nation has in the twentieth century grown spectacularly, and the average household enjoys many material and leisure benefits that would have seemed the height of luxury at the start of that century. And yet there is a catalogue of trouble too. The boom years have led to bust. Full employment is just a dream, so many are long term unemployed. Housing is ugly, and ill planned and 1960s tower blocks are ghettos of crime and intolerance.

Drugs have become prevalent, and truancy and illiteracy have increased. Respect for authority has declined. Prisons are full to bursting. Inflation has been an ever-present spectre, and is only held in check by maintaining a 'natural' level of the population out of work, and defining it solely by the RPI measure and ignoring asset inflation.

The Conservative party does not seem to have an answer to all these many problems. Palliatives perhaps, but their answer deep down is to hope that by encouraging the capitalist to create wealth it will somehow trickle down to the lower levels of society.

The blind spot with the Conservatives has been the distinction between land (a natural resource) and capital (man made wealth): the former is an essential but passive element, the latter is an enhancer of the output of labour being put to work to create more wealth. The risk-taker employing capital is to be applauded. The land speculator is not. Even the Conservatives' own politicians have referred to the 'unacceptable face of capitalism' but have done little to analyse why that unacceptable face was allowed to flourish. Many inside the party may not have such a blind spot. Analytical they may not be, but they know from years of practice that land works for them. These are the people with the vested interests, and cannot be expected to give up their privilege without a fight.

Change is required of the Conservatives if they want to be in government again. New Labour has shown it can do much of what they did, and can with honesty say they want a welfare state. The public perceives the need to address the effects of inequality, but does not see the causes, and so rather likes an efficient New Labour government that promises to keep the economy on course, and ameliorate the lot of the disadvantaged. Whether the promises will be kept is another matter.

Can it be that the young Conservative elite, now largely disassociated from landed interests will see the need to free all labour to use capital for their own interests - making in total the healthiest and wealthiest economy ever? Indeed, 'the wealthiest ever' might not mean materially surfeited with unnecessary goods, but wealthy in space to live and work, time to be and play as well as work, flexible so that each member of the family can be in work or not as circumstances change, cultured with interests in all the arts which would flourish at local as well as national level. This mix of wealth rather than mere goods is being sought after by the middle-income strata of society already, as material standards of living reach a certain level. But very often their high incomes demand a punishing commitment to work - running to ensure they stay abreast of the competition.

One of the hopes of Conservatives has been that all should become owners of the 'capital'. We were encouraged to be a 'property-owning democracy'. Privatisation shares were to be held by millions. But while economic progress has advanced these goals for many, so long as the opportunity is denied to the majority to work by not having equal access to land, the lowest (which in any pyramid structure is the majority) will be disadvantaged. And the disadvantaged sell shares that may be thrust upon them; and get into trouble keeping up mortgage payments. The result is the ownership coalesces round the 'haves' and dissipates from the 'have-nots'.

History has proved that society cannot perpetuate an injustice and then hope to spread the benefits of the injustice around so that all are equal again. For a start doing just that looks pretty stupid on paper. If that really were the intention why not simply eliminate the injustice in the first place? Secondly, it is pretty poor logistics: to create a problem and then go to great lengths, and to great cost, to counterbalance the effects of the problem. Thirdly, it is analogous to pushing water uphill. Nature will soon ensure it goes to the bottom of the hill again. The natural law of Rent is no different. If we create a community we will create a Rent. If we do not collect that Rent for the community, we will allow some few individuals to control the lives of the many. The socialists see the resulting problems and set up state machinery to smooth and soothe the problems of the masses - or try to. The Conservatives see the problem and think everyone can be a part of it, and gain from it. Yet they still advocate a free service providing health and education to prop up, not just the fallen, but also the vast majority of the population. That doesn't sound very convincing. Neither party seems to see the causes.

The 'Third Way'. This phrase has been bandied about, but no one seems to understand what it means. It is by no means a coherent ideology, but rather a fudge invented by the Left who can't admit they were wrong on socialism, and try to pursue socialism with the methods and practices of the Right. A recent survey of what people think it means and what they want out of it reveals the patchwork nature of the term. The work ethic...environmental concerns...welfare for the unemployed and the elderly....Welfare to Work....mothers should stay at home while children are pre-school age....protection of the countryside....reducing taxes on motorists....liberal stance on personal morality....electoral reform. And behind it all Mr Blair just saying: "what works". For all the fine rhetoric, and already books have been written on the subject, the Third Way is at best an incoherent wish list.

Trying to make some sense of it and trying to guess what the voters thought they were choosing New Labour for at the 1997 election, I could put forward a party that wanted improvements in public services, financed by increased taxation. But without penal taxation rates that frighten abroad high earners and corporations. A 'better' balance between the individual and public bodies performing the wealth-creation, reversing the imbalance of the Thatcher years. However, in office Blair has found it impossible to achieve these objectives and so far has succeeded only in increasing the centralizing role of government, which was already too much a feature of the Thatcher government. In addition he has attempted to control the political process in selecting candidates for the London and Welsh elections, and has shown contempt for both Houses of Parliament. Finally, he is renowned for seeing the image as more important than the substance. No government can perform effectively with such criteria.

How long the voters of this nation, or any nation, will have to wait for a government that recognises their past failings, the reasons for them and what needs to be done is anyone's guess. I am afraid it may take a very long time. But the fault, and the answer, lie not solely with the politicians, but also much more so, with us.

CHAPTER 29

Monopoly: Just a Game?

It is strange that every child of age seven upwards has played Monopoly. Some for the last seventy years or so, and some of these adults are addicted to it, yet the clearly obvious principle - indeed natural law - on which it is based appears to be irrelevant when those children, now adults, set about ordering their own affairs. I may be wrong about this in one sense; perhaps the property millionaires of today were addicts of Monopoly when they were young. Perhaps it would be more accurate to say those who set about ordering our public affairs ignore the game's principles.

The game of Monopoly does exemplify the result of non-collection of Rent on housing and other buildings in London, and this subject has been fully aired in earlier chapters. In this chapter, I examine the other monopolies that can develop in today's conditions. I also look at the true monopolies that might still be a problem, even when Rent is collected.

Monopolies are a problem in economic life because a single supplier to a market can dictate prices and terms, and so make profits in excess of that which in aggregate would be made in a market supplied by two or more true competitors. This in itself does not necessarily mean that the customers pay more for the goods or services than they would otherwise: the splitting up of the market may increase the total costs because of loss of economies of scale. However, there is a presumption against monopolies.

It has been said that all monopolies derive from the monopoly in land that is itself only created by the non-collection of Rent for the community. There is certainly a tendency for enterprises that have an established position of advantage because they have many years of access to special natural resources or locations to keep competition out. The strong position once established is re-enforced by many other factors detailed in standard economic text books, such as the economies of scale in production making a potential competitor's small scale production uneconomic; exclusion of all others by having control of some vital factor in the chain of supply; legal restrictions on all but the established producer; maintaining of goodwill by heavy advertising. The newcomers find it an uphill struggle to compete. In this sense the monopoly derived from non-collection of Rent encourages quasi-monopoly structures in industry and commerce. The oil barons of the early twentieth century in the USA are one example. A monopoly that, in theory, took legislation to break it. But recent commentators note that by the time the legislation had achieved the break up of Standard Oil, competition from newer oil companies such as Texaco and Gulf Oil had made the legislation superfluous. Many of the problems of monopoly - and whole books have been written about the problem – for example, the whole expensive saga of oil production and refining in the USA, would therefore disappear when and if Rent is properly collected.

Monopolies can be created by the astute filing of patents. And recently the ethics of allowing the knowledge of genetic material to be patented has sparked a controversy. The point being that patents should exist to defend the owner against exploitation of their inventions from others copying the product without the competitor having done any of the research work. But the genetic material itself is not an invention. For the purposes of this discussion clearly inventions do not rely on space to be effective, and therefore such monopolies created by inventions are in a different category. The laws on exploiting patents differ in different countries and can obviously be reviewed and challenged.

While a few inventions may make their owners and exploiters fabulously rich - a classic example is Singer and the needle with a hole at the sharp end - they do in fact do nothing to disadvantage the working population as whole, as do the monopolies arising from the control of land or natural resources.

The shenanigans of the owners of businesses attempting to create a monopoly position in the market make their action look like a complicated game, but a game in deadly seriousness, and where the stakes are high.

It used to be thought that the utilities of electricity, water, and gas supply were inevitable monopolies because it only made economic sense for one enterprise to supply all the needs of all the consumers through one network. The Thatcher revolution changed all that, through privatisation coupled with appointment of a Regulator who acted in the consumers' interest to keep costs and prices in some kind of reasonable relationship. However, that is all the Regulator can do. In reality if there is only one supplier there is a monopoly. To some extent there is bound to follow monopolistic profits, which the enterprise will do its best to hide from the Regulator.

Recent governments have tried to encourage price competition by artificially creating many companies pricing gas and electricity even though the product is universally the same and supplied through a common network of pipes or cables. Telephone services were the first to be privatised, and competition easier to introduce, because although the wires were common, the service provided could be quite different, and pricing structures varied and tailor-made to suit different customers. Variable pricing at different times of day can to a lesser extent create competition in the electricity supply industry too. And of course there has sprung up a variety of suppliers of electricity generation, based both in this country and abroad.

All these moves toward competition can be applauded, and are nails in the coffin of monopoly. In many ways the Thatcher government chose the difficult task first. These utilities were monolithic public corporations that it was difficult to break up. As I have noted already many quasi-monopoly situations are perpetuated by the non-collection of Rent. Rent collection would be an easier change for a government to make, and would do more to encourage competition than changing the structure of the public utilities. However, the vested interests were, and still are, powerful and many. Many of course were and are supporters of the then Conservative government.

Although cartels are illegal, there exist many formal industry federations, which are careful not to discuss pricing formally, but in practice operate to maintain oligopoly in many industries. As I observed earlier entry into established industries by newcomers is made virtually impossible by the established advantage of ownership. An advantage that would be much reduced if Rent were collected. To take another obvious example, the sand and aggregate extraction industry is dominated by few players none of whom pay Rent for using the natural resources they are extracting. The same is true of the now almost obsolete coal mining industry, and the North Sea oil and gas extraction industries.

The waste disposal industry is a big land user, and sites for disposal are running out. Proper charging of Rent would have an immediate effect on our wasteful society, as well as increasing competition in the industry. "Where there's muck there's brass" and to the extent that there is little competition there is more "brass"!

New Labour has woken up to the fact that there exists an oligopoly of the big supermarkets, a situation that arose wholly from failing to collect Rent on the supermarkets when they were built. It could be said that that fault was coupled with a poor planning procedure, but the planning procedures were no match for the big guns of the huge food retailers who stood to gain millions from the planning permissions as described in more detail in the chapter on planning.

While it is by no means an absolute that all monopoly derives from the monopoly in land granted by society's failure to collect Rent its influence is so widespread that a change to Rent collection would be the most beneficial change to root out monopolistic tendencies.

International free trade is another important factor in keeping competition alive in the supply of many goods, and will be very important in large scale production. Industries such as steel, cars, aircraft and shipbuilding are examples where if protection is afforded to national producers there will be a tendency for monopoly pricing to develop. The problems of free trade when Rent is not collected in all the relevant nations have already been discussed.

In addition to the supply of utilities discussed above, the supply of other services such as broadcasting of radio and television, railways, roads, air traffic control, all need to be at a national level, and provided by one or few suppliers. Each has its own particular nuances, but general principles can be outlined. Where space is important, Rent must be assessed and collected. This is the best method of utilising space as we have seen when applied to all land use. In some cases operators, which in all cases should be private, can be kept competitive, by offering franchises for a fixed period of time. This works adequately for Independent Television, and the National Lottery. In other cases the use of a government appointed Regulator for an industry works reasonably well.

The sale of licences to six suppliers of mobile telephone network services is the most recent and striking use of franchising to keep competition healthy, and to make the users pay for limited space. However, it is not clear that the space of those air-waves need be limited to six. If the government has chosen to do so artificially then the government is imposing an artificial price, and creating a 'tax' revenue for itself in addition to a legitimate fee for the franchising.

The BBC as the publicly financed radio and television broadcaster may seem an exception to the call for privatisation of everything that can be privatised. Television channels seem to be of a quality in reverse proportion to the number of channels, each chasing ratings for adverting income to be maximized. Certainly a service that is outside the race for advertising ratings is a step towards maintaining programme standards, particularly the maintenance of minority tastes. Since a remit has to be given to the BBC as a public corporation, there seems little reason not to franchise the operation to a private corporation. The income would still be funded from a subscription whether this is mandatory, as now in the form of a licence fee, or optional. This raises the question of access to the 'ether'. In some ways it is a space like geographical space on land and sea. In a sense it is infinite, but in practise it is impractical to offer more than a fixed and small number of radio channels and TV channels. The user of these, which is on the supply side the broadcaster and on the receiving end the view and listener, can be asked to pay a charge very analogous to a Rent. This is simplest to collect from the supplier. The selling of franchises for a limited period of years would achieve this. The scale of the charge being reflected in the demand for that type of channel. There is clear distinction to be made between a 'commercial' channel with advertising revenue, and a higher quality channel offering minority tastes as part of its remit.

In the latter case the income from the public to the broadcaster could be a low subscription set when the corporation bids for its franchise. If it is kept low then it is likely to have a high uptake. Quality would be maintained by its remit, and by its desire not be excluded from bidding at the next tendering. Given these parameters, the 'Rent' raised by this channel might be much lower than the lucrative commercial channels. That is a reflection of society saying it wishes to have a quality, advertisement-free, service in addition to numerous commercial channels.

Still considering broadcasting, the use of scores of satellite and cable channels should be no different. Unless they are specifically for one type of broadcasting such as sport-only, news-only, etc. the number of channels franchised should be kept to a reasonable number. It will be interesting to see how the recent proliferation works in practice. So long as a BBC-quality, non-advertising service is maintained, maybe it will not matter that the amount of junk on other channels is multiplied many-fold. Advertisers will only patronize the successful in any case. And there will come a point when the poor quality outputs will be unable to afford even the minimum franchise fee if one is set. Setting a minimum franchise fee would seem therefore to be a way of cutting off the over exploitation of channels through the new methods.

I have discussed broadcasting 'space' whether it is from a land based mast, via satellite, or through cables. Similar arguments might seem to apply to 'cyberspace'.

In the recent past, at the height of the 'dot com' boom one could be fooled into thinking that all the economy of the planet would happen in the computer-linkage of the internet. However, it has to be remembered that the internet is just a big and soon to be universally-used tool. It does little other than oil the wheels of commerce that existed anyway; in the same ways as advertising agencies - all the buzz in the 1960s - were a growth industry way back then.

It is true that services not previously available are now available. E-mail replaces post and telephone services to some extent. Information formerly only available in reference libraries is available in a disseminated way. These services are wealth and replace or run alongside the wealth inherent in the older versions. It is also true that advertising, choosing, and ordering goods and services through the internet is providing a service that is itself wealth, but it reduces and maybe replaces the former methods. On the other hand the book you order, the holiday you choose, the car you buy, the food you have delivered, are all just the same as they were before. They all still happen in the real world, and the internet is a tool for publicizing them, and getting orders into factories and offices. The factories and offices are still needed. They may or may not need more or less people as a result of using the new tool.

Does any of this create a monopoly for any corporation? Microsoft has been criticized, but its pre-eminence will not be long lasting in my view. (It relies for its pre-eminence on patents, and its established place in the market re-enforced by advertising. And in all probability the legislation against it will turn out to be superfluous as was the earlier oil anti-trust legislation.) Nor is the cyber channel like a broadcasting channel. The medium may not be of infinite capacity but it might be to all intents and purposes: time will tell. At present any number of connections by millions of people can be accessing millions of separate items of data. By contrast broadcasting channels may be limited to a few score, or at most a few hundred. It may be that broadcasting channels will eventually disappear, forced out of the market place by television on demand through an internet type of distribution. If this does happen I would hope to see a BBC-quality provider of programmes that would create the material in the first place. And it is this service that could and should still be franchised in the way described above, even if the method of distribution has changed.

CHAPTER 30

Cyberspace

The twenty-first century will certainly be one where the developments in the last decade or so of the twentieth century will be exploited to the full. How fully the internet will be part of our lives, most of us have yet to see. What other new devices and methods will be developed we can imagine, but cannot with any certainty predict.

The 'dot com' companies making their appearance on the stock markets of America and Europe give the impression that they will be all important, and the old-fashioned trading methods used by older feet-on-the-ground companies will be pushed aside by the brave new world. But many have been humbled somewhat by the collapse of some early entrants, and the severe decline of share prices generally.

There are real new tools on offer from the internet and allied technologies that make useful information available in ways that were undreamt of twenty years ago. Information of certain kinds is valuable. Information made available quickly can be more valuable than the same information that might have taken days or weeks to transmit by older methods. Some companies sell this information, and some companies sell the expertise to make this information exchange possible. Both types of company will prosper if they offer a real service.

There are other more frivolous uses of the cyberspace world that seek to offer games or fads. We can expect these to be with us no longer than fashions and fads of earlier decades. In their short timescale they may be routes to a fortune for the entrepreneurs or investors, or they might not.

The opening up of cyberspace might suggest that the limits of the physical world have been removed. Companies can trade in the invisible world of bytes and offer all manner of goods and services without ever being based in one country rather than another. They therefore owe no allegiance to one nation, nor need pay any tax to a government. This indeed to some seems like a whole new world. But is it? Is it not just another clever tool of mankind?

If a new printing technique arrives on the scene as has happened regularly throughout the last five centuries, books and papers can be, and have been produced quicker and cheaper using the new technique. The development of first steam and then internal combustion and finally jet engines transformed the transport of people and goods throughout the nineteenth and twentieth centuries. In the same way the techniques now appearing and coming to fruition ever more rapidly in the information age, and using cyberspace, are doing just what early technologies did for earlier generations. They all helped the wealth creating process. They all have given opportunities for clever or far-sighted entrepreneurs. Like transport, information technology is only a means to an end. Even mass-produced print was needed not for itself but as a means of oiling the wheels of the wealth creating process. It may seem more tangible than the other examples, and some books and other printed matter have endured as works of art. But the bulk of printed matter of today and former centuries is and was as ephemeral as a train journey: useful while happening but gone tomorrow. Information may have a 'shelf-life' measured in seconds or weeks, or much longer. But its economic value will decline and eventually fade to nothing or almost nothing.

Cyberspace is not a new world. It is an imaginary space where useful technologies can help us in the real, on the ground world. We will have life, and have it perhaps more abundantly, where we have always had it: in the places we inhabit, the clothes we wear, the games we play, the arts we enjoy, relationships with each other, the few possessions we really need and care about enough to look after. The new abundance, if the new technologies help us with abundance, will still be poorly distributed and the pattern of poor distribution will be skewed the more as there is a more sophisticated population - or a larger population - and the more there is abundance of goods and services. If the need to see natural economic law was necessary for justice in the enclosed worlds of the nineteenth and twentieth centuries it will be the more imperative in the twenty-first.

CHAPTER 31

Immigration

In an ideal world all would be free to choose where they lived. That choice would involve an assessment of the costs and benefits of living in more or less favourable places. Naturally favourable would be as significant as socially favourable.

It will be clear from what has already been written that all individuals would by their presence contribute to the chosen society. It would be impossible for an individual to live and work in a place that commanded a Rent without paying that Rent. Each would therefore be gainfully employed to be able to pay the Rent. Being a wealth creating member of the community he would help to enhance the overall vitality of the community. If he chose to be involved in a less favourable area commanding no Rent, i.e. a marginal position, he and others coming there would begin to build a new social structure.

I have earlier referred to the fact that the world is not overcrowded. It is never likely to be if it is socially developed. Developed communities tend to have falling populations.

Immigration for even a crowded island like Britain would therefore cease to be a problem. The magnet that draws immigrants to Britain at present is the stability of the country, the opportunities, and the welfare on offer.

In a new Britain where Rent was collected, and individuals looked after their own needs because they had been empowered to do so, immigrants would not be motivated to come merely to collect welfare - there would be no free handouts. This is usually cited as the reason undesirable immigrants try and gain entry to Britain, legally or illegally. But in a new Britain under Rent collection economics, and as a stable place where there are opportunities to provide for oneself, new immigrants might be tempted to come. The fault in the world order would then be that other countries were unstable and did not offer any similar opportunities.

Good economic migrants are usually welcomed by developed nations. These are people seen to be well qualified and able to fill job vacancies where there are shortages of suitably qualified persons in the indigenous population. What is also clear, but never acknowledged is the fact that an increasing population increases the overall Rent in the nation. This is clearly of benefit to those who control, by appropriation, the Rent, as is the case in today's Britain – and elsewhere. But the problem is manifested by competition for jobs between the indigenous workforce and the new migrants. Wages are depressed by competition when Rent is not collected. The people who fear immigration are the already disadvantaged.

If Rent were collected properly in Britain and other developed countries immigration would present no fears, but would by contrast present all members of the society with greater aggregate wealth. But could there be a danger that even without the prospect of a free handout from welfare the number of immigrants would be so large as to make the indigenous population feel unable to absorb the changes? Changes in culture being the key point. Cultures grow up over centuries. We hope to feel comfortable with the culture we know and understand being unchanged, or only evolving slowly. That can be disrupted by a sudden influx of foreign people, with their different looks, different standards, different ethics and different religions. A limit on the numbers as a percentage of the population would seem to be necessary. Such a step would only be necessary if the differences in economic and social pressures were acute as between one part of the world and another.

The goal for humanity is therefore to enhance the attractions of other parts of the world by persuading governments to set fair systems in all parts of the world. The international structures such as they exist should be pushing this forward. It will need further world-embracing organizations to do so. I do not mean to imply the need for massive new bureaucratic structures, merely forums in which representatives of all nations with a serious agenda can agree how to proceed.

It is not my intention to postulate in detail how we move from an imperfect world, to one based on liberty and opportunity. But it is my intention to explain the goals that each of us need to strive towards. Only by understanding can we know how to elect democratic governments that will with other democratically elected governments move towards a better global system.

I would expect that geographic areas such as the EU would push out their boundaries. There is a strong danger that will happen with the wrong parameters. The difficulties of EU enlargement have been discussed in chapters on Europe and the EMU. But the one thing the EU does have is the freedom of movement for all its citizens. If that expanded to include all the Eastern European countries; and if the same process were to happen in Asia and Africa and South America, it is conceivable that the world would have six or eight equally matched, or at least roughly equally attractive, free trade and free-movement areas. It ought then to be possible to break down the barriers between these areas, and have complete freedom of movement between all parts of the world. I do not expect to see this happen in ten years, but it could happen in a hundred. But, only if we begin to understand how now. Trying to force it to happen in the EU or elsewhere before the basic concepts of Rent collection are understood and practised will cause problems on a larger scale of the kind that not only I have identified, but have been the subject of so much anguish for most contemporary observers.

If and when the right conditions are set immigration, which in Britain we see as a problem today, would cease to be a worry. It is unlikely to be any more of a problem than we have now of mobility between Germany and France, or Greece and England. In other words we do not perceive a problem within the EU because while the conditions are not exactly the same in each country, there are strong reasons why the majority choose to stay where their roots are.

From what I have already said about the EU in Chapter 20 it will be clear that I am only holding up the EU as an area where free trade - of a kind - and free mobility of populations exists. Moves towards federation would both be unnecessary and undesirable both in Europe and in other parts of the world. Each nation must remain as a nation. The nation defines the area in which the people elect a democratic government. Each will be different even when they all have adopted a Rent based economy. Each country will therefore be on offer to men and women from all parts of the world, and will need to set the appropriate conditions. The population would otherwise throw out the government, or as a last resort vote with their feet by moving elsewhere. It seems to me inevitable that some countries will set better conditions for freedom than others, and some will be at the mercy of dangerous men. It is up to the populace as whole to see the dangers and reject the dictators and silver-tongued charlatans. The price of freedom is eternal vigilance, and of course, an educated and discerning electorate.

CHAPTER 32

War and Peace

One of the essential functions of government is to maintain a military force to defend the community from armed attack from outsiders. Such attacks have been commonplace throughout history. Since the history of settlements, that is. Nomadic tribes may have sparred with each other, but rarely so, and such bouts could hardly be called war. They had little to fight about, and nothing to gain from winning or to fear from defeat. Perhaps not quite nothing: the competitive nature of man may have seen virtue in fighting merely for the sake of being a victor in the complete abstract. More likely there were the spoils of women to be abducted.

Nomadic tribes might have sought to keep other tribes off the territory over which they were accustomed to forage. But already then they can be seen to be territorial and not truly nomadic. As true settlements established, characterized by buildings, corralling of cattle and growing of crops, so fighting was likely to be more worthwhile for the victor. Not so much to take over the settlement, though that happened later in the history of civilization, but to take over the peoples who would then be subjugated to the conquerors. And again women were desirable prizes and functional in building up the population of the dominant tribes.

In the earliest civilization of the Old World, ancient Egypt, wars were few. This was partly because the Egyptians had few civilized neighbours, and more probably because the religion of the Egyptians insisted that men were buried on Egyptian soil. Thus no one wanted to wage war abroad for fear of being killed and buried in foreign lands. They would then not be able to enter the after-life, which was a crucial part of the beliefs of the ancient Egyptians. The early Egyptian civilization had its internal battles for supremacy, and in its very long history the country has suffered from invasion and control by Greeks, Romans, Arabs, Ottomans, and much later French and British. Egypt was of interest to these foreigners for its gold, its fertility and the wealth that could be derived. In recent history for its shipping route through the Suez canal to the Red Sea, and to the Far East.

Moving through history we have seen the Greek and Roman empires conquering territory and not only subjugating the people but occupying the territory as a controlling elite. Their methods were military might, and physical coercion, making the conquered race actual or virtual slaves.

The economy of the Romans rested on conquest and slavery. The great wealth of the Emperors, the priesthood, the senators and other elites, which took the form of buildings and lavish adornments for those buildings and themselves, resulted from the use of slaves as workers in the construction of the palaces, civic forums and streets, theatres and temples. Slavery was also used to produce food and wine, and work with metals and minerals. Pillaging treasure and later taxation of foreign colonies were methods used to bring wealth to the centre, Rome, and other important cities in the Roman Empire. The pattern with modifications was repeated in later centuries by the Arabs, the Ottomans, and the British, and other European nations. In the Old World space was not itself at a premium, but strategic sites were. Water was essential for settlements, and the Romans were builders of incredible aqueducts to bring water from its source to the towns and cities where it was needed. Such sources were therefore eagerly sought, developed and defended. So too were sites of military significance. Hills dominating valleys on all sides were ideal places to build. Ports were developed where the coastline, the prevailing wind and the seabed were all favourable. Whole tracts of land were designated as routes for commerce, for example the King's Highway in the near east in what is now Jordan which was an essential route for goods travelling from Turkey and the areas further east bound for Egypt. Such routes were possible because the land was not mere desert, and had food and water at settlements along the way.

The strategic and economic importance of all these ports, hills, tracts of land and water sources were fought over throughout the history of the Old World based on the shores and islands of the Mediterranean Sea. Control of such features meant prosperity for the tribes or nations controlling them. Hill forts and castles may have been mainly defensive to keep control of an area once it had been conquered, but extracting tariffs from traders using narrow passes through the terrain were also common, and the wealth of such ancient settlements as Petra were solely derived from such tariffs.

As religion crossed the boundaries of tribes and nation states wars have taken the form of religious feuds, notably the Crusades in the early Middle Ages, when Christian armies fought Muslims for supremacy in the Middle East. From our perspective nearly a thousand years later, it seems the wars were anything but Christian acts. If we can imagine ourselves in their timeframe we might feel more clearly the economic necessity of waging war. The flags under which they marched were then, as so often in the following centuries, banners under which like-minded peoples could unite to defend their way of life, and very likely their very existence. Like all military strategists the Crusaders, and indeed later warmongers in Northern Europe, sought to control the key natural features I have already listed: the hills, the water, the ports and the islands. The same battles are being waged today. The Golan Heights on the border of Syria and Israel are disputed because they are the sources of water that feed the Jordan River. As a result the waters of Israel are vulnerable if there were any interference by hostile neighbours. Jordan too would be vulnerable, but being Muslim like Syria, there is less likely to be hostility. Israel of course being only fifty years old and having had to establish its people in that part of the world, and being Jewish not Muslim, feels vulnerable.

But old battles and old banners persist long after they serve any purpose. The divisions in Ireland are along the lines of religious sects, even though sects of the same religion, are phoney battles: phoney anyway as far as worshiping any God is concerned. As a minority "tribe" the Catholics in Northern Ireland can feel aggrieved because the majority "tribe" discriminates against them, and there is a nasty history of persecution to be forgotten as well. Twentieth century governments in Ireland and other parts of the world where minorities are discriminated against were at fault for failing to set democratic principles, and perpetuating privilege for the ruling elite rather than opening up opportunities in the territory for all whatever their religion, colour or background. This function and duty of government has of course been made harder by the long period of resentment. But where so often the problem has seemed intractable, because change might seem to be giving in to unlawful pressure, had governments seen a way to economic freedom that leads to democratic equality, then the feuds might have withered more quickly. What seems clear is that failing to address the problem of privilege has made the resolution of disputes that much harder.

The Basques in Northern Spain are equally adamant that they want to rule themselves, and have their own territory. They too use terrorist activity to make themselves heard. Quite rightly the Spanish government will not be pushed by such methods.

The Basques have no more absolute right to be in Spain than you or I. If we were there we would hope to be living under some democratic government that would look after all our interests. As I have explained in earlier chapters of this book, our democratic and economic interests, which go had in hand, can only be safeguarded if we all, Basque, Irish, Christian, Muslim, black or white, male of female, or any other group or combination of characteristics, have an opportunity equal to every other member of that democracy. Indeed, as I have also argued, the world order can really only be harmonious if all the democracies play by the same rules. But even if all countries do not do so, it is essential in a proper democracy that the people understand the economic mechanism, set fair conditions which are immutable whatever the colour of the government - preferably in a short written constitution - and operate free from any imposed outside superstate. Then if conditions are not to the peoples' liking the government can be blamed and if blameworthy removed.

Now under these conditions, will the Basques be content? Will the sects in Northern Ireland be content? Will the Palestinians in Israel be content? If not, I suspect the answer lies in the resentment of past hurts. It may take a generation of fairness to wash away those hurts. There have been many others in other parts of the world in recent history. Blacks and Coloureds in South Africa; Serbs and Croats in the Balkans; Kurds in Iraq; the oppressed peoples in East Timor: they have all had their conflicts. If not wars, certainly not peace, and peace and prosperity is what they really want. Societies allow warmongers to surface from time to time only when there is an injustice that rallies the people to a leader promising liberation.

In our modern world it is hard to remember that slavery was only exorcised from European and American life in the nineteenth century. The subjugation of huge numbers of people to slavery or virtual slavery from Greek and Roman times to virtually the present day has structured our societies in a way that has re-enforced the pyramidal layering of society: a mass of underprivileged at the bottom supporting a small elite at the top, with a limited structure of freemen in the middle some of whom become privileged attendants to the elite. The abuse of humans imported from Africa as slaves led to a real war: the American Civil War.

Whilst it is not the case that all European nations had slaves from Roman times until the nineteen century, it is fair to say that the feudal system perpetuated an underclass, and conscription to armies and navies amounted to a de facto slavery for the conscripts. It is also apparent that the nations who made use of these methods had the most powerful ruling elites, and tended to dominate their neighbours, often battling to move boundaries in favour of the stronger nation. There were frequent wars between England and France, and also Spain. Up to recent times the boundaries in Eastern Europe were very fluid. Russians, Prussians, Germans, Slavs, Poles and others have had a turbulent history. The boundary disputes were of significance to the ruling classes because they could raise taxes from the economic activities of the people they had annexed. Taxes were often in kind: agricultural produce or manufactured goods. The collection of taxes was likely to be very imperfect. Some small artisans no doubt escaped the collector. But the more prosperous, established, and therefore visible, landowner would contribute significantly. He in turn would set the conditions accordingly for his workers on the estate. The conditions were hard, but not unbearable. There was an alternative until all land was enclosed. That alternative was for the worker to use unenclosed land to feed himself.

We have seen in this chapter how from Egyptian, Greek and Roman times the elite at the top of the pyramidal structure had great wealth, and used this wealth to expand their territorial control. Empires came and went, as the motivation to expand is strong when nations are vigorously led and hungry for aggrandisement, and weak when the spoils of war and appropriation are in surfeit. We have seen how slavery, absolute or various forms of coercion have been used to maintain the wealth of the ruling classes.

The wars of the Old World have been over strategic natural resources as well as and alongside the expansion of territory. Peace has been rare even for the island race: the British. Conflicts have been most frequent where there are many small neighbours, and one or more powerful nations.

I should also mention the American War of Independence as the largest break away of a nation from its rulers, the British. Other conflicts that sought or seek independence have been mentioned: the Basques, Northern Ireland, and the Balkan states. Clearly the massive size of the United States now, and probably even of the American colonies then in the eighteenth century, necessitated its independence as a democracy free of any outside influence. Size is important to a democracy, for a very small nation cannot function by itself. Also, it can be argued, nor can a very large one, and the fact that the USA is a collection of semi-autonomous states is crucial. It is possible that some of them or groups of them should be more autonomous. I do not get the feeling that the USA today is one nation.

In the struggle for independence of ethnic groups within modest sized nations I advocate the adoption of fair economic structures within the whole nation to address the problem, not independence. My view is that the concepts of economic justice contained in this book would have had a bearing on the conflicts of recent history. The conflicts of longer ago were often if not always manifesting the importance of natural resources that are at the heart of economic justice now. We should not be surprised if conflicts arise when economic injustices are extreme. While this book clearly sets out how injustice in the nation state is harmful to that state and its citizens, it also should be appreciated that if there are minorities within the nation state who are oppressed by the injustices there will develop a potentially dangerous situation.

Also if in the world order rich nations prosper and poor ones stay poor, and the economic models we are content to use re-enforce injustices between nations we can only expect there to be conflict between nations.

Nations large or small who have rulers of immense power and wealth tend to be more bellicose than democratic nations. As I have explained in earlier chapters the ruling elite is maintained either by subjugating the citizens physically as virtual slaves, or economically, as mere wage-slaves - and grossly underpaid.

Bellicose nations led by tyrants are rare in today's developed world. Iraq would be a current example. However, there are examples in Africa frequently: Ethiopia, Rwanda, Mozambique, Nigeria, Zimbabwe, and others.

Whilst the old rulers had to rely on taxing their colonies or conquests, and enslaving their own or imported peoples, and did so in both cases by coercion, let it be clear that the same result is achieved by today's rulers by denying equal access to land and natural resources. It has been truly said there is no need to enslave and spend energy on keeping a person restrained yet working if the people do not have freedom to work for themselves. If many people rely on a few to give them employment the few need do nothing. The many will be obliged to come to one of the employers and will work harder than any slave, and will seek only enough reward to keep themselves from dire poverty. No amount of government tinkering can change that fundamental fact. As we have seen, to the extent governments try and alleviate poverty without addressing the root cause the more harm is done and the more expensive the government machine becomes. Gross economic injustices have created wars in the distant past, the recent past, and the present. The same will happen in the future. Peace is likely, though never guaranteed, by prosperity and freedom within nations, and justice between nations. The price of this freedom and justice is the vigilance to set and maintain a society based on fundamental truths, and the vigilance to kick out any government that flouts these truths. On an international scale, governments need to agree through world-wide treaties and trading agreements to set fundamentally similar patterns of justice in each nation state.

CHAPTER 33

Terrorism

As the twenty-first century dawns we are seeing that old inter-nation wars are being replaced by terrorist incidents and prolonged campaigns that are much harder to contain, or see a start of or an end to. The most dramatic of these to date has been the September 11th 2001 attack on the twin towers of the World Trade Center in New York and on the Pentagon in Washington by hi-jacked aircraft.

Terrorist activity is so effective against an urban civilization. Having made a threat felt by a dramatic incident, words or subsequent actions have a disproportionate effect. After September 11th, the few, and on the whole non-fatal, incidents that the terrorists subsequently perpetrated with the dissemination of packets of white powder, some of which contained Anthrax spores, disrupted life in the USA and other civilized countries. It takes only a little imagination for the possibility of what might lie ahead for the bulk of the population to be fearful of going about their daily business. The authorities feel obliged to draw up expensive and disruptive procedures and contingency plans.

The IRA has waged war in a similar way for decades. The cost to economic activity in terms of disruption has been incalculable. After so long a time the populace may be inured to some extent to the latent threat, but the costs of anti-terrorism action, and even the mind-set of the whole population, has been woven into everyday life.

These costs include the erosion of liberty. The freedom for individuals to go about without interference from other citizens and from employees of the state is curtailed in times of crisis. And each crisis measure, while bemoaned by a few champions of liberty, tends to become permanent in one form of another. The carrying of identity cards, for example, is excused by the majority on the grounds that it ought to deter or detain the criminally intent. They say that the innocent have nothing to fear. They forget that the criminals will find it easy to forge, or obtain by other illegal means, such cards. More importantly they forget the potential abuse of power handed to petty officials. They forget the cost of setting up and administering such a universally applied measure. They forget that it will become impossible to undertake even the most routine transaction without identity cards. They forget the possibility that 'swiping' cards through terminals linked to central computers will log the movements of all, or selected, individuals.

In Chapter 32 I outlined the history of wars through the ages, and concluded that economic injustices were at the root of all conflicts, both inter-nation, and those characterised by terrorist or guerrilla activities such as in Northern Ireland and the Basque country. We have learned to live with these irritations however much politicians may pour out rhetoric abhorring them. As I have pointed out these disaffected peoples would have tired of their struggles if the conditions under which they lived were truly democratic and economically free. This can never be a certainty, but contented people are hard to recruit for terrorist campaigns. History is peppered with would-be tyrants who apparently seek aggrandisement, but in each case they needed to recruit disaffected peoples who could see a cause. Even Alexander the Great had the excuse of liberating Greek peoples from foreign control in his Persian expeditions. But it is probable he conquered for the sake of conquering in his later campaigns.

In more recent centuries, and certainly in modern times, the foot-soldiers required for military action, even guerrilla and terrorist activity can only be recruited where there is either conscription, coercion, or a 'just' cause. The foremost is only available to nation-states when they wage war. Coercion is only available when a powerful tribal leader has a physical or economic stranglehold on a population that is close at hand. And the last - the excuse of a 'just' cause - is only likely to be found when a powerful leader highlights real or imagined injustices for a disadvantaged group. That is not to say small sects of religious or quasi-religious fanatics have not seduced numbers of people to join them in strange cults, some of which end in tragic mass suicide or other horrific acts. But these are not terrorist acts in the sense that they are not acts against the state, or authority of some kind.

Other fanatics have been able to use the promise of eternal life to employ individuals in suicide missions against symbols of authority. This most nearly fits the picture of the Muslim-extremists' attack on the World Trade Center and the Pentagon. But would even these fanatics, who are worlds away from normal Muslim teaching, have found such exploits possible if they did not have an 'evil' target to attack?

Individuals can become deranged and some will perpetrate horrors on society. But major acts of terrorism require organization, money, recruits, and sustained campaigns. To feed the minds of the recruits the leaders need to spell out a scenario of evil to which they can bend their minds.

Now it is not unknown for certain people to object to the way of life of modern society. Sexual mores, for example, which are lax in most Western countries nowadays, may provoke the opprobrium of more traditional religious sects or societies. However, while such behaviour may provoke adverse comment it is not likely to lead to outright physical attack. What is likely to provoke terrorist organizations is the economic supremacy of one nation over others. In this sense it easy to see that America, as the arch advocate of free enterprise and globalisation, would be the target for such thinking and indeed recent action. It may not be clear to everyone why that should be so. Americans have no excuse for being blind to the injustices they perpetuate. A proper analysis of the Rent generated by free enterprise, and the compounding of that Rent effect by broadening the market by free trade – nowadays called globalisation – will clearly elucidate the impoverishment of the already disadvantaged nations and societies, and the enhancement of wealth of the already fortunate. Chapter 18 on Free Trade and Chapter 19 on Agriculture have shown in some detail what happens when there is not a level playing field between nations who seek to trade with each other.

Terrorism is no way to address these problems in a civilised world. But the rich nations of the world are uncivilised if they cannot move ahead from nineteenth and twentieth century *laissez faire* economics and see the need for collection of Rent. And if some nations can see that and others cannot or refuse to acknowledge it, they should not expect to be able to trade with each other.

American politicians, and indeed those in Britain and other European countries, are seen to be seeking to stamp out terrorism by making it difficult for the terrorists to operate. This is an impossibility. A desperate individual or group of individuals, particularly those led by fanaticism of one sort or another, and who are prepared to give up their lives for a cause, will always be able to inflict terrorist acts on an urban society. Of course those who flout the law and commit murder should be brought to justice. But it is not enough to do that. In fact it will often be difficult to do even that. Indeed it is impossible to do so when the perpetrator is already dead. The urban and so-called civilised West therefore has no choice but to alter its ways.

Ironically, the campaign to bring to justice those responsible initiated in the aftermath of September 11th 2001 was titled Enduring Freedom by President Bush. This provoked no comment, perhaps because he himself was focussing on freedom for Americans to continue to go about their business unhampered by there being enemies of America present in the world. But he was blind to the lack of freedom inherent in the American way of life. In the way even Americans treat each other. In the way all of the nations of the world have the same flaws. In the way trade between each of these countries is impossible without exacerbating the problems.

Economic justice, which is only made possible by the proper collection of Rent, is essential if such societies really want to minimise the risk of terrorism.

As will be clear from the whole range of changes that result from the proper collection of Rent, which have been examined in this book, the perception of all members of society will be so different that there will be no genuine serious grievance for even extremists to attack. I have tried to show elsewhere that there is no Utopia. The challenge of a just society for us to live in is for all members of society to want to see a just system. There will still be people in the world who do not want it. Either because they are blind to the need for it, bigoted about their own conception of economic justice, or determined that a system similar to the status quo is in their best interests, even if they see that it cannot suit all the people of that society. But if enough people can see the justice of Rent collection, and can see that no other method of economic organization will achieve justice, then the majority will by democratic means always elect their representatives in government to ensure that Rent collection laws are in place. When that is achieved, and hopefully enshrined in written constitutions, then the threat of terrorist attacks will diminish. When that is achieved throughout the world then the populations of all countries can enjoy the prosperity that is due to them from the application of human effort to an abundant world.

CHAPTER 34

Partnership

There are a number of commonwealth entities operating in the UK, but they do not enjoy a popular image and they too often have an ethos of communality - almost communism - that gives them lack of leadership. There are however, some high profile examples such as the John Lewis Partnership.

What gets in the way of ordinary trading companies being friendlier to a joint interest in the outcome for all employees is the taxation system. In various ways both Conservative and Labour governments have tried to give incentives to companies to encourage employee share ownership. They have either been not attractive enough or so attractive that they have been withdrawn. In a situation where income tax was a thing of the past (it was meant to be temporary), companies would be free to offer shares instead of salaries.

In the pure situation all employees would be entitled to shares. The number of share issued by the company would be governed by the trading results of the company. Since salary costs would be nil, the trading profit would be large by normal standards. Scrip dividends, i.e. free issue of shares, would therefore be given to all employees. Each employee would get the same scrip dividend, but the hierarchy would determine how many original shares each employee held. The CEO would have more than the junior employees.

Having no salaries as such, each employee would need to sell back to the company shares he held, and would do so on a regular basis. (Or if the employer was a plc, employees could sell in the open market. In this case the company having cash reserves representing the new shares issued would need to buy them back from the market place unless the directors could better re-invest the cash in building up the business.) However, in a successful company, it would be seen that the share price was, over time, increasing. It would therefore be in the interests of those who could do so to defer selling. Different employees would be at different stages in their careers. Young single employees might then be able to save for housing or later family commitments. Young parents might be selling more than they received, i.e. selling some saved earlier. Older employees would be saving for retirement, so would sell less than they received each year.

Why all these changes from the way things have traditionally been done? The answers have partly been given by the governments of both Right and Left. They see that commitment of the people working in the company lead to successful businesses. Indeed the long established John Lewis Partnership thinks the same way, though its scheme is a very diluted partnership.

Those involved know best whether a company is on the right track. Rapid selling of the shares by employees would give a clear signal to management that all was not well. Finance directors would need to balance funding from banks, from employees and from outside equity holders.

It can be emphasised that both income tax and capital gains tax are barriers to this kind of involvement. A Rent orientated economy, which does away with these taxes, opens the way for this kind of stakeholding in companies.

It can be argued that workers should not hold all their eggs in one basket and should not rely on one company for both their livelihood, and their savings. Nor would they. It would be up to each to decide to hold shares in their company, or to sell and re-invest in another. Just as any investor might do.

But it is probable there would be a large body of 'stakeholder' shareholders. This would work to everyone's advantage. The directors would have a committed workforce. They would also in a publicly quoted company have cash resources to re-invest in growing the business, leading to a rapid development of a market. The employees would have a share in the efforts they made over and above that which a normal employee has in today's large company. Employees would have savings that would be likely to grow at a faster rate than money in a bank or building society account. Employees as shareholders would have a say in some of the key strategic decisions made by the directors. One of these might well be where the workplace was located. Rent would be high in congested areas. Employees would probably 'vote' for cheaper and more congenial locations.

In summary, by using shares as currency with which to reward workers, the conditions of the very small firm or family partnership is simulated. This has the advantage of sharing in both the success and failures of the company. While no trade can survive when trading conditions have fundamentally changed (as an example, oil and gas have replaced coal as the economic fuel), companies will be able to better withstand temporarily poor trading conditions, and will be quicker to adapt to new conditions.

It might be of interest to compare this shareholding acting as currency, for all those employed in the company, to the national economy where the actual currency is a 'shareholding' of each citizen vis-à-vis the rest of the world. In the chapter on currencies, one could imagine the debate as if the nation were one large plc. If we trade successfully with the rest of the world our 'shares' or currency are highly valued. If others around the world perceive our currency is a good investment they will buy into it and it will increase in value in terms of other currencies. When this happens we, all of us, enjoy a 'strong' currency when we are abroad, and enjoy lower prices for goods made by others abroad. We are in fact able to take less out of the economy for consumption when we measure the amount in terms of these strong units. This allows for more investment in new enterprises. I am using terms that can be seen to be interchangeable; on the smaller scale, considering the individual companies and their shares, and on the larger scale pertaining to a nation and its currency.

CHAPTER 35

United States of America – a Failed Dream?

There is indeed abundance in America, but there is also widespread poverty, and misery. Nevertheless capitalism as practised in the USA is held up as a model of how the world should be, and European, Second and Third World countries, even the mighty China, now see it as a pattern to emulate. There are dissenters, of course, as seen at most major conferences on world trade and similar occasions, but their numbers are still relatively few. These people do highlight – although never very clearly – the fact that America is a protectionist bloc. The administration may talk of free trade, but only on American terms. The present state of affairs in far removed from free trade, as I discussed in Chapter 18.

America has had a chequered history in its few centuries since being colonised by Europeans in the seventeenth century. When the Pilgrim Fathers landed they had a strong sense of justice and very early set up the elements of democracy in stark contrast to the prevailing notion of the 'divine right of kings' from which they had fled when they left England. The Puritans with their background of conflict with the Roman Catholic Church in England were keen to establish not only their own self-governing church but also self-government for their whole existence. Church and everyday life were for them intimately intertwined. America was at that time still a colony of England, and therefore government of any kind needed approval from the English King, Charles I. In Massachusetts a charter was granted under which the Puritans could be virtually self-governing.

It is not necessary to detail the exact workings of these early democratic moves, but it is germane to the 'American

Dream' that these early Councils and Courts, which were largely established to sort out the everyday disputes of the small population, developed rapidly into Upper and Lower chambers; the members of the Lower House being elected.

Each of the English colonies and after independence (1775) the fledgling independent States had their own constitutions. The federal constitution followed rapidly after independence developing out of the Articles of Confederation (1781) and was drafted speedily in 1787. It is a model of brevity unequalled by other written constitutions. Amendments are possible, but need wide consensus, and thus there have only been seventeen after the first ten, which introduced the Bill of Rights in 1791. And of these seventeen two were needed to introduce prohibition, and its repeal.

Contrary to popular perception the constitution does not mention the pursuit of happiness. What is does say in its pre-amble is "We the People of the United States, in Order to form a more perfect Union, establish Justice, insure domestic Tranquillity, provide for the common defence, promote the general Welfare, and secure the Blessings of Liberty to ourselves and our Posterity, do ordain and establish this Constitution for the United States of America." Domestic tranquillity…general welfare…the blessings of liberty. These together with justice might be expected to ensure happiness. However, these fine words were not interpreted in the articles of the constitution, which primarily sets out the structures of government. The interpretation relied and still relies on the elected members of the various bodies.

In the early days of the federation the administration of the economy verged on the *laissez-faire*. The greatest interpretation of the 'blessings of liberty' and of justice was over the question of slavery, culminating in the Civil War, and eventually an amendment to the constitution making slavery illegal. As has been pointed out in earlier chapters, the early development of manufacturing and commerce in the various states could proceed apace without much governmental control for the simple reason that there always seemed enough natural resources for the population to exploit. The population was expanded rapidly by refugees from poverty or persecution in Europe, and uncontrolled immigration continued to be allowed well into the twentieth century. The Founding Fathers and their early successors were therefore barely concerned with economic justice. Their concerns were to avoid religious bigotry and to establish independence from any influence of other nations, or indeed from any regal figurehead in their own country. The mood in Europe was changing at about the same time with the overthrow of the aristocracy in the French Revolution and federalism of the German states.

It is fair to say that with each generation Americans may pay lip service to their past in celebrating their liberty, just as they celebrate their bounty on Thanksgiving Day, but it is largely only their democracy that has come down the generations. Not that that should be belittled: democracy was a fearful concept to the elite in England, and even after the French revolution France, while trumpeting *liberte, fraternite* and *equalite,* has continued for the next two centuries with a centralist and elitist administration.

Democracy has triumphed in America, and the federal administration is in constant check by the terms of the constitution, leaving the State legislatures to set their own laws unless constrained by that constitution – which as we have seen is very difficult to amend. The 2000 election for president whilst almost a dead heat, and in the eyes of some a fiasco of the first order did show clearly and plainly how the democratic process is constrained. It is true that the electoral college does not function as it was set up to do. The states were each to choose men or women of high repute and beyond reproach, and they would each cast their vote as they thought fit for the man they thought would be the best president. Now what happens is that the men or women sent by each state to the electoral college merely vote in accordance with the majority verdict of their particular state. But this is in accordance, perhaps, with most people's idea of democracy nowadays. It would in any case not be of major significance unless, as in 2000, the overall vote was neck and neck.

What has not triumphed is the *laissez-faire* economics internally coupled with protectionism externally. Or rather, I should say it has triumphed for the wealthy and been disastrous for the minorities, the disadvantaged and the less talented amongst the USA's own peoples. And disastrous for many of the poorer nations of the world, who have become in debt to America.

Champions of the American system may argue that the development of the USA into the global superstate in the twentieth century enabled the world to be a more peaceful place, defeating the forces of darkness in two world wars, and holding back and eventually defeating the tide of communism and socialism as practised in Soviet Russia, China and too many parts of Europe as well as the Third World countries. But it can be argued that the USA with it vast natural resources and strong domestic economy would in any case have been a powerful nation, and by exploiting rather than trading fairly with developing countries has been the cause of some of those lesser nations falling victims to socialism.

So where has the dream faded? Where are sweet dreams now nightmares? What was the dream in the first place? In theory all Americans can aspire to become president. And by implication can achieve any other exalted position in the economy or the affairs of the nation. In practice, the candidates for the highest office needs a deep pocket, even to enter the race for it. Those who have entered the race have either inherited great wealth or accumulated it. In each case the role of Rent has been of great significance.

So the dream that all Americans subscribe to is that the sky is the limit for each of them personally. But it is also the inheritance of the Founding Fathers that all should live in a free and just society, where the chance to achieve to the fullest potential of each individual is not dependent on the subjugation of anyone else.

I referred elsewhere (Chapter 20) to the fact that Americans have some understanding of the principle of Rent. They do, or some do, and many more should. The principle, and its effect on society, was lucidly explained by Henry George the American writer at the end of the nineteenth century. He lectured and wrote many books the most famous of which is Progress and Poverty, published in 1879. Americans are still aware of his work even if other nationalities are not, though many should be as his work was translated into at least fifteen languages. Since Henry George's time progress in the economic sense has made Gulliverian strides, each huge step succeeding the next with ever increasing rapidity. We should therefore not be surprised that the poverty, which he explained would be the concomitant of progress if the principle of Rent were not understood, has continued with equal rapidity. Society both in America and internationally has failed to learn from his studies, and instead has administered palliatives. Some of them draconian: communism, Marxism, and socialism have blighted the twentieth century in virtually all nations of the world at some time or other, and even those on the right of the political spectrum have had to embrace palliatives such as welfare-state-ism. Far worse for many in the 'Eastern bloc': their liberty has been completely taken away for generation after generation.

As to the USA itself, it has first exploited its own natural resources, allowing an influx of people to develop its economy, then denied access to the USA for anymore immigrants when the evils of progress' partner, poverty for many, appeared to threaten the stability of the nation. And finally as the twentieth century settled into further progress in the post-war decades has progressively exploited the peoples of other nations by making their poor service America's wealthy. The mechanism by which this happens being outlined in the chapter on free-trade: free-trade without recognition of Rent in inter-nation transactions leads to accumulation of 'wealth' (in the form of capitalised Rent) in the powerful centres and poverty for the peripheral and already disadvantaged.

CHAPTER 36

Charity

The poor are always with us.

All people should have equal opportunities. This book gives some insight into how that can be and why it is not so in the modern world. We can also see throughout history the reason why it has not been so.

We may struggle towards a workable democracy in Western affluent nations and eventually come to accept that the way to do this is to give each of us equal access to the God-given natural resources. And I hope we will see this being done by the collection of Rent. There is in fact no other way.

But the world is populated much more so by other nationalities living in countries in which conditions are more akin to our middle ages. Or depending where you look to the conditions equivalent to our society in seventeenth, eighteenth and nineteenth centuries. There is little if any real democracy. There is little education for the majority; there are strong tribal rivalries. There are poor communications, and the infrastructure generally is undeveloped. The climate too may be harsh and the means to protect man-made works against it are poor. Probity in public affairs is rare, there is corruption in the governments and the civil services, such as they are.

Couple all these things with a feudal system, or more likely a society modelled on some Western colonial heritage with all its wrong ideas of property rights, and the result will be plenty of poor people.

Looked at across the world therefore there is the need for charitable giving from individuals in rich nations to the people of poorer ones. But let us first not forget the disadvantaged at home. There will always be some who do not or cannot make a satisfactory living for themselves even if they have the same opportunities as everyone else. Fortunately there have always been charitable societies who have helped to pick up the pieces.

Happily also there are some individuals, who having made for themselves great wealth, will proudly give to established charities or will set up special charities for purposes which particularly interest them.

We should have no fear that this will cease to be the case if we make the whole population of the rich nations equally entitled to the opportunities of production. Equal opportunity does not mean equivalent outcome. There are talented individuals in the arts, for example, who will be sought after and handsomely rewarded without setting out to become wealthy. They just want to paint, or sing, or whatever their metier is. The market will do the rest. They will be hard working - perhaps driven by an inner voice - to spread their talent around the community. And the thirst for good art is likely to be even greater in a society that allows the whole population to be free to develop in the way they wish.

So with artists, so with business entrepreneurs. Their talents are different. We may not call them 'talented' as we say of performers and artists, but some by the standards of the average will be exceptionally talented and will create wealth far in excess of the average, and far in excess of their own requirements.

Surprisingly, the UK and other countries' tax laws allow us to create wealth and give it away to charity without being taxed; without any limits. Not that the government is consistent, because VAT is applied to everything the charities spend. (There is expected to be partial relief by reducing the

VAT to a lower rate, but unfortunately not to zero.) But if there were no taxes in the UK we would not all stop our charitable giving. Our tendency to give is strong, and although charities' income was knocked temporarily when the national lottery started in the 1990s, the level of giving soon recovered to pre-lottery times.

In re-modelling any society we should therefore not expect everything to perform without a hitch. But nor should we forget that charitable giving is inherent in us. And affluent people will be 'freed' and enabled to give. The very wealthy will very probably be very generous, though obviously not all will be.

Reverting to the poorer nations, we as the rich Westerners can help by giving, and in times of crisis, natural disaster, famines and the like we are particularly generous. If we have our doubts about giving they centre round the organizations channelling the funds. There may be unnecessary costs or even corruption. We also are concerned about the use of the funds when they arrive in the poorer countries. We do not want corrupt governments, or petty officials to be benefiting when we wanted to relieve hunger or provided much needed medical supplies. We do not want to make gifts that undermine the normal trade in the foreign community. We should also have concern that our charity is directed to communities that are based on justice, and ones where equal opportunity is part of the structure of the state.

It may seem daunting to expect new nations to develop into societies as fair and open to equal opportunity as our own in a short period of years. It has taken us centuries of slow development, and we are not there yet! But in some ways it is easy to start with a simpler society. We should target our giving on places in the world that have been receptive to fairness. It will not escape the peoples and governments of other nations that they are not being favoured. This responsibility falls on each of us to ask the questions of the charitable organizations, who in turn must be expected to put pressure on the receiving communities. More particularly putting pressure on the communities that might benefit but who do not because of their illiberal regimes. This may not sound very charitable. Should we not give without strings attached? In extremes of famine perhaps yes, but the follow through should be selective, surely.

CHAPTER 37

Churches

".... thou shalt love the Lord thy God with all thy heart with all thy mind and with all thy strength. ...... Thou shalt love thy neighbour as thyself. There is none other commandment greater than these."

Those of us who regularly attend church services and have done so perhaps for many decades, are struck by the ever present themes. We find ourselves encouraged to love our neighbour above all else. We are also expected to be compassionate to the disadvantaged in the world. We are frequently reminded of the troubles in the world around us, and we pray for solutions, or at least alleviation of the suffering.

We may meet as discussion groups outside formal church services. We may have invited preachers who have special knowledge of some of the intractable difficulties in the modern world, and we may add our own thoughts and knowledge to discussions following such preachers.

There are of course charitable works going on which alleviate suffering. These are often founded by the churches, and are certainly partly if not wholly funded by church going people. I have written about the work and the role of charities. In this chapter I want to ask the questions about the teaching of the church beyond charitable giving.

"If God didn't exist we would have to invent him". The memorable, and paradoxical, words of Voltaire remind us that there are many religions, but in all the ancient religions of the world, which have stood the test of time, there are similar doctrines. The existence of a God or gods, humility, compassion, a moral code by which to live one's life. It is true that religions have also been bigoted and dictatorial but these phases have been aberrations from the teaching of the prophets or founders of the religion.

Unfortunately, the hierarchy of the churches has also been responsible for a structure of privilege that has kept an army of bishops and sycophants in a regal life-style quite alien to the teaching of Christ (or in other religions, of their founders). It would be not unfair to say this has been a problem throughout the 2000 years since Christ was born, but as the influence of the church has waned in the twentieth century, the church leaders have to a large extent been obliged to cut their coat according to their cloth. And to be fair to them, they are nowhere near as wasteful or self-serving as most commercial, governmental, or other organizations of similar size.

But the key question is do the churches do enough? If we as mankind are sentient and thoughtful and as a consequence are able to acknowledge the existence of higher beings or forces above the mere human condition what is this spirituality able to tell us? What does it do to control and improve the human condition?

Through the centuries it has - concentrating on the positive aspects - given us a magnificent heritage in art and architecture. Also, the churches have promoted education, both at a primary level and in a more limited sphere secondary and tertiary levels. Missionary work overseas has 'civilized' many parts of the uncivilized world; though there were certainly unfortunate results as well. To a small extent the church has modified the workings of the state, but it can be argued the church leaders have not been vocal enough. It has in the broadest sense given us a culture: structuring our milestone moments in life; enriching our beginnings, marriages, and departures. Its words have given us a universal richness of language that has aided cultured dialogue. Or at least it had to those born before the 1960s. Many people of the younger generations are poorer for being unable to refer to this rich heritage, having had little religious education in school.

As the fundamental focal point, religions have given many generations a mode of living through their moral codes. Sometimes these were embodied in absolutes such as banning the eating of pork, or beef. The prohibitions were in ancient history a method of avoiding disease in the community. The customs often outlived their original purpose. The churches have been slow to adapt and change their teachings to suit changed conditions. But on a more spiritual plane the teachings of the various churches has enhanced the life of their followers.

Considering the civilizing influence of Christianity in earlier centuries it seems to me that the churches of the Western world have been slow to analyse the problems of the world in the twentieth century. They cannot be lacking in intellectual capacity, yet they so often seem to be defeated by the problems before them. It is not of course for the churches or their leaders to make secular changes. They have no power to do so, indeed. What they do have is the moral authority to say what is right and wrong in a human context. They can with moral authority speak of justice and injustice. Not in a legal sense, but in a broader sense of natural justice.

They could and should identify the causes of poverty in the midst of plenty in the rich Western nations. They should then speak out.

They could and should identify the causes of poverty in the undeveloped countries. The bishops of Africa do indeed seem to have a closer affinity with their people than elsewhere, and they have commented on the injustices, oppression and conflict where this is obviously being manifested as wars, or imprisonment, or apartheid. But, I ask the bishops and leaders and congregations of the richer nations to see the whole gamut of injustice in the world in their own countries and in the disadvantaged. Then they should speak out.

The churches have as much right to be heard by political leaders as other non-governmental bodies. The churches can speak with the backing of millions. This cannot often be said of other pressure groups. However, they should be sure that the membership do indeed understand the moral and intellectual stand-points if the leaders wish to present cogent arguments to politicians. This requires an openness and willingness to communicate, and teach, within the church organizations.

Throughout this book it has been my object to show how the privilege wrongly derived from holding property without payment of Rent to the community impinges on every aspect of human existence in all countries at all times. The church itself might find this inescapable fact unpalatable because, for example, the Church of England holds large portfolios of property unconnected with the workings of the church. It might be said then that its feet are set in blocks of concrete. It cannot speak out when it is clearly privileged itself by this wrong.

Let us be clear about the church property. In England, as elsewhere we have a magnificent heritage of cathedrals, churches, abbeys and monasteries. All of these should be exempt from payment of Rent, as they are now exempt from rates. So should mosques, synagogues, etc. All these buildings are created by the people and for the community. There seems no need to extract Rent from them, the community, to give it back to the community. It could be said that the religious communities are not the community as a whole. Even if that is a legitimate point the scale of the exemption is not such as to be significant to the community as a whole. More difficult would be to define bona fide religions. But charitable status would be an essential qualification and each religion would have to apply for exemption, and could appeal to the courts if necessary.

It is well known that the Church of England has a very large property portfolio. It has traditionally argued that this pays for the salaries of the clergy, and for their pensions. It may be recalled that in the early 1990s the church lost a sizeable proportion of the value of its property through the decline in property values, and some poor handling of its portfolio. In later years the losses were recovered. But in the shock of discovering it had suffered major losses, there was set in train a process to make the parishes pay for the clergy they employed. This change has stuck. However, pensions are still funded centrally by the church commissioners.

There can be no objection to any organization having a fund of investments with which to pay its pensioners. But the church could and should liquidate its portfolio of properties that have no connection with its churches or other religious buildings, and re-invest in gilts and equities like any other pension fund.

By contrast, the church commissioners will not invest in any equity share that they perceive as being unethical: companies trading in South Africa under apartheid, shares in tobacco, gambling and the like. All these are shunned, yet the powers that be in the church seem oblivious of the ethics of holding and gaining from the title to land which they must think will appreciate in value over time - otherwise it would not be a profitable investment. While the concept of Rent is not widely appreciated, it is by no means unknown, and the churches have made it their business to look into and comment on the crises and misfortunes in the world. The intellectual thinking that has gone into analysing and addressing the spectrum of poverty and misfortune cannot have been wholly blind to the causes. Yet there has to my knowledge been no discussion in church circles of the role of land tenure or Rent collection. I may be wrong. In which case

I would like to know why the church has not spoken out against this widespread wrong. Can it be that the wrong is seen and the only reason it is not addressed is because of the benefit the church itself gains from its property holdings?

As I have written in Chapter 27 the churches throughout the world are pressing for a jubilee of debt relief to give the disadvantaged nations a new start for the new millennium. Now would be the time to put their own houses in order and speak out with moral authority on the causes of poverty. Poverty caused inside every nation by the laws of each nation, and across the world by the ever more vocal demands for free trade. 'Free' trade that is only free in the sense that it calls for absence of barriers to trade. But wholly illiberal because it perpetuates and expands ever wider globally the system of commerce which uses a very un-level playing field, disadvantages the already disadvantaged, and lavishes undue wealth on the already wealthy.

Here indeed is enough to re-vitalise the churches of all sects, indeed of all religions, in the third millennium of Christian teaching.

CHAPTER 38

Collecting the Rent: how to assess it?

Any imposition of government should be fair, be seen to be fair, and should have a transparent method of revision and appeal. It should also be easy to collect and impossible to avoid.

We have seen that Rent is only the result of communities coming together to live as communities rather than as isolated or nomadic peoples. The Rent is therefore manifestly due to the community. And it provides revenue for the essential functions of government. This revenue is uniquely the fair and reasonable money to collect from the members of a community.

As Rent arises on small and large parcels of land, and is varied not only by the size and complexity of the community, but also by the uses that the community allows on each different parcel of land, it can therefore not only vary gradually with changes in the structure of the community, but also rapidly, indeed instantaneously, with new decisions of the community. Most obviously when planning permission is granted.

All land changes hands from time to time, but in some cases the time interval can be protracted. Years, even generations, can pass before some land comes onto the open market. Nevertheless there is an active market in land at all times. It is likely that land with low capital value (lower values will result from the introduction of Rent collection) will change hands more often than under the present system, where high capital values tend to fossilize the market, making new entrants to the market pay dearly through mortgages to get a foot on the ladder.

Today's market would be sufficient, and a more rapidly moving market would be even better to assess the Rent due on all land. Not just the land changing hands but also, by comparison, all similar land, in that location.

The market as always finds its own level. If land at a particular location with typical improvements is changing hands for a price that is out of line with, and higher than, the market price for the improvements alone, then the Rent historically attached to that land is not high enough, and will be reassessed. The market itself tells the assessing authority by how much. Conversely if the land changes hands at less than the market value of the improvements, then the former Rent assessment is too high, and should be reassessed downwards.

Critics of Rent collection have long argued, and still argue that it is difficult to assess the Rent on land. But it is clear from the previous paragraph that the only assessment needed is the value of the improvements on the land. And this is being assessed constantly by the construction industry and all its professional associates such as architects and surveyors, agents and insurance brokers. Each of these professionals needs to know to the nearest few pounds what it cost to build a particular type of house, factory, office block, supermarket and even less common buildings such as railway stations, car parks, ice rinks, sports stadia, etc. Each needs to know so as to insure existing buildings, to build new ones, to advise clients as to purchase value, to advise bankers as to loan security, and for other genuine commercial reasons.

The Rent then becomes a simple mathematical equation. If a piece of land already having a Rent assessment attached to it and improvements on it changes hands for £1m., as a whole, and the improvements are valued at £1m., then the Rent already being assessed is correct. If the total price at auction is £1.1m, the Rent needs to be moved upwards. By how much will be determined by experience, and each new sale will help to determine the answer, because some similar sales will be happening at around the same time. When the historical Rent is too high, property will change hands at a value less than the value of the improvements.

Also appeals from titleholders who think their Rent is too high will bring forward their arguments, and by determination of the appeal new Rents will be set all the time for land that changes hands or is subject to appeal.

Every few years each titleholder will be assessed, but with computerization of records the assessing authority will be able to constantly reassess the current market Rent by feeding in data from sales as they happen.

This is not to suggest that the authority should reassess the Rent for everyone every year, except perhaps in special circumstances. This would provoke too many appeals from titleholders who did not understand the reason for changes, and unless the market were changing very fast a gap of around five years would be comfortable. However, if the authority were to have a computerized model reacting to market sales, there is every reason why this list should be in the public domain so that anyone could assess the position as it affected them and others. They might want this information to see where they might re-locate, and also so as not to be caught unawares at the next revision date.

Capital values, determined by actual sales, above or below the value of the improvements will indicate the need for a Rent adjustment. There will be a direct relationship between capital values and annual Rent payments. This will be determined by experience. A bidder aware that he is paying the vendor more than the value of the improvements will need to take into account that the Rent will be reassessed, and will temper his bidding accordingly. But he will also be aware of other potential purchasers so if the "package" is worth more to any of them than the value of the improvements, a higher bid will still be forthcoming in spite of the fact that a higher Rent should equate the value of the improvements with the market price for the whole.

It may be the policy of the collecting authority that Rents for most property changing hands will not be adjusted until the next revision date. In this case the premium paid by the purchaser will reflect the value of the Rent difference for the number of years until the revision.

The important Rent changes, which must be implemented immediately following the event, will, of course, be on change of planning use: the agricultural land becoming building land; the disused railway yard becoming office blocks, both will command very large changes in Rent as soon as the planning permission is granted. A revision of the Rent is required immediately. No concession should be granted for the time it might take to change the actual use. It must be in the interests of the community as a whole that the proper Rent is collected at all times, and titleholders should not be allowed to escape the Rent by delaying their improvement programme. To do so would invite what happens now: land both with and without planning permission is held out of use. This leads to speculation and a tightening of the land market. It is a fundamental condition that the Rent is collected on all sites whether used or not, and is collected at the rate appropriate to the planning consent granted.

CHAPTER 39

Acceptance of Ideas

It may be recalled that Charles Darwin was the son of a doctor, and studied both medicine and theology at university.
He was from a privileged family, well-educated, observant, interested in natural history, hard-working and determined in his travels. He was able to postulate a hypothesis, examine it himself, and raise his own doubts. He had no knowledge of the chemistry of life: chromosomes, genes, DNA, all had yet to be discovered. He published his book 'The Origin of Species' and immediately provoked a vigorous public debate and some considerable opprobrium, from church leaders in particular. He had offended the established thinking of the day like great scientists before him. Galileo and his explanation of a round earth revolving around the sun, being one example.
Darwin's ideas are still challenged today, and many can still find it impossible to imagine how complex organs such as the human eye can evolve. To some it just seems impossible for chance to configure something so complex. Hundreds of books have been written and are still being written to explain and progress Darwin's one hundred and fifty year old ideas.
Much of what Darwin thought and wrote about was invisible to him. But he could observe in minute detail what was happening around him. For example, discrete differences in the island finches each adapted to the life on their own island.
But biology is a natural science that can be examined closely and is always there for further and further

examination, with better and better tools. We have in the last century seen chromosomes, discovered the characteristics given by genes, exposed the chemistry of DNA and in many, many experiments, which are still very much at the centre of scientific discovery today, elucidated the basis of life and the mechanisms by which any living organism is uniquely itself.

Some of the skills Darwin possessed are needed today in a science that is not one of the natural sciences: Economics. Yet, even though it is not seen by the public as a science, and even economists are proud to differ from others who call themselves economists too, there are natural laws. We cannot, unfortunately expect to get better microscopes to see what is happening. We have to rely very much on observation, just as Darwin did. He looked painstakingly at the evidence around him. He then put together a theory that fitted his observations. We have to do the same in the economic world; a world that is fast changing. Not just in the sense that the tempo is fast, but in the fact that the variables that can affect the outcome are so numerous. Yet underlying all the variables are some constants. In the same way as I drew attention to the fact of sex - two sexes - and the multitudinous consequential effects on human behaviour of this fact, so the fact of economic laws, and in particular the Rent that so clearly exists solely and undeniably from the existence of the community, affects our human lives too. We cannot deny it any more than we can deny the influence of two sexes. We can suppress our natural sexuality. The Victorians did. The homosexual community was forced to because it was illegal until the mid twentieth century. Heterosexuals still frequently find homosexual activity unacceptable. There are strong views expressed today about the morality of displays of heterosexual activity, too. But no one denies it exists. Sex is a fact of life. So is Rent.

Darwin discovered hostility to his ideas with a vehemence that I am sure surprised him. He after all had studied theology. He could make the leap he had to make, even with his background and training in theology. He was up against the vested interested of the church which was as powerful in his day as the multinational corporations and the legal profession in our day. The church today, with perhaps some exceptions, accepts the Darwinian argument and is a very much humbler church than in the nineteenth century. The vested interests of state, government, big business, lawyers, and the elites surrounding them are far more numerous and far more powerful than the church that Darwin had as opponents. On the other hand the disadvantaged who can be introduced to the concept of Rent, perhaps for the first time, are numerically multitudinous.

The developed Western economies may not be the first to recognise the theory of Rent, and if recognized, not the first to act. We are in a way all dancing to the music of the vested interests as if we were all courtiers dancing a quadrille in the courts of the seventeenth and eighteenth centuries. Because the Western economies have the Second- and Third-Worlds in their grip - so far - and we collectively have purloined some of the Rent due to the third world, because of that fact, there are better prospects for acceptance in the countries of the world like India.

In India they have the necessary history of democratic structures - however imperfect. Equally importantly they have around 700 million people living in or around villages; some 70 to 75 % of the population. Some of these villagers are money lenders and men of property with their own vested interests, but the vast majority are not. The now disadvantaged could triumph in India if their governments (there are state governments, as well as the national government) developed their nation in the twenty-first century by recognizing the power of Rent. If India with one sixth of the world's population led the way, and in so doing demonstrated the power of an economy of free people, the rest of the world would feel disadvantaged. It is a dream at present. I only point to India as one fertile ground.

America lost its way at the end of the nineteenth century. But America is nothing if not innovative, and fast changing. They may re-invent what they lost a century ago if an educated people given the stimulus perhaps through internet industries which do not so much rely on land take the ascendancy. Vested interests will still be there but not so powerfully as the oil and steel barons of the early twentieth century.

It could be said that the twenty-first century will be forced to discover the laws of economics and particularly the law of Rent. The alternative is a return to ever-building pressure that led to inter-national conflict in Europe and Asia in the 1940's. The conditions in Europe are different now, and history won't repeat itself in just the same way. But the pressures will build. The peoples of North Africa are only across the Mediterranean Sea from Europe and already pose an immigration difficulty for southern Europe. They are being confined to a non-European existence, but on the other hand twelve or more eastern countries may join the free trade bloc that is the EU and the EU structure is singularly ill equipped to deal with them. And who would have predicted the Balkan conflicts of the 1990s?

The word Rent and the concept of Economic Rent is forgotten and rarely understood even by the cognoscenti. Yet it needs to be constantly repeated in the annals of serious thought, and popularised by numerous easier to read references in the mass media. It was remarkable to me to read in a novel published in 1936 a reference to Rent - yes and with a capital R there, too - merely in passing, with the assumption that everyone would understand the meaning the author had in mind. Of course, therefore, I say we as a society have forgotten. The concept was well understood in the early part of the twentieth century, and the latter part of the nineteenth.

Repetition is essential if concepts, particularly concepts that are not liked by the ruling elite are to take hold and have effect in the population at large. "It is not the simple statement of facts that ushers in freedom, it is the constant repetition of them." Words borrowed from another battleground, but equally relevant to this one. Repetition can be boring of course, but debate is usually lively. And it takes enlightenment by someone like Darwin to spark a lively debate. He was lucky that he was upsetting the religious establishment. Controversy by definition sparks a debate. The causes, which are read about by the power elite and then ignored, are the ones doomed to wither. The challenge then is to the many more who are not the elite. They - probably you - are the ones who should take up the debate. Raise the questions at every opportunity, write articles and give talks that address our everyday questions in terms of the fundamentals following from the fact of Rent. Ask awkward questions when politicians seek to lead us down ever more sophisticated paths based on the wrong assumptions.

As the apocryphal Irishman so wisely put it when asked by a stranger how to get to Dublin - "Ah, well, if I were you I wouldn't start from here". Indeed to have a sensible world economic order we would be well advised not to start from here. We have unfortunately inherited a mess. But we have to first see what should have developed and accept that major errors were made for a wide variety of reasons. Nothing is irreversible, though no one should pretend that changes will be achieved without difficulty and without much effort being exerted and time being taken.

CHAPTER 40

Patronage

Are there any benefits of the system under which we now live that we would miss if all men were equal? By which I mean, of course, have equal opportunity in society. All men are not the same and are not inherently equal. Not in how they develop, nor in the choices they make. The nightmare of cloned half-beings as in Huxley's Brave New World are no part of human society. To hear and see a musician play, an opera singer sing, a sportsman perform, even the effect of a magician's legerdemain is to appreciate human diversity.

But might there not be a nagging doubt that if we no more allow some to wield great wealth by appropriating capitalised Rent there will be no grand architecture, no fabulous collections of the arts, no parkland estates - no Blenheim Palace, no Chatsworth? The royal palaces have arrived over the centuries of monarchy, but I do not want to be either for against the privileges of royalty. The functions of royalty in a mature sovereign state could be safeguarded and rearranged in a republic, particularly if there is an unalienable clause in a written constitution, but I have a strong desire to see royalty championing the 'real' as they were always intended to do.

The single greatest progenitor of our artistic heritage has been the church. It is true that the church has been a great beneficiary of capitalised Rent, but more than that the Christian church – and other religious orders – have been the source of our communal efforts resulting from spiritual yearning. Each period in history has manifested different results. The cathedrals of Western Europe, including Britain, are fine examples, as are the Pyramids of ancient Egypt. But so too are the parish churches built anytime between the

Norman Conquest and the present day. Charities have played their part in the generation of fine artistic expression and will continue to do so in changed circumstances.

I have mentioned but a few of the treasures from the past. The sense of heritage is such that except in the most philistine periods of our history there is a strong desire to preserve the beautiful for posterity, even when it is manifestly unsuited to today's circumstances. So it is not that we might lose these treasures. I raise the question of whether we will see new creations in our century that will lift the spirits of those who come after us.

I have already noted the diversity of human existence and human talent. In a free society these will flourish. The performing arts, the visual arts, music, and sport, all of which are expensive to produce and bring before the public will not be wanting for outlets. A well paid self-sufficient populace hungers for artistic expression, and to see others perform. Each production is expensive but can be paid for if marketed well in the right place, and to an informed educated public.

As for private collections of art and sculpture, there will be some, because there will always be some very wealthy talented individuals. Some of them will want to make private collections. But while private collectors may be an ingredient of the art market, locking wonderful paintings and sculptures up in private non-accessible collections is not good for the rest of us. What then of communal collections?

In a world of abundance, free people are unlikely to be so preoccupied with wealth creation that they have no time for communal affairs, and part of those communal affairs will be concerned with the beautifying of their community. Parks, concert halls and theatres, art galleries and monuments. All can be private, and have been, and could always be brought into being by entrepreneurs. Equally all can and have been in the past funded from public money. And could still be again; not from state funding but from community funds at the level where those making the decisions are the people who will be seeing and using the facility they have wished for and paid for.

It would be unwise to underestimate the wealth in private hands when all have equal opportunity. Wealth above the normal will accrue to the talented artists, the very successful entrepreneur, and the sportsmen just as great wealth comes from their earnings today. They will not be taxed so they will in all probability have greater funds at their disposal. Some will extravagantly live the opulent life. Some will pass wealth to their children, and some will be patrons of the arts.

Absent from the patronage league will be government. This is no function for central government. Also out of the picture will be companies and individuals who have accumulated great wealth solely from exploiting the property sector on the back of appropriated Rent. No tears over losing those two unworthy patrons. In will come not just the very wealthy, but also the whole population who now have sufficient means. Not by themselves, perhaps, but as groups of like-minded people get together amazing feats can be achieved.

I conclude that any fears regarding the demise of the heritage from the past or the artistic outpouring we can hope for in the future are ill-founded.

Patronage has a darker side in the modern world as well. Large monetary or other donations to political parties can be interpreted as bribes. Even if no overt favours are given in return there is inevitably currying of favour: a certain entry into a circle of influence; a reserve of goodwill which will smooth the path of some future difficulty in high places.

It would be too much to expect for such behaviour to disappear even under ideal conditions of equal opportunity. Man, a social animal, will always which to make connections, and in so doing make both friends and enemies. What we can hope for is that if privilege deriving from the appropriation of Rent, either directly by controlling valuable space, or indirectly by being at the top of the industrial hierarchies based on Rent, is absent from economic life – as it should be – then the manipulation of wealth will be lessened. Not just because there will be less villains able to wield large amounts of money, but also because in a fairer society, there will be less need to climb the greasy pole of privilege. Those in advantageous positions in society tend to think that they need to advance to the next exalted position. Many such positions are either politically based and in the gift of the government or if economically based are derived from a degree of monopoly or oligopoly. These economic vantage points are in turn based on the appropriation of Rent.

I therefore am confident to conclude that changing the economic nature of society to a fair assessment and collection of Rent will both allow artistic patronage to flourish and reduce the amount of political shenanigans.

.

CHAPTER 41

Liberty

"Man was born free, and everywhere he is in chains"
- Jean-Jacques Rousseau, 1712-1778

There is no greater ideal than liberty. Without it man is nothing. He may be resilient and be able to survive long periods of hardship, deprivation and even incarceration. But man has a spirit, and that spirit can only soar when man himself is free to do so.

How strange that in the recent past the word liberal has come to sound almost like a word of condemnation in political circles. The tough he-men of politics regard their lesser colleagues and adversaries as less robust than themselves if they perpetrate arguments that appear too generous or woolly. They may then be labelled 'liberal'. But liberty is something quite different

Every student of morality, or even of basic citizenship, knows and readily understands that men and women in society are not absolutely free. They are constrained by the rights of others just as they have their own rights. As noted earlier my enjoyment of being able to walk down the street without being molested is balanced by my acceptance of the right of others to do the same. In exactly the same way we are all obliged to obey the laws of the land whatever they may be as passed by parliament. From time to time laws have been passed by parliament that are so flagrantly at variance with the popular mood that after a shorter or longer period of unrest they are repealed. But in England and most other civilised societies the unrest is very often more verbal and written than physical. Newspaper editors write leaders or publish letters from readers;

broadcasters make documentaries; discussion programmes highlight the injustice. Even when physical demonstrations are held they are largely peaceful, in the sense that no harm is done to persons, although public and private property may get caught in the cross-fire, metaphorically. On the whole we support such happenings in the name of freedom of speech.

Very often the wrongs that provoke the public to respond in such a way are new laws, or new discoveries that appear to threaten the status quo. So, for example, the Poll Tax of the Thatcher government; as also the nuclear arms and the campaign for nuclear disarmament (CND). It is a saddening observation to make, but the population at large is much slower to react when long established wrongs are perpetrated by governments. This is to say the government can only pass laws that do reflect public perception of what is acceptable. Homosexuality was for a long time a crime, and most people believed it was wrong. So also in earlier centuries it was generally regarded that the world was flat. This may not seem a great wrong, but the assumption made it impossible for men to contemplate a circumnavigation of the world to cite one example, and inhibited them from navigation generally.

History has shown us that wrong science and wrong principles have moulded society and been widely accepted until plainly revealed by some new thinker who has clearly illuminated the true principles. But illumination may come very slowly to the people of a society in sufficient numbers to make a government change any law. Certainly in the paternalistic societies that are the characteristic of most Western societies, it would need the educated elite to understand the need for change. But what better way to perpetuate the elitism than to deny to the hoi polloi the opportunity that the elite has enjoyed?

If, and it is a big if, we now regard societies as less paternalistic, and think that having sent a high percentage of our young adults to tertiary education we have a populace ready and willing and able to understand how and why they are who they are, and why and how others in society are who they are, then the rights and wrongs not just of justice in the sense of human rights but also in the sense of economic duties and rights will become evident to a wider and wider group of people. Regrettably many of those with ability may learn of true economic liberty, which is desirable but still lacking, and be tempted by the rewards of scaling the heights of the existing system instead. There will however be many more who can expect a better deal for themselves and their families from a change to true liberal democracy, and we must look to the strength of numbers collectively to use the rights they do have, particularly the right to vote, to bring about their economic rights.

CONCLUSION

It would be unrealistic to expect to address all the wrongs and evils of the modern world and miraculously to see universal acceptance of a changed order of man's affairs. What I have tried to do in this book is to present a different way of looking at the way man does associate with his fellow being.

We saw how men and women are 'hard-wired' to be sexually attracted to each other, and how this fundamental human condition can dictate behaviour in many acts and manners of both men and women. I also referred to the many natural science laws that dictate what is possible, and what is not, in the ordering of man's endeavours.

Having referred to the civilising of society into a pattern of behaviour that replaces the court house for the might of the individual and the tribe in order to settle disputes and to recognise our human rights and duties, I contrasted this with the failure of society to recognise the economic rights and duties we owe to each other.

Early settlers in any community may fight, but more often will cooperate, and we have seen how specialization and cooperation lead to trade. It is noted that in primitive societies men do not need money or tokens of exchange but can get by with barter and pledges, where a man's word is his bond. Crucially I explained how very early Rent becomes a natural consequence of a society trading and cooperating. And furthermore this Rent becomes a larger and larger factor as the community develops. Real, another word for royal, describes how in former times monarchs arrogating to themselves the divine right (and duty) from God were, or should have been, guardians of the Real and hence the Rent which is, it is now explained, as fundamental a fact of human existence as sexuality, and other natural laws. We can no more operate without its existence than we can without breathing or eating.

How we let the fact of Rent's existence influence our dealings with each other determines a wide range of other matters, which are usually perceived as intractable by today's politicians, and most of the populace who have had no knowledge of the workings of a power that enters into their every move, their every decision, every day from their earliest upbringing to their twilight years living on a pension. These intractable matters are the Real questions that I have explored in this book.

The legal status of titles to land has been wilfully misunderstood from Roman times, and addressing the wrong done by this so that Rent is collected by accountable governments would, and in some places does, address the many ills that spring from neglecting to do so. Inflated land prices, withholding land from productive use, over-crowding, inner city decay, corruption of the planning process and peoples, and many other ills associated with the world of property can readily be appreciated by a clear understanding of the role of Rent. I would not be the first and I sincerely hope I will not be the last to draw attention to these matters.

I have aimed to go further in this book, and explore how the conditions of our economic world that appear to have nothing to do with land or property are distorted by the failure to recognise Rent and the need to collect it by accountable governments. The money we use to trade is corrupted by failing to collect Rent. The wages of the majority of the population is depressed by failing to collect Rent. The governments we elect are programmed to legislate by our failure to collect Rent. The choice of political parties we are offered is limited by society's failure to understand what is Real and the part played by Rent. The tendency towards federalisation and our loss of sovereignty is pushed ahead as inevitable because we fail to collect Rent.

Our wars, our internal strife and terrorism, our breakdown of law and order are all both caused by failure to collect Rent and exacerbated by the palliatives governments devise rather than addressing the problem.

Protecting the boundaries of our nation states from undesirable immigration is made necessary by the failure to collect Rent on a world wide basis. Globalisation of trade, which is a euphemism for the supremacy of huge corporations over less fortunate countries, is only seen – by some – to be a good thing because we fail to collect Rent on a global basis.

The crisis of world debt and the seemingly impossible task of bringing first relief of poverty and then real quality of life to Third World peoples is a direct result of failing to collect Rent both locally and nationally, and also globally.

In a relatively short time, in the twentieth century, taxation has been transformed from a relatively simple – if misguided – charge on a few to an invasive network of taxes and allowances on every member of the community. It is not only unwieldy but wrong in concept and debilitating in its effects on industry and commerce.

The need for a welfare state and the concomitant waste and mismanagement of the nation's schools, and hospitals, both of which should naturally be functions of private enterprise if peoples' wages were to be high enough to pay for their own requirements, is another evil consequence of failing to collect Rent.

The sclerotic effect of trade unionism on industry in the mid twentieth century was a direct result of low wages caused by failing to collect Rent.

The cycle of boom and bust is not just an extreme form of natural business cycles. Whereas demand for products and services varies according to changing conditions, and decline in one economic activity will be replaced and developed in a new industry, the small cycles of activity will overlap, and general economic activity may be expected to increase as overall demand and prosperity increases. By contrast, wholesale boom and bust, on a national or nowadays on an international scale, has been shown to be a phenomenon of the failure to collect Rent.

So, each of these questions are not only real questions but are Real questions. I look forward to a better understanding of all these matters by enough people to make the difference. We owe it to ourselves to understand, we owe it to each other to make a difference, or to enable those that come after us in this new century to make a difference. In former centuries, those frustrated by iniquity could re-locate themselves to a new territory. In this century, we have to learn to live together on a small planet. Our children and grandchildren will need to know what has held us back, and learn how to live with a fair and equitable collection of Rent.

Appendix 1

The Power of Rent

Imagine a range of individuals working at some trade, each separately and in diverse locations, but otherwise all equipped to the same standard and of equal ability and energy. The one at the best location (A) will produce, say, 100 units of value after paying all input costs, and at the worst location (E) 60 units. The others, (B, C, and D) will produce let us imagine, 90, 80, and 70 units respectively.

The Rent on the worst location will, by definition, be zero, since Rent is the added output at locations better than output at the least favourable site in production. The Rents therefore are 40 units at the best location, 30, 20, and 10 at the others. In aggregate therefore the Rent in the community will be 100 units over a total production of 400 units produced by the five people. In this example it is 25% of output.

Imagine now that wages throughout the community are much lower than E can produce at his marginal location. Less because he has been forced to compete with others for jobs. Land is all owned by a small percentage of the population and many millions make up the workforce competing to secure jobs in the economy. E may be glad now to settle for 20 units while others are unemployed. This is the unhappy situation in modern economies. The five people still produce 400 units but the wages are only 20 units for each person employed at each location. The Rent therefore has increased from 40 to 80 units at A; 30 to 70 units at B; 20 to 60 units at C; 10 to 50 units at D; and at E from zero to 40 units. This in total is from 100 units formerly to 300 units now; and in percentage terms from 25% to 75%!

The laissez faire entrepreneurs in earlier centuries did very well by fully harnessing this power of Rent for themselves. Wages were often way below the 20 unit level in the above example, and Rents therefore were extremely high.

In modern times unionisation and legislation have intervened to keep wages at a 'reasonable' level, but they are still extremely depressed, not just by the misappropriation of Rent, but also by the heavy burden of taxation.

Let us imagine proper Rent collection. Wages would be at the 60 unit level throughout the economy because all men and women would be free to emulate the worker at E, or alternatively be employed by others who would have to pay similar wages to attract new employees.

After the struggles of unions and legislation have stopped wages falling to poverty level, in today's economy the level of wages throughout the community might be, say, 50 units. But taxation will reduce this substantially to, for example, 40% of the gross level. This will equate to 20 units again. No wonder a Welfare State is needed when only 20 units is the take home pay, and when it should be 60 units. And note that taxation in this example has taken 60% of the nominal wage. That is 30 units, and in aggregate for our five people the 150 units equals 37.5% of the total production. That sounds bad enough, but in fact the taxation take of the UK government is normally in excess of 40%. And that 40% is as a percentage of GDP not just of aggregate wages!

I have highlighted the greatly depressed level of wages in a modern economy. It may be perhaps a third of what it should be, as demonstrated by the above example. So, government then tries to address poverty, or at least inadequacy, by propping up the majority of the population using welfare, instead of seeing that each individual with three times the income could provide for himself, or herself.

Meanwhile the Rentiers have creamed off not just the Rent that would have naturally accrued to the better locations, but also extra Rent resulting from wage levels being depressed.

The proper collection of Rent would have yielded 100 units in our example, being 25%, which would be much more than enough to run government. The government machine as outlined in Chapter 15 might legitimately absorb 7%, even perhaps 10%, adding a few extra percent for international concerns. But the remainder can be returned to the community, as individual payments. These should be regular annual, or more frequent, payments. There will be temptations to retain these in government and hand out sums as pensions, vouchers for education or for health care, and other schemes reminiscent of the nanny state mentality that we have grown up with. But all such schemes should be resisted. The individuals in the population should be able to choose exactly what it does with its wages and what it does with its share of the Rent collected. While earnings will vary according to ability and occupation, the division of Rent collected and not used by government should be the same for all. Each adult in the community should receive the same. Children might receive – through their parents – a lesser sum, which might be graduated according to age. Prudent families will use part of their earnings and their share of Rent to provide for the future, the proverbial rainy day, and for their old age.

Appendix 2

Population

There are approximately 6 billion people in the world. It can be seen that they could comfortably all fit into Wales, and be considerably less crowded than at the average social function. The area of Wales is 20,768 square kilometres. That is 20.768 billion square metres. Each person would therefore be able to occupy just under 3.5 square metres.

City densities are not as high as this on average. But Tokyo allows only 77 square metres each for its 8 million inhabitants - in 618 square kilometres.

Manhattan, New York, is home to roughly 1.5 million in only 57 square kilometres, an average of 38 square metres per person. The average will hide much higher densities in some areas. Remember that much of Manhattan is only sparsely populated in low rise accommodation, particularly in the poorer areas, and the high density skyscraper landscape of the central, east and downtown areas are subjected to an influx of many non-resident workers each day. The occupation density of a multi-storey skyscraper office block will be far greater than one person in 3.5 square metres when this is calculated on the ground area, as opposed to the floor area, occupied.

Appendix 3

The Enclosure of Land

The pressure on the availability of land is not an issue when there is land aplenty, and any person wishing to use it only has to stake his claim. This phrase derives literally from the practise of pioneers in the Americas banging stakes into the ground marking out the area of land each claimed as their own. Quite clearly there is a limit to how many people can do this, and as populations increased and exploration of new territories exhausted all workable land, there came a time when no new person could simply stake a claim.

Much earlier the pressure mounted in more populated parts of the world, and in Europe the lands were effectively claimed from a very early time. In Britain the process was first a physical process as described above, and then under successive Acts of Parliament enshrined in law.

It can easily be appreciated from what happened in the Americas, that new arrivals would not stake out what they actually needed, but an area of land that they thought they might need or more probably an area they thought that they could control, even defend from others. In other words, a land-grab with the most powerful claiming the largest areas.

In England from medieval times there were in existence from many years of custom and practice common lands that were available to all for grazing of livestock.

Even arable cultivation took place on common land with the control of land being for the growing season only. After the crop was harvested strips of land controlled by individuals became available to all for grazing of their livestock.

The history of land tenure in Europe is convoluted, and varied considerably from country to country. While there were allodial holdings (the holder having absolute rights of tenure) in many parts of Europe and in England before the Norman Conquest, they were completely replaced by the feudal system in England after that date. The agricultural economy, which effectively was the basis of all commerce, was structured around the manorial system, and from the twelfth century onwards the process of enclosing land to increase the amount of land available to the manor continued. The times when enclosures were most active were the mid fifteenth century to the mid seventeenth century and again from the mid eighteenth to the mid nineteenth centuries. By the latter date there was effectively no unenclosed land in the United Kingdom, though there are still very small areas of common land that survive, as community amenity land for the most part. In 1972 it was recorded that only approximately half a million acres of common land remained. Very little of it is of economic use.

It can be easily appreciated, and it is well documented in history, that when a peasant family, which had been used to scratching a living in the countryside, was excluded from the land being enclosed, that family would have to migrate to the towns. This migration became acute as the landed area of the nation became fully enclosed. The alternative – not an attractive one it is true – to making a living as a peasant was to seek employment in the towns. In the industrial revolution that became possible, if unattractive, in most provincial towns as new mills and foundries were set up. But in earlier times the choice was often to go to the major centres where the wealthy needed services of all kinds, and if employment was impossible, begging or stealing from those more fortunate was a real if grim and hazardous last resort.

Even employment in the new industries was far from congenial. Wages were extremely low for the reasons explained in the main body of this book. Accommodation was inadequate, unhealthy, and in relation to wages expensive. The healthy peasant life, which was certainly no life of ease, was exchanged for a far less congenial existence where looking after oneself was nigh on impossible. Looking after a family was full of hazards in the extreme. Many children died. Once they had moved to the cities and towns, many women, isolated from friends and supporters that might have been part of a rural community perished, often in childbirth, alone and in sordid conditions.

And yet the migration went on. Was there an illusion about the wealth of the cities? When London was days if not weeks of journeying away, there may have been rumours of the potential to succeed 'where the streets were paved with gold'. But in truth there was, for the displaced, no alternative. The attractions of cities were not so great that the population of the rural areas chose to migrate when they had a choice. Only when they were literally forced off the land did the depopulation become a flood to the cities.

Acronyms and Abbreviations

I have introduced most acronyms and abbreviations at the relevant point in the text, but their use later in the text may be unfamiliar to some readers. I therefore list them here for easy reference. And also include the ones in common use at the time of writing, which may not have been introduced, and that may not be obvious to all, or that may be less in current use at later dates.

ADAS	Agricultural Development and Advisory Service
BBC	British Broadcasting Corporation
BSE	Bovine Spongiform Encephalopathy
CEO	Chief Executive Officer
CGT	Capital Gains Tax
CND	Campaign for Nuclear Disarmament
CV	curriculum vitae
DEFRA	Department of Environment, Food, and Rural Affairs
DNA	Deoxy-ribo-Nucleic Acid
ECB	European Central Bank
EMU	European Monetary Union
EU	European Union
GDP	Gross Domestic Product
GM	Genetically Modified
IMF	International Monetary Fund
MAFF	Ministry of Agriculture Fisheries and Food (now defunct)
MPC	Monetary Policy Committee (of Bank of England)
NIMBY	Not in my back yard
RPI	Retail Price Index

UK	United Kingdom of Great Britain and Northern Ireland
UN	United Nations
USA	United States of America
VAT	Value Added Tax
WTO	World Trade Organization

Continued from back cover

But this is not a political book, nor an economics textbook. It is deliberately written in a non-technical style to appeal to a wide readership.

It is a book for all time. Its message applies to all nations and all societies. The questions raised are real questions that every member of society asks themselves and each other. We all need some new light on these questions to elect better and more appropriate governments, and to move forward to a more prosperous and stable society. Because politicians are focused only on the short term, the electorate itself must keep in its collective conscious the long-term goals, and elect governments that measure up to their high standards at each election.

THE AUTHOR

Encouraged to think liberally at an early age by parents, and enlightened headmasters at both The Dragon School and Bryanston, the author went on to read both Natural Sciences and Economics at Trinity Hall, Cambridge. He then studied philosophy privately while working in London – part of twelve years in large scale manufacturing industry being based successively in many parts of the UK, and for two years in India. As well as writing, he is involved in agriculture, which has included some years with related food industries, and is now involved in the financial management of small companies. At many junctures he has been frustrated by and critical of inappropriate institutions. Seeing through vested interests to the moral dimensions, he has come to the realization that there will be little change for the better until enough people comprehend how and why they are bound to the fate that controls their lives. His book is intended to reach a wide spectrum of people: ordinary people and those in diverse professions, many of whom will feel challenged by it.